Fishing Dry Flies for Trout
on Rivers and Streams

Illustrations by Gordon Allen
Photographs by Kris Lee

Fishing
Dry Flies for Trout
on Rivers and Streams

ART LEE

ATHENEUM NEW YORK 1983

LIBRARY OF CONGRESS CATALOGING IN PUBLICATION DATA

Lee, Art.
Fishing dry flies for trout on rivers and streams.

I. Trout fishing.   2. Fly fishing.   I. Title.
II. Title: Dry flies for trout on rivers and streams.
SH687.L37   1981   799.1'755   81-66449
ISBN 0-689-70662-6   AACR2

Text Copyright © 1982 by Art Lee
Illustrations Copyright © 1982 by Atheneum Publishers, Inc.
All rights reserved
Published simultaneously in Canada by McClelland & Stewart Ltd.
Composition by American-Stratford Graphic Services, Inc., Brattleboro, Vermont
Manufactured by Halliday Lithograph Corporation, West Hanover, Massachusetts
Designed by Mary Cregan
Color section designed by Robert Michaels
First Atheneum Paperback Edition

This book is for Chett Osborn, naturalist and teacher,
and the only friend I always called Mister.

Contents

ACKNOWLEDGMENTS

FISHING DRY FLIES FOR TROUT is largely a solitary experience. Producing a book about it, though, is a team effort, and I would like to introduce you, the reader, to the team that made this one.

First, last and always, there's Kris, the only person in the world who knows how bull-headed and temperamental I really am. She works while I play, and she works while I work, and despite it all, still loves me and is ready to work some more.

Then there is Gordon Allen whose work with pencil, pen or paint I admire, and whom I predict will be one of America's most celebrated artists someday—soon. Thank you, Van Gordy, for trying so hard to make me look like Errol Flynn.

Special thanks to Ed Van Put, a singularly talented dry fly fisherman, who labored tirelessly to dress each fly for this volume just so; to Ken Bowden, my editor, who knew where a thousand "thats" ought to go; to Mary Cregan for designing the thing; to

Arnold Goodman, my agent, who has seen me at my worst and is still around; to Mike Kimball whom I respect mightily as an angler and love like a brother; and to my brother, George Scott Lee, who is also my best friend.

Untold thanks to Walt Dette, Poul Jorgensen, Ed Sutryn and Lee Wulff for their assistance in doing this book.

Thanks, too, to Winnie Dette, Mary Dette Clark, Leon Chandler, Francis Betters, Ernie Maltz, Curt Gowdy, Ted Simroe, Ron Bensley, Harry Darbee, Pierre Affre, Larry Solomon, Rudy Romania, Lefty Kreh, Bill Conrad, Charlie Fox, Jim Cook, Ron James, Jack Hemingway, Joan Stoliar, Al McClane, Budge and Dot Loekle, Ralphie Graves, John Randolph, John Barstow, Joan Wulff, Ed Shenk and Art Flick.

Thanks to the publishers of *Fly Fisherman* and *Sports Afield* magazines in which some portions of this book appeared.

And a private prayer of thanks to my parents, Arthur and Florence Lee, to Elsie Darbee, Chett Osborn and Dave Danzig, all of whom had to go while this book was in the making.

Prologue

KRIS AND I LIVE IN A COTTAGE on the banks of Willowemoc Creek in New York's Catskill Mountains. The cottage badly needs paint, and all around us foliage that might make a lawn has grown tall and tangled and, we think, beautiful. Permitting such anarchy of landscape does nothing for the market value of our little home. But we don't care. We don't intend to move.

All this has a lot to do with trout fishing, the subject of this volume. In fact, it may just be that I'm qualified to write it, because Kris and I learned long ago that each day gives you only so much time, and ours has been spent fishing. Fishing and exploring, experimenting, photographing and writing. Other chores widely judged "necessary" have had to wait and will continue to do so in the foreseeable future.

For more than a decade I've been asked when I'd write a book. I've offered numerous answers, all of which have boiled down to,

"When I know I'm ready." It took considerable discipline to keep from cashing in on the fishing-book "boom" of the 1960's and early '70's, a period during which only sex got more of a going over between cardboard covers. But I waited, and to those who waited with me, I can only hope the wait was worth it. You will soon know.

Being a professional fisherman is much like being a professional athlete of any sort. (The major difference is, of course, that fishing is the one sport I know in which the athlete is usually his own press agent.) First, there are the formative years during which you master fundamentals. Then comes a period of honing, when those fundamentals must become almost automatic and you concentrate on the fine points, the nuances—the tricks if you will—that inevitably set you a little bit apart from most fellow anglers. Finally, there is the time of decision and commitment. That time past, there is seldom any turning back.

When fishing becomes your life, it is very easy to lose perspective. To you the sport is a question of livelihood, something about which only a fool could be less than serious. You are, in fact, doing it for money, playing a game to survive. You are different, just as a major league center fielder is different from the fellow who runs home from the office, grabs a bat and glove and heads for the baseball diamond to represent a local used-car dealer. For the professional to lose track of this distinction, I think, is a terrible mistake. Unfortunately, I'm convinced too many of us do.

My notes confirm that I fish during some 250 days a year. Writing and film assignments take me to many parts of the country and the world. Basically a hedonist, I admit I love it or I wouldn't do it. I fish hard—harder, some friends insist, than anyone they've ever fished with—and, like many professionals, I tend to regard each outing, each fish cast to and hooked as if it might be the last. I try not to forget, however, that most anglers do not, cannot, fish 250 days a year, and that most probably wouldn't want to if they could. A fishing companion, Dave Danzig of Schenectady, New York, told me recently, "I love trout fishing, but if I felt I had to do it every day the way you do, I'd die of boredom." To each his own, I guess.

"The charm of fishing," wrote John Buchan, quite correctly, "is that it is the pursuit of what is elusive but attainable, a perpetual series of occasions for hope." Above all else, though, I'm convinced it should be *fun*. And it is of that essential spirit, I fear, that my colleagues and I too often lose sight in our efforts to inform and excite.

During the last decade I've scanned, perused and read scores of angling books—big ones, small ones, specific ones, general ones, tidy ones, tedious ones. Some have been useful, a few even inspiring. As a body of work, however, they have left me troubled, primarily due to a pervasive bias toward portraying America's favorite form of outdoor recreation as much more complicated and difficult than it really is. "I caught so many more fish before I knew so much about it," the devoted reader might complain. He'd get no argument from me.

A nice thing about angling is that a *sport* can make as little or as much of it as he or she wishes. A person can learn a few basics, and, that done, have a glorious, lifetime hobby. Or, the same person might devote a lifetime of study to angling and die happy, if still a little mystified by the fickleness inherent to all games played on Nature's court. Between the two extremes, of course, the options are virtually limitless.

I haven't sought here to write the "complete book" of fishing, or even of trout fishing. Those who try such things, like Santiago, the proud Cuban fisherman of Hemingway's *The Old Man and the Sea,* soon learn they have gone out too far. This isn't a primer either, however. Rather, I chose a subject I believe represents the most rewarding adventure for the freshwater angler, whether the fish involved are six inches long or weigh six pounds, and tried to convey in practical terms the battle plans that have served me best. Once mastered, I believe they will also serve most other fly fishermen, novice or advanced, in most situations.

This volume deals exclusively with three trout species—the

brown trout, book trout and rainbow trout—those favored by most dry fly fishermen worldwide. It doesn't cover, for instance, Arctic or European grayling, both species I like very much, primarily because environmental defilement has shrunk the grayling's range to insignificance in my native United States, while elsewhere the species has been relegated to second-class status. Suffice to say the techniques applied to species treated here also fool grayling, landlocked salmon, cutthroat trout, and Rocky Mountain whitefish, among others prone to surface feeding.

It's also worth noting that this book treats only those fish of each species that live entirely in moving freshwater. Fishing dry flies on ponds and lakes is another matter altogether. Likewise, anadromous fish—those born in freshwater which feed at sea before finally migrating upriver again to spawn, such as steelhead trout or Atlantic salmon—constitute a separate study, one I'll probably write a book about someday . . . if the "crick" don't rise.

Some critics are sure to complain that much of this book isn't very scientific in contemporary fashion. They will be quite right. Those who seek, for instance, yet another dissertation on aquatic insect life rife with Latin names, or an engineering manual on the comparative recovery rates of rod-making materials, will have to look elsewhere. Such stuff has its place, of course, but I've encountered too many avid readers of it in recent years who talk a great game on the bank while they're lost on the water where it counts.

This book is based largely on experience, the best teacher in the end. When you have enough time to fish as I do, you are inclined to experiment with that time, and what is dished up here is casserole concocted from hundreds of such experiments, and then well simmered. In many ways it is a throwback book, not the one I might have written just a few years ago. It is a bit reactionary, in fact. Fishing dry flies has carried me almost full circle, beginning with a simplistic view when I was innocent, through a period pregnant with erudition, and finally back again to a vantage point much closer to the former than the latter. I may not always be observed doing what I say, but that is an occupational hazard that should be of concern only to fellow professionals. The essential purpose here is to make fishing dry flies for trout more *fun* for all by making it only as difficult as it really is, which is *not at all.*

The title of this book, *Fishing Dry Flies for Trout on Rivers and Streams,* was chosen very carefully. Within it lies the essence of my angling philosophy: technique over technology. I saw the need for a "how-to" book aimed at restoring some horses to their proper places before the carts, and when I felt I could fill the need, I was finally ready to sit down and write.

Besides, have you checked the price of house paint lately? . . .

Fishing Dry Flies for Trout
on Rivers and Streams

~~~~~~~~~~~~~~~~~~~~~~~~~~~~~~~~~~~~~~

CHAPTER ONE

Trout

THE GREATEST ERROR many fly fishermen make is to give trout too much credit. Over the years I've heard anglers attribute all manner of intellectual wizardry to the fish, often to lengths that would have made Walt Disney, king of anthropomorphism, blush. Fact is, trout aren't wise or clever as we understand those mental capacities. Strictly speaking, they aren't very smart at all. When a person accepts this premise and sets out to take advantage of it, he's got a big leg up toward becoming a better angler.

If sporting enjoyment depended on an intelligent adversary, a person would be better advised to take up bridge or chess than trout fishing. The "village idiot," after all, has greater native intelligence than the smartest trout that swims. The difference lies in adaptation. As game fish, trout are superbly adapted to a host of varied environments, both in the U.S.A. and abroad. Trout are, in fact, among the most widely distributed coldwater fish on

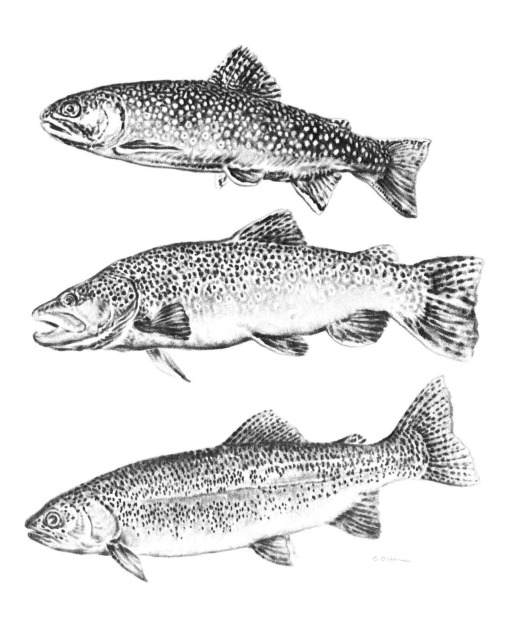

The Eastern brook trout (top) is characterized by the so-called "scrambled eggs" on its back. Generally green in hue, the brookie is nevertheless the most colorful of trout, often showing bright orange streaks along its belly and orange pectoral, pelvic and anal fins, edged by black and white. Deep red spots on its sides are haloed by pale blue. For the pure joy of catching trout, many anglers still like the brookie best. The brown trout (center) may vary in color from almost uniformly ochre with black spots to a myriad of burnished browns, oranges and yellows with bright red spots, depending on locale. Wonderfully adaptable to a host of water conditions, browns sometimes attain weights exceeding thirty pounds, and no matter where they happen to appear, the big ones are usually hard to take. The brown trout is my personal favorite dry fly fish. Note the small bullet head of the rainbow trout (bottom) and the sleek body that just guarantees it loves to run. Rainbows are native to the Western United States and are still the staple of dry fly fishing there. Their trademarks, of course, are those streaks of color, ranging from pink to bright red, along the middle of their sides.

earth, being native or having been successfully introduced to all continents except frozen Antarctica. Only three of the United States don't host trout—Florida, Mississippi and Louisiana—and all three border more than one "trout state." (Yes, there are trout in Hawaii.) Therefore, most Americans can test their skills against the fly fisherman's favorite quarry with a minimum of time or travel.

Despite substantial propaganda to the contrary, I believe it's singularly self-defeating for dry fly fishermen to become preoccupied with the endless material biologists have dredged up about trout during the past two centuries. Although it sounds great, learning the exact number of pores along a brown trout's lateral line, for example, makes about as much difference to the *practical* angler as a geological analysis of dirt from the mound would to a major-league pitcher. It helps to know, of course, that each fish has a lateral line—a series of receptors along its sides that pick up

5

vibrations in the water—not for its own sake, but because with that knowledge an angler will understand why he can't ram around a pool like an egg-beater in a bowl without spooking his quarry. The key, then, is to clutter the mind with only that which can be put to use to make you a better angler.

In that spirit I attack each fishery using the hypothesis that *a trout's a trout* until it's proven wrong. Trout take dry flies, I'm convinced, for two reasons only—chiefly to eat, but secondarily out of excitation, that being perhaps akin to playfulness or hostility. Of the stimuli in the latter case I can't be more precise, but I also feel that further precision serves no fundamental purpose to the angler. Of one thing I am absolutely certain, though. *All trout are opportunists,* patterned by nature for survival. Each reaction, therefore, represents a quick and automatic response to that patterning, carried out without resort to any consideration whatsoever. Therein lies the essential matter for successful dry fly fishing.

This is not to say there aren't some characteristics more prevalent in one species than another. Not that it should make much difference to a fisherman, but the Eastern brook trout, also called the speckled trout, squaretail or native trout, isn't a trout at all. It's a char, catalogued in Latin, for anybody who wants to know, as *Salvelinus fontinalis.* Often found in the headwaters of streams, brook trout require cold, clean water, a major reason why changing land use in many areas has dictated they be supplanted by more hearty browns and rainbows. Of the true trouts, the brown (*Salmo trutta*) tends to be territorial and a ritualistic feeder, particularly in waters of dependable fly hatches, while the rainbow (*Salmo gairdneri*) is apt to be a cruiser and less discriminating in its eating habits. Brookies, sometimes dubbed "dumb" by sophisticated fly fishermen, as a species generally respond readily to the excitation phenomenon, and thus may seem to earn their uncomplimentary reputation.

Yet, if you have fished enough places long enough, as I have, you're sure to catch too many exceptions even to these rules to take them very seriously. I've caught a lot of ritualistic brookies and rainbows and some very excitable browns, all big enough to have conformed to the mold if they were ever going to. Therefore, it's my rule to pay less attention to notions about species *per se* than to (1) a fish's pedigree, that is, whether it was spawned in the wild or hatchery bred, and (2) its relationship to its environment, that is, the river or stream in which it lives and coexists with all its fellow creatures. If you're nosy enough about a trout's lifestyle, it's hard to go wrong.

If I had my "druthers," I'd never catch another hatchery trout. In these days of easy access to less water by more anglers, of course such a sentiment is a pipe dream. In fact, if it weren't for stocking, in conjunction with expanding management by "catch and release" or "fish for fun," I doubt we'd have even our current tenuous hold on quality sport. To some experienced fishermen it's chic to openly disdain hatchery systems. In deference to those mandated to manage our fisheries with a minimum of money and a maximum of political pressure, it's fair to say, I think, that such a view is impractical at best and at worst counterproductive. Trout stocking is essential today and probably will be so long as there is to be trout fishing.

Considering the scope of trout stocking, it's surprising how few anglers can differentiate between hatchery fish and those born in the wild, or "wild fish" as I call them. Of the trout in the Willowemoc–Beaverkill system, for instance, about eighty percent are of hatchery origin. Yet I've met few fishermen able to tell them from the streamborn strain. I'm particularly awed by eastern friends who travel west each season and return with stories of gigantic "wild" trout they've taken on Rocky Mountain waters. Somehow they're convinced large trout necessarily mean wild trout, which just isn't true. Several western states, including Colorado, Montana and Wyoming, operate among the world's most ambitious and efficient hatchery systems, cranked up to rear fish to large size before planting. Imagine the shock of a pal of mine who was working a pristine stretch of Montana river when a state hatchery truck suddenly pulled up and unloaded enough sixteen-

Signs like this one on the busy Beaverkill in the Catskills of New York are showing up along American trout waters in increasing numbers every year, thanks largely to the efforts of organized fly fishermen. Special regulations, including fly-fishing-only stretches, are unquestionably the key to the quality angling of tomorrow.

to eighteen-inch rainbows practically at his feet to keep a New York restaurant in *Truite Bleu* for a month. Unfortunately, my friend returned home badly disillusioned.

It would be nice to leave ignorance with bliss, if learning to sort hatchery trout from wild ones weren't integral to becoming a first-class angler. This is so important, however, that the first question I ask when I approach a fishery is, "Is it stocked?" Heretic though I may be, by comparison I don't give a damn what fly is hatching, or even if the trout are browns, brooks or rainbows. No, siree. First tell me what I'm up against. Then I'm on the way.

The obvious means to find that out, of course, is to ask someone who knows. Barring that, there's no alternative but to catch a fish and see. Perhaps a dozen anglers have confided their detection secrets to me through the years, ranging from body coloration and condition of teeth to the rise form shape on the water's surface. None have proven universally reliable. The most reliable measure, I've discovered, is a quick look at a trout's pectoral fins. Regardless of species, wild trout generally have long, arrowhead-shaped pectorals, while those of hatchery fish are inevitably rounded and stubby, no matter how long they've carried over in the wild (see illustration). The difference is usually so marked that only seconds are required to discern it. I'd like to inform the

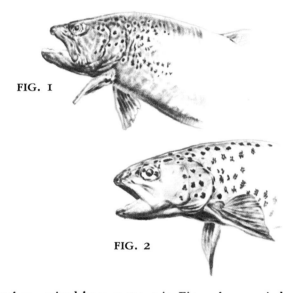

FIG. 1

FIG. 2

The hatchery-raised brown trout in Fig. 1 has carried over in a stream for several seasons, and yet its pectoral fins continue to be blunted and somewhat ragged. Note, by contrast, the smooth, tapered pectorals belonging to the wild brown in Fig. 2. Such comparison is the surest way I know to distinguish between hatchery and wild trout of any species.

reader why this difference occurs, but I can't. Biologists, it seems, don't agree, although the front-running theory is that young hatchery trout blunt the nonrestorative tissue of their underbody fins on the linings of holding tanks. That's good enough for me, I guess, because the *why* isn't important to the angler anyway. To the fly fisherman on the water it's the *wherefore* that really counts.

Learning whether a fishery is stocked tells the angler plenty about its trout, whether the fishery is a big river or a small stream. Experienced Beaverkill dry-fly fishermen, for instance, frequently return humbled from tackling Vermont's Batten Kill. Batten Kill browns and brook trout are reputed to be "tough," while those of the Beaverkill are sometimes called "easy." Similar comparisons are made about waters across the U.S. and abroad. Having once lived near the Batten Kill, however, I maintain there's nothing extraordinary about its trout. They're no tougher certainly than upper Delaware River rainbows and browns, or the legendary fish of Pennsylvania's Letort. Some anglers have a terrible time with them, however, essentially because the trout are wild, and the anglers just don't understand them. *Wild trout are virtually always unpredictable.* They simply refuse to play by our rules.

The opposite holds true of hatchery fish. While wild trout survive only by contending with raw nature from birth onward, man has chosen to shelter hatchery fish from that struggle, thus substantially increasing the odds for survival from birth to maturity. By so doing, however, he inalterably disrupts nature's program of selection, insuring that his charges are institutionalized or patterned to accommodate his plans for them. We know that almost any animal, no matter how primitive, reacts to certain positive stimuli if they are repeated often enough. Birds talk. Dogs do all manner of undignified tricks. My father had two full-grown alligators behind his winter home that swam to him anticipating food when he clapped his hands. Free from predators unless a cat sneaks in, and regimented by the controlled environment, hatchery trout are fed at appointed hours, usually in tune with popular fishing periods, until they are patterned (1) to accept man, and

(2) to feed *en masse* when food is readily available, as during hatches. It's little wonder, then, that hatchery personnel refer to stockers as "catchable trout," because, once patterned, the trout's behavior seldom changes radically in the wild, no matter how far removed in time from a hatchery environment. To paraphrase the old saw, therefore, *you can take the trout out of the hatchery, but you can't take the hatchery out of the trout.*

Predictability, then, generally makes hatchery trout easier to take than wild ones. So, fish them accordingly. On stocked waters, for instance, smart anglers pinpoint major aquatic and terrestrial insect hatches, because hatchery fish feed dependably during them. Wild trout may just ignore them. The mass of Beaverkill browns, for example, seldom fails to react to the river's renowned springtime hatches, while I can testify to Delaware River fish passing up a carpet of flies at the very same hour of the very same day. Similarly, stockers feed uniformly up and down river, even as wild trout may feed ravenously on one pool and ignore flies on another. We'll understand these contradictions, perhaps, only when we come back as fish. In the meantime, however, it's reassuring to me to find that Mother Nature still keeps things most interesting.

Knowing if water is stocked also helps in deciding where to fish. Although cover and feeding lanes are always important, trout are normally well distributed throughout unstocked streams. Because they get less pressure, however, least accessible stretches frequently prove most productive. On stocked streams, by contrast, when hatcheries are short-handed and volunteers hard to find, trout are often dumped from highway bridges or toted only to popular pools near roads. These concentrations of fish seldom wander far during their first season. However, in fall, late winter or spring, depending on species, even hatchery trout flesh out a river by migrating upstream and down. Remote waters, therefore, are dependable for holdover fish, i.e., those which survive more than one season in the wild. Amid mixed populations of stockers and wild trout, I seek wild ones near potential spawning grounds or within a quarter mile of small tributaries which are ideal natu-

Dry fly fishermen who want to take wild trout from stocked waters do well to pay particular attention to stretches near the mouths of small tributary streams, such as this one entering Willowemoc Creek near the author's home. Tributaries act as nurseries for young fish spawned in the wild that drop down into main flows as they approach maturity. Trib mouths also make excellent places to try when waters along main streams are low and warm, since the generally cooler temperatures of these feeders tend to attract trout in times of stress.

ral nurseries and which funnel growing fish into the main stream. On busy waters I've inevitably located the best angling where sport is managed by special regulations, such as "fish for fun." It stands to reason, after all, that creel limits tailored to maintain optimum carrying capacity is insurance of quality fishing for all.

All this shouldn't suggest that wild trout are necessarily smarter than their hatchery-bred cousins; by human standards, predictability, or the lack thereof, doesn't measure intelligence. Perhaps in human terms hatchery fish may actually have more savvy, this stemming from their symbiotic relationship with their keepers. I won't quickly forget catching a wild trout from the Delaware twice in the same day, just as I've caught a Beaverkill stocker more than once during a single outing. Where the two experiences parted company, however, was that I would have been ready to bet the Beaverkill fish would be feeding when I returned to try it.

Any learning about trout by determining their hatchery background is limited to the information outlined above. More precise characteristics must accrue by gathering knowledge of trout populations, regardless of species, and their positions in the ecology of fisheries in which they operate. Briefly quoted are a few common stereotypes about trout species, followed by how I believe such misconceptions break down through experience:

"Rainbow trout jump when hooked." *Not always so when streams in which they fight are shallow and boulder-strewn.*

"Brown trout don't jump but seek obstructions that foul up anglers." *Again untrue, when water is deep, expansive and relatively obstruction free.*

"Big browns don't rise to tiny flies." *Try a size-22 dry on a stream short on small bait fish and large insects.*

"Brook trout hit almost anything." *Show an old rubber boot to one in a feeding rhythm during a hatch.*

"Wilderness trout are reckless." *You've never encountered them with full stomachs, if you think so.*

The litany could fill a volume.

Learning about trout, therefore, which is a prerequisite for learning to fish, ultimately involves learning about the waters they inhabit. "Learning" waters—that is, perceiving them as individual worlds governed by a myriad of physical and biological principles both from within and without—should not be confused with the purely optical act of "reading" waters, a subject covered elsewhere in this volume. Reading waters, in fact, is but a single facet of learning them, although one crucial to the angler on a day-to-day basis.

No two fisheries are entirely alike, and therein lies the rub. It's

Seldom in fly fishing history has a trout stream received the undivided attention from an angler that the famed Letort has from its dean, Charles K. Fox of Carlisle, Pennsylvania. For decades Charlie has studied the behavior of this stream's finicky feeders from benches he set up along its banks, until he has come to know the trout so well, he has even given many of them names. Just moments before this photo was taken, Charlie had pointed out a feeding trout to the author who then proceeded to put the fish down with a "bum pitch," as Charlie would call a poor presentation.

knowing the subtle to dynamic differences between waters that accounts for virtually all local "experts" who appear to be able to talk to trout. These anglers *belong* to their rivers and streams to such a degree that they're likely to know them better than they do their children, perhaps even their spouses. In their fishing, luck is seldom if ever involved, although sometimes you might like to believe otherwise. Be advised, however, that it's *knowledge,* not luck, that grips the rod of each truly expert angler.

There is no short cut to such expertise. Totally mastering a single fishery demands undivided attention. It comes down to choosing one and sticking with it almost exclusively. Frankly, I lack that kind of dedication or discipline. There is too much gypsy in my soul, I guess. Thus, my trout always get a handicap—and I'm not certain it isn't more fun that way. It sure keeps life interesting, anyway. This handicap business, however, can be taken too far, and all that can get you is skunked. It's like a blind man who hopes to decipher *Finnegans Wake:* he'd better know enough to buy it in braille.

The motto of my high school was *Facere et Docere,* Latin for "to do and to teach." Whoever dreamed it up must have had a good feeling for priorities. To *do* is the best way to master most things, and it is certainly the best way to learn trout water. All that writers can realistically hope to *teach* the angler are a few helpful guidelines to follow.

A trout takes advantage of the best its environment offers. Always opportunistic, it develops behavioral characteristics attuned to what its neighborhood provides—water volume, cover, food. Metabolically, for instance, the feeding impulse of trout is keyed to water conditions, the most important of which is temperature. Thanks to Mother Nature, trout require the most food when food is most available. All fishermen should obviously take advantage of those times. For the dry fly fisherman, however, it's critical to recognize that trout are sluggish and reticent to rise during periods of extreme water temperatures, hot or cold, but that they loosen up when water temperatures moderate. Fortunately, nature has worked things out to accommodate these periods to hatches of aquatic and terrestrial insects.

Too many dry fly fishermen, I believe, never look *beneath* the surface of a river or stream. Although the sport is, by definition, played entirely "upstairs," many elements which regulate its quality are determined on the lower stories where trout live. The propensity of trout to rise at a given time requires that floating food be more attractive by virtue of, for instance, abundance, bulk or vulnerability than anything available nearby. The dry fly fisherman must, therefore, probe the dynamics of each fishery to turn the habits of its trout to his best advantage. Considering that trout, like most wild creatures, are innately lazy (the bigger the lazier), that they rise at all sometimes seems to me a minor miracle. Ideal dry fly water would put food only on the surface, giving trout no alternative but to rise or starve.

If you ever locate such a place, please call me. I'll sell my soul, gypsy and all . . . and cheap.

CHAPTER TWO

~~~~~~

Rivers and Streams

WITH TYPICAL AMERICAN AFFINITY for statistics, I briefly had a mind to compute how many miles of flowing trout water there are in this country. In no time, however, through my study window I spotted swallows working over the Willowemoc, and so the embryonic notes joined other momentary lapses into academics in a full file entitled *Called on Account of Hatch* (*Not to Be Continued*). Minutes later, with rod in hand, I waded into the stream whistling, "Love the One You're With." Can't say the information gaps which result from preferring fishing to figures have cost me a single trout, either.

Although I'd never wowed 'em at cocktail parties, I knew quite enough about the sum of trout water to serve me as an angler without dragging out a calculator. There is more of it in America than battalions of fishermen could cover in a lifetime wearing jet-propelled waders—about 17,000 miles of rivers and streams in

New York State alone. Most stirring, though, seems a claim shared by professional fishery managers across the nation that ninety percent of anglers fish but ten percent of available waters *with regularity*. Allowing the managers a one hundred percent margin for error (the minimum I recommend for any official estimate), those who seek "the quiet places" to tangle their backcasts may still have eighty percent of America's trout water to choose from on any given day—barring a case of *irregularity*.

Choice of fisheries is normally a question of personal preference, although many anglers must concentrate only on waters close to home. For purposes of general discussion, I sort all moving trout water into two purely subjective classifications—rivers and streams—regardless of their official designations. (I wonder, frankly, if our forebears weren't a tad prone to hyperbole when tagging waters near their homes. "River" was big in their lexicon and ended up attached to an awful lot of trickles. Perhaps out of respect, however, it's best to assume our ancestors all moved in during spring runoff.)

As I see trout water, if I can't comfortably cast across it, it's a *river*. If I can, it's a *stream*. Waters requiring chest waders are apt to be rivers. Chest waders look ridiculous on many streams. If "stream" sounds like British understatement, *please* call it a "river." When questions about "the river" get you quizzical looks, try "stream." Rivers are big water; streams, smaller, small and smallest water. I always lump *creeks, brooks, kills, rills* and *runs,* incidentally, as streams, unless instructed otherwise by my host or a Neanderthal toting a two-bladed axe. What's in a name, anyhow? Trout couldn't care less.

I admit preference for big water—rivers, the bigger the better—although I've learned through the years that each fishery, big or small, presents the dry fly fisherman with unique challenges. If it's true that *a trout's a trout* when viewed in the abstract and thus detached from its environment, then those material differences which drive even the most competent angler crazy throughout his life must derive from eccentricities peculiar to the water the trout inhabits.

Danish angling writer Preben Torp Jacobsen makes a long cast to a rising trout on the upper-main-stem Delaware near the author's home. When he first sighted the big Delaware, Preben sounded somewhat awed as he said: "Now, that is a river."

Hip boots were all that television broadcaster Curt Gowdy needed to wear to keep dry while fishing this stream in his native Wyoming. Soon after this photo was snapped, Curt hooked a fine brown that was feeding tight to the opposite bank.

Each river and stream is as different from the rest as human fingerprints or snowflakes. No angler can presume to know one entirely. There are, in fact, no two pools, riffles or currents exactly alike, and it seems axiomatic that as you become convinced you're master of one, nature springs new and ingenious wrinkles—the fallen tree, a gravel bar, spate or dry spell—to humble you, like sudden caprice from a trusted lover. The successful angler, therefore, I believe, must have an incurable, if joyful, case of masochism.

I don't want omniscience about trout water, because it would translate into knowing *too much* about trout. The mystery gone, fly fishing would be like watching television reruns—a colossal bore. Ultimately, a chance to fail is altogether as essential to angling pleasure as the promise of success.

Only once have I encountered a river where taking trout was just *too easy* to be fun. The fish wouldn't refuse a dry fly regardless of pattern or presentation. Twenty-one took consecutive casts. I was like the reckless drinker on New Year's Eve, at first liberated, perhaps giddy, then irritable and sullen, going through the motions of consciousness. Each night I'd tell Kris, "A little bit of this goes a long way." She agreed.

Finally, though, something occurred that really made the trip. A hidden force, or complex of forces, with authority as old as the river itself, told the trout to quit. It was as if, magically, there wasn't a fish in the river. I couldn't buy one. I won't try to explain what happened and perhaps it would be better not to even if I could. Suffice to report that I've loved trout fishing all the more from that day to this because I'd been taught a lesson I'll never forget: the reward of fishing dry flies is more in the water than the fish.

It's possible, indeed fashionable today, to become obsessed with the biology of trout streams. While much of the scientific data stored up may be incidental to catching fish, I will say this: If a person is determined to study something, better trout water than, for instance, aquatic entomology, or even the fish themselves.

Thorough knowledge of stream ecology peaks awareness of water quality among other properties paramount to trout survival. Healthy trout unquestionably provide the best sport, and therefore, the contemporary fly fisherman has little choice, I believe, but to accept a conservationist's role, if only for self-interest.

It might be swell to pigeonhole trout water into neat compartments, if that weren't an impossible task. The problem must be viewed, however, as a mixed blessing, since it springs from the remarkable diversity of waters across the land, ranging from tea-colored streams wandering between spruce-lined ponds in Maine, to brawling rivers that rush to sea fed by eternal snows on western mountainsides. No comparable diversity exists within the trout's ancestral or adopted range, which in great measure is why I maintain that well-traveled American fly fishermen are the most accomplished practitioners of the sport on earth.

Although imperfect, a last resort for probing general characteristics of rivers and streams to examine their influence on resident trout is to dress them in two unavoidably baggy suits: (1) those originating and largely maintained by subterranean water, and (2) those sustained primarily by surface water, including rainfall, snow runoff, and spillage from natural and manmade ponds and lakes. (I refuse to string along with popular "limestone-freestone" labels which, my limited knowledge of linguistics tells me, do nothing more, and sometimes less, than beg their definitions.)

The former group, much the smaller, encompasses hundreds of so-called *spring creeks* of underground origin, including many renowned names like the Au Sable of Michigan, California's Fall River, and the Gibbon and Firehole rivers of Wyoming, as well as generous overflows from limestone faults such as Pennsylvania's Letort, New York's Spring Creek, the Castalia Club of Ohio, and Idaho's Silver Creek. The world's largest spring creek is, in fact, a "limestoner," Henry's Fork of the Snake River, located in eastern Idaho. Also worth mention are thousands of small seepages that hold trout and serve for spawning and as nurseries for immature fish.

Silver Creek, which slithers through Idaho ranch land, is a classic example of a big river that originates and is maintained largely with subterranean water. Note the S curves and almost unbroken flow that are typical of so-called spring creeks. Extremely rich, the river supports an almost unbelievable number of rainbow trout that regularly feed on the surface.

The latter group, by contrast, represents fisheries many reckon look most like *classic trout streams,* from wee mountain brooks to rugged rivers that drain vast and varied watersheds at latitudes and altitudes hospitable to one or more species. Notable among these are Maine's Kennebec and Penobscot rivers, the Beaverkill and Ausable of New York, Vermont's Lemoille, the Brodheads of Pennsylvania, Maryland's Big Hunting Creek, the Brule of Minnesota, Colorado's Frying Pan and Roaring Fork, the Yellowstone of Montana, New Mexico's Rio Grande, the McCloud of Califor-

The famed west branch of the Ausable River in New York's Adirondack Mountains drains a vast and beautiful watershed, including the slopes that hosted the 1980 winter Olympics. A typical surface water fishery: note its turbulence and preponderance of pocket water. Despite heavy fishing pressure during peak periods, the Ausable remains one of the most challenging brown and rainbow dry fly fisheries in the East.

nia, and Oregon's spectacular Deschutes. Some impressive waters in this category, called tailwater fisheries, result from releases below manmade dams. Important examples include the Delaware River along the New York–Pennsylvania border, the White River of Arkansas, Arizona's Colorado River in Grand Canyon National Park, and the San Juan River below Navajo Dam, New Mexico. In many instances tailwaters provide excellent angling where no trout existed before dams were built, while in others cold water released downstream has vastly improved marginal trout water.

The big Delaware, I know so well, is a sterling case in point.

Lest things appear too orderly, I'd best note that many fine fisheries fit neither suit comfortably. Influenced equally by underground and surface water, some assimilate significant characteristics of both. Vermont's Batten Kill is a good example. Another is the majestic Madison of northwestern Wyoming and southern Montana. It emerges from mingling flows of the Firehole and Gibbon rivers, both spring creeks, and the Gardiner River, fed by snow melt from the looming Rockies. Other streams, such as New Jersey's Musconetcong (Musky) River and the Bois Brule of Wisconsin, rise as spring creeks but soon take on enough surface water to alter their characters entirely. The reverse also occurs. Pennsylvania's Yellow Breeches, for instance, begins as a small surface-water stream into which abundant springs flow from lowland limestone formations. Thus, popular downstream stretches create the impression of a classic spring creek.

Water supply is singularly important to all life, including trout, that inhabits a river or stream. Simply put, fertility—the quantity of dissolved nutrients—dictates a fishery's food chain, while its water source governs flow and temperature. The ideal fishery, therefore, is one rich enough to promote plentiful food for each link in the chain through a course of stable water flow that maintains temperatures within the range at which trout tend to be most hungry.

Bearing in mind that nature never designs without exception, it lies within accurate limits, I believe, to rate spring creeks, especially limestoners, as our richest trout waters. Alkalinity, or the hardness that raises hell with soap suds, engenders within spring creeks prolific organic communities, from primitive plant and animal plankton to sophisticated aquatic vegetation—and, of course, fish. Unless polluted by, for instance, careless agricultural practices, a fertile spring creek teems with insect larvae, served up as hatches in generous courses according to a timetable ordered by the seasons.

Because their function isn't drainage, except perhaps during brief periods each year, spring creeks require only gentle gradient, thus minimizing velocity and visible current. A spring creek is often said to meander, snaking through virtually flat country and appearing to head for no place in particular. And since it's prone to wind back on itself, anglers may find several miles of fishing within a single tape-measure mile. Rich water, plentiful alluvium deposited over centuries, and the character of the flow, frame an environment ideal for aquatic vegetation—elodea and watercress, among other species. The vegetation, in turn, fosters copious animal life, particularly crustaceans such as the scud, snail, crayfish and sowbug. By the process of photosynthesis, vegetation also manufactures oxygen, vital to all a stream's living things. So bountiful is a healthy spring creek, in fact, that its trout population per acre of water, and the annual growth of that strain or strains, may be nothing short of stunning compared to typical surface water rivers and streams.

Spring creeks sacrifice little life to the devilry of unstable water conditions. While levels of surface water rivers and streams may fluctuate dramatically with the vagaries of weather, underground supplies generally remain constant, making damaging spates a rarity and deadly low water virtually unheard of. In fact, it's a curious mark of spring creeks that they can actually appear fullest during the driest times of year as vegetation bloom displaces voluminous quantities of water which are pushed outward toward the banks. Throughout the season, then, eggs deposited by aquatic insects, including many species of mayfly, are rarely flushed from a fishery by heavy rains or left to parch in dry spells. Therefore the number of immature insects—like mayfly nymphs—that survive to emerge as duns, later to transform to spinners, may represent a remarkable percentage of the eggs deposited by parents, insuring profuse hatches that cause surface feeding to be integral to most trout's habits, no matter how generous alternate underwater sources of food happen to be.

Since subterranean water is unaffected by external conditions, another constancy of spring creeks is likely to be temperature. An

Whether the setting is stark, as in this picture, or lush, as in the spring and summer, the Letort, a limestoner in Pennsylvania's Cumberland Valley, can always be depended on for a fine day's fishing. Upstream springs insure ample water to maintain levels year round and relatively stable water temperatures to keep the fish feeding, even when the air temperature becomes very hot or very cold.

underground reservoir should be perceived as much like a cave or cellar, warmer than the atmosphere in winter and cooler in summer, and thus an ideal job of climate control. Although exact temperatures may vary somewhat from region to region, when a given spring suddenly sallies forth to form or feed a stream, its temperature will remain dependably constant despite the season. Pennsylvania's Letort, for instance, surfaces at about fifty-five degrees Fahrenheit year-round. At a point a couple of miles below its source I've taken water readings in the high forties and low fifties on winter's coldest days. (Three Letort browns took my size sixteen Adams one afternoon, although the air registered just fourteen degrees.) However, at the same point on the stream my water thermometer has reflected temperatures only in the low- to mid-sixties on the hottest summer days. Much better circumstances for trout and, therefore, for fly fishermen, couldn't be rigged, not even by Nature.

Temperature, perhaps more than any factor including insect abundance, governs "the breaks" of dry fly fishing. Water too cold or too warm makes a trout logey and unlikely to stir, as the fish's depressed metabolic rate calls for little or no food, sometimes over extended periods. I've seen thick hatches on chilly waters go untouched by a single trout except for a few unfortunate flies washed into little eddies near the banks where revolving water is warmed by the sun. Conversely, sparse hatches are reacted to aggressively throughout the length and breadth of a stream when water temperatures reach levels more suitable to trout feeding. Thus when a dry fly fisherman encounters trout of any species exhibiting apparently extraordinary behavior, regardless of season, he'll seldom go wrong to use a thermometer to help determine the cause.

The merits of spring creeks aside, surface water rivers and streams remain the favored haunts of most American dry fly fishermen, including yours truly. A contributing factor is, of course, that in the U.S. they outnumber those of underground origin by hundreds-to-one. But there's more to it than that. What surface water streams may lack in richness or predictability, as a rule they make up for in spice and diversity. Tamed only at enormous cost, these irrepressible natural drainage systems disdain all obstacles to get where they are going. Surplus water running off the land tumbles, falls, cuts through narrows and swirls around rocks and boulders, digging deep holes beneath them, eroding and depositing. In minutes it can drop a tree that took a century to grow. It makes music, as if carrying a million bells. It glides. It even seems almost to stop at times to drink sunshine—but seldom for long. Surface-water rivers and streams are indomitable living things. You can perceive in them character and gusto and spiritual determination. They will thrill you one day, break your heart the next. Only a person without a snitch of the romantic could fail to love them. They are the soul of trout fishing.

Except for some tailwater fisheries which can be dependably managed by pushing a button or turning a wheel, the quality of life in surface-water rivers and streams is a function of varying external conditions. Most significant is certainly weather, and in particular precipitation, its sum and distribution. Few anglers are spared occasional visits to favorite streams when they're running too high or too low. Unfortunately, that's part of the game. Through decades of pounding the waters of my native East, I remember few seasons I'd call *ideal,* either for fish or fishermen. The ideal requires moderate winter snowfall and little sub-zero weather, a spring season of warm days and chilly nights and only gentle rains, and a cool, wet summer followed by plentiful autumn rainfall—a tall order, indeed. Generally we settle for less, recalling the best years with a kind of veneration, consoling each other after the worst. A capacity to make bad years better, incidentally, is one mark of an accomplished fly fisherman.

While trout born to spring creeks may have it pretty good, life for those inhabiting surface-water rivers and streams is seldom easy, a fact frequently overlooked by anglers. Lean fertility may inhibit a food chain, for instance, thus limiting the effective carrying capacity of trout per acre of water. It would be a rare steep mountain stream, twenty feet wide, that held trout so numerous or large as one of comparable size fed by rich springs. Usually pollution isn't the problem, as fishermen like to think. Food is the key. When too many trout are suddenly introduced to such a stream—the result, perhaps, of misguided management principles—nature eventually compensates in one of several ways: (1) a stable population of runts, (2) universal malnutrition, or (3) mortality to a level in line with the stream's potential to provide at the time. Of the alternatives, the third is unquestionably most desirable. All too often, however, we discover lovely little streams hosting trout with big heads and skinny bodies, or, worst of all and hardest to correct, unchecked populations of sexually mature fish barely four inches long. This doesn't argue that surface-water streams make lousy trout habitat, because quite the contrary is normally true. It does, however, illustrate that the do-or-die job of trout adaptation requires ready adjustment to tricky though inevitable changes, about which neither fish nor angler has anything to say.

Water running off the land, of course, isn't necessarily inhospitable for trout. Were it so, the earth would have few trout streams. Despite all uncertainties between "boom" and "bust," vast regions throughout the fish's range depend almost entirely on drainage from highland to lowland for cold water, fertile or not, and I find it fascinating how remarkably nature compensates for deficiencies that might otherwise imperil trout survival. Mankind, of course, although frequently a despoiler, can be one of nature's most useful and reliable tools for maintaining and enhancing the world of trout.

Important examples of compensation are found in stream structure and adaptation to it by trout and insect alike as flows fluctuate. Adequate oxygen for fish and insect larvae is absorbed into a stream by agitation as water churns over large and small rock scattered on the stream bed. The effect of a waterfall upon a stream, for instance, isn't unlike that of a compressor pumping air into an aquarium. Loose stone also provides cover and shade. Evolution has taught some aquatic insects to seek safety against receding water levels in deeper channels, while others burrow into sand or silt which holds sufficient moisture to sustain life except, perhaps, during the most severe drought. Nor is it sheer coincidence that the flies that emerge in traditional low water periods will be the season's smallest, requiring the minimum amount of water to survive the larval stage.

Whenever changes occur on surface-water rivers and streams, it seems, something happens to minimize the crisis. No fishery, large or small, is exempt from this process of cause-and-effect, and the perceptive angler does his best always to stay current. Observation and experience teaches that each change, no matter how subtle, is reflected to some degree in subsequent trout behavior. For instance, during protracted dry spells when waters drop and aquatic insects suffer, dry fly fishermen are wise to use terrestrial insect imitations—grasshoppers, beetles, crickets and ants—representing species that flourish under such conditions. Similarly, when pollution takes its inevitable toll on some fragile mayfly species, the pragmatist immediately does two things, although not necessarily in this order. First, he digs into fly boxes for patterns to represent more tolerant caddis flies that are likely to proliferate to fill the void, and second, he organizes with fellow fishermen to curb the source of the destructive pollution.

CHAPTER THREE

~~~~~~~~~~~~~~~~~~~~~~~~~~~~~~~~~~~~~~~

The Book on Water

WHEN YOU LOOK AT FLOWING WATER, what does it tell you? If you think you can answer that question in few words, you probably can't *read water*. Simple as that. Don't "take the bridge," though; you're not alone. In a couple of decades of dry fly fishing, I haven't met two-dozen anglers who read water well. Few even seem to recognize its full significance, although reading water is a must to effectively attack rivers or streams. Without the technique you're working blind.

The reading water concept, as it should be understood, recalls a yarn about Emily Dickinson, a brilliant nineteenth-century American poet. Miss Dickinson lived with a sister in Massachusetts. Returning home one wintry evening, Emily discovered she'd forgotten her key and so sought to rouse the household. When her sister finally unlatched the door, she found Emily covered from head to toe with snow. "Gracious," exclaimed the sister. "What happened?"

"I fell in the snowbank," Emily answered evenly, pointing to drifts outside the fence.

"But didn't you *see* it?" cried her sister.

"I *saw* it, yes," replied Emily, brushing by and into the house. "The trouble was I didn't *perceive* it."

Reading water, it so happens, isn't a simple matter of recognizing fixtures, such as riffles and pools, along a stretch, although that's essential to it. It requires interpreting characteristics and conditions and their positive or negative potential for fish and fishermen. At issue, then, *isn't reading at all, but analyzing what is read.* Besides vigilance, it demands curiosity, plenty of patience, imagination, judgment, and a liberal quota of common sense. Ultimately, it's a *discipline* the angler better know at the outset he won't master overnight.

Without subjecting readers to a lot of technical bilge about molecular structure and the like—except to say that water has greater density than air, for instance, and less than sand or stone—it should be noted first that there's no such thing as a river or stream that stands still in its natural state. Each one, by definition, from source (beginning) to mouth (end), is composed of water moving over, under, between, around and through an infinite variety of the physical properties that constitute a riverbed or streambed. The movement of the water is called its *flow,* and this flow, governed by and reacting to all things it encounters along its way, provides the medium for an angler to analyze a fishery.

Fishermen seldom have the opportunity to poke around a pool, unless they're willing to spook its trout. Rivers and streams aren't built like fish tanks (thank heavens), nor are there many vantages, such as bridges or high banks, that command more than limited overview, even when the sun is right. Thus the clearest streams hide most secrets from novice and expert alike, leaving no alternative but to size up what we can't see below the surface as it's reflected in the behavior of the flow on top.

Figure 1 on page 33 is a short stretch of a hypothetical surface water stream from which the illustrator has kindly drawn off most

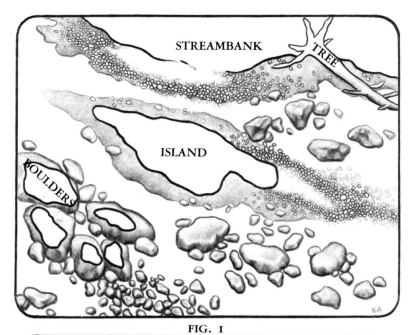

FIG. 1

FIG. 2

of the water. Note that the flow from bottom to top would be altered by many objects scattered about the scene if the water remained—small stones and rocks, a bank, some boulders, a downed tree and a small island.

Responding to gravity, the water would be pulled along at a speed known as *velocity*. Because water has greater density than air, on one hand it would fill all the voids along its course, such as the spaces beneath rocks and boulders, depressions in the bottom, and the gap between the submerged tree and the streambed. On the other hand, the water would be displaced by all articles of greater density than itself, including the rocks, boulders and tree, thus diverting the direction of flow over, under and around them. With each flow diversion, in turn, whether to fill a hollow or bypass an obstacle, currents would be created that would shift temporarily, stabilizing only when the effects of modifying forces subsided.

A miracle of moving water is that each influence on flow from the streambed upward is telegraphed to the surface. The greater the modification of flow below, the more dramatic its reflection on top. Viewed through the practiced eye, therefore, a stream's surface becomes a mosaic revealing the character of virtually all underwater conditions. The surface of the stretch of hypothetical stream shown in Figure 1, then, would appear as in Figure 2.

Several qualities define the surface picture, among them water velocity, depth and the dimensions of forces modifying the flow. For example, when slow-moving water approaches a boulder, the water can be expected to slide gently by, thus telegraphing only a minor flow adjustment to the surface. Increase water velocity or the size of the boulder and the magnitude of surface disturbance increases accordingly. Greater depth, however, dictates greater vertical distance through which the message must be telegraphed, thus diminishing its impact on the surface when it finally gets there. So, while a stone the size of your fist may generate considerable surface commotion in six inches of water, the same stone six feet down should cause no mark at all on top. Similarly, nobody could miss spotting the impact on water six feet deep where it rushed by a rock the size of a station wagon. Yet, only experienced observers might detect the same rock at a similar depth were the water barely crawling along.

The potential for variation seems infinite, especially when reinforced by the fact that fisheries change from season to season, occasionally to a degree that you won't recognize a favorite stretch from one season to the next. The changes keep life interesting, although often they wash out fishing, buggering trout cover or eroding streambanks beyond the capacity of water supplies to maintain adequate flows during dry spells. Changes are frequently subtle, however, altering perhaps only feeding lanes, so that untrained anglers are caught casting where trout *were,* not where they *are.* Or maybe shifted currents frustrate realistic presentation of their flies. Skilled fishermen, by contrast, adapt to changes easily, thus avoiding energy wastage on unproductive water.

A nifty way to study habitat is to give a real dry streambed a good going over. Mid-summer is normally the time that they're easy to find. Don't worry about size, since both the smallest stream and biggest river have enough in common to make the exercise worthwhile. A tiny brook, in fact, is often the perfect microcosm of a great river, and is certainly a whole lot simpler to work with. Once one is chosen, you might as well stay home as stick to the banks, though. To learn all a dry stream will teach about where trout live, eat, hide and fight when hooked, getting into it, like a prospector sniffing for gold, is the only way.

Lacking even one drop of water, for instance, you can ascertain the direction of flow by standing midstream and looking right and left to find which is uphill. Water always travels from the uphill direction toward you at a speed determined by the angle of incline, or *gradient,* as scientists call it. To verify your conclusion, note how the water has worn streambed stones, leaving them smoothest on upstream surfaces.

Now check the banks. Are they undercut? If so, grab a stick

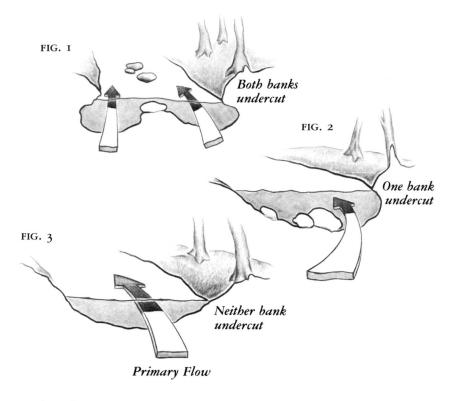

FIG. 1

*Both banks
undercut*

FIG. 2

*One bank
undercut*

FIG. 3

*Neither bank
undercut*

Primary Flow

and probe their recesses. You'll find many tailor-made to hide trout. Whether one or both are undercut, or, in fact, neither are, discloses streambed *slope*. That is crucial information because trout tend to favor the zone of primary flow, except perhaps during periods of extremely heavy water (see illustrations). Two undercut banks indicate either unbroken water or a stretch divided by midstream high spots, most often gravel bars. (Fig. 1) Such double slopes are common. One undercut bank reflects either the outside of a bend or a straightaway through which the bottom slopes decidedly toward that bank. (Fig. 2) When neither bank is undercut, the bottom will be found to slope inboard toward midstream—the most prevalent situation, incidentally, on many Catskill streams. (Fig. 3) Whatever the slope, however, anglers should anticipate most trout on the down side except during peri-

36

odic hatches and spinner falls when they'll slide from deep water onto shallows for easy pickings.

Next, examine the streambed's physical characteristics, including distribution of stone. Some rocks, you'll notice, would break the surface were there water, while others would remain submerged. Visualize how each might deflect flow to form a myriad of currents requiring that the fisherman compensate to insure a dragless drift of his dry fly. Inspecting the stones, you'll find scores of crevices at their bases, dug by years of water flow. Many, you'll discover, would make ideal trout hideouts. It's also fun to speculate which spots might be claimed by the largest fish, bearing in mind the criteria of optimum cover and easy access to the most profitable feeding stations. Trout, like all territorial predators, establish pecking orders based on strength and ferocity.

Also scrutinize anything left along the stretch in high water—like, for instance, a log wedged between two boulders. Note that debris gathers on the log to form a kind of leanto under which trout could rest unobserved. Ponder your best location to deter hooked fish from running to this and the other snags that are certain to be scattered about. Nor should you ignore natural dams where small stones have lodged against big ones to provide a gamut of holding water from deep pools to plump pockets. In the end you'll realize your favorite stream would look very much like the dry stretch, were all its water to disappear.

Finally, standing on a bank, survey the overall scene. You should be able to imagine how the stretch would appear when its water flows high, moderate and low. It's a good idea, indeed, to return to check your images against the real thing. You'll be a more knowledgeable angler for the time you spend simply looking and learning.

Nowadays, it seems, life is rife with nomenclatures, and there's no reason to suppose fly fishing should be exempt. Our sport, for that matter, may just be the most over-nomenclatured of them all, a dubious distinction. Doubters might like to consider a single *fly pattern*. At very least it has a *tail, body, wings, hackle* and *head,* not

to mention the probability of a *tag, tip, butt, rib, cheeks* and *topping.*
Similarly, what's a *rod* of *bamboo, graphite* or *glass* without a *screw-lock reel seat, cigar-shaped cork grip, butt and tip sections, a fly keeper, male and female ferrules, a ceramic stripping guide, stainless snakes* and, of course, a *tip-top?* You schlepp it around in an *aluminum case* containing a *poplin bag* containing the *extra tip.* Remembering everything would guarantee master's points in Scrabble. Yet, no-where have I found a comprehensive nomenclature of a *trout stream,* although of the sport's many nomenclatures, it would be most useful. Given one, when somebody tried to tell you precisely where he caught and released a big one, you might just have some inkling as to what he was talking about. Or, wouldn't it be ter-rific to be able to accurately communicate your analysis of a piece of water? You bet.

So, while I loathe nomenclatures no less than I have since I met the M-14 rifle, dedication dictates I now add one more. Portrayed in the illustrations on pages 40 and 41 is a "model" trout fishery with a nomenclature of its component parts.

There's nothing new about many of the names compiled for the illustration. A *pool* has been called a pool as long as sport fishing has existed. Other names are regional, yet adapt well to universal fishing situations. A *sweeper,* for example, has for generations de-scribed a fallen tree jutting into a midwestern stream. Some names, including *rip-rap* and *deflector,* were borrowed from stream-improvement jargon, while others, such as *outcropping* and *bedrock,* are standard to geology. Some are derived as extensions of each other, for instance, a *riffle* as water tumbling over relatively few rocks or stones, *riff* as a series of riffles, *rapids* as big riffs through which great volumes of water speed over large rocks and boulders.

Size determines what I call *pebbles, stones, rocks* or *boulders.* Some names I have coined for descriptive writing through the years. A narrow gorge through bedrock, for example, I see as a *gut,* while a fast flow with little surface disturbance is dubbed a *slick.* Water breaking narrowly between two objects I call a *shoot.* A hollow in a gravel bottom is a *depression,* the fore end of it a *lip,* the back side a *hump.* I have also tried to organize names I deemed sloppy when they were used interchangeably. A *bank,* for instance, has vertical distance to water, while land sloping gradually to meet water constitutes a *shore.* A *beach,* by contrast, is a shore below the high-water mark. And so it goes. Mastering this nomenclature should make you a better angler to the extent that it clarifies discussion between you and fellow fishermen, which is a matter of no small concern.

Whether my nomenclature is adopted or not, the reader must be aware that every phenomenon to which I've assigned a name has its effect on trout positioning. Externals, such as *overhanging trees* and *bank grass,* lure fish by dropping terrestrial insects onto the water while providing shade. The tree overhanging a stream today should also be viewed as a prospective *sweeper.* Each flow modification, governed by conditions within a stream and represented by names like *run, slick, side eddy, dead water, stickle, jabble, shoot, riffle, rush, surge, pocket, boil* or *backwash,* appears in a unique form to the trained observer, and it's crucial to know where among them trout are most apt to rest or feed.

For instance, it's fair to expect that a trout will leave a calm *pocket* to intercept flies floating on the surface of a *shoot,* but you wouldn't look for the trout to lie in the shoot's heavy current when not on the prowl. Similarly, trout may wander from *channels, pools* or *pockets* into *side eddies, dead waters* or *shallows* to make fast work of helpless midges, although these regular feeding places lack adequate cover to provide secure homes for the fish. You may find that trout frequent the *belly,* or mid-section, of a pool, run to its *head* when spooked and drop back to its *tail* to eat.

1. RIP-RAP: A man-made structure, usually of logs and stone, covered by fine wire, designed to "hold" a streambank, thus preventing erosion. 2. BANK: Land that drops sharply to a river or stream.

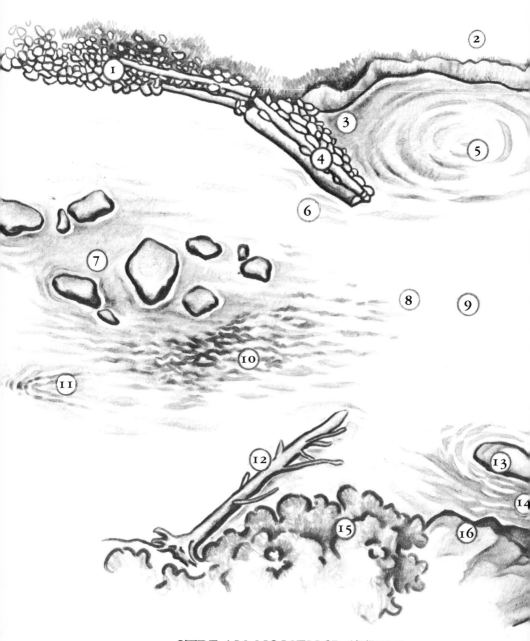

STREAM NOMENCLATURE

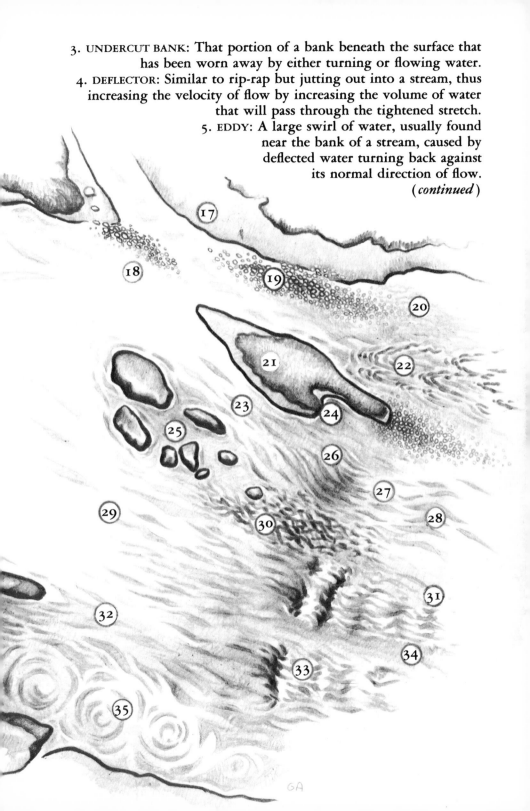

3. UNDERCUT BANK: That portion of a bank beneath the surface that has been worn away by either turning or flowing water.

4. DEFLECTOR: Similar to rip-rap but jutting out into a stream, thus increasing the velocity of flow by increasing the volume of water that will pass through the tightened stretch.

5. EDDY: A large swirl of water, usually found near the bank of a stream, caused by deflected water turning back against its normal direction of flow.

(*continued*)

STREAM NOMENCLATURE (*continued*)

6. SHOOT: Water breaking narrowly between two or more objects.

7. POCKET: A place of relatively calm water, the force of which has been broken by the presence of several boulders or rocks.

8. HEAD OF POOL: The uppermost limit of a pool.

9. BELLY OF POOL: The mid-section of a pool.

10. RIFF: A stretch of water tumbling over rocks or large stones.

11. BOIL OR BACKWASH: That calm spot found in the wake of a single boulder or rock.

12. SWEEPER: A fallen tree jutting at a downstream angle into the flow of a river or stream.

13. BEDROCK: The exposed stone of which the entire area of a stretch of river or stream would be composed if all the material deposited over it were stripped away.

14. GUT: A narrow gorge through bedrock.

15. OVERHANGING TREES: Trees found on many streambanks that lean out over the water.

16. BEDROCK OUTCROPPING: A ledge of bedrock that is so situated that it becomes, in effect, the streambank.

17. SHORE: Land that slopes gradually to meet flowing water.

18. BEACH: A shore below the high-water mark.

19. STICKLE: Sloping small gravel over which a thin veil of water flows.

20. SHALLOWS: A relatively flat stretch of gravel and small stones over which very little water gently flows.

For dry fly fishermen all the above is superfluous when you can't spot rising trout. Seeing rises is even more fundamental to success than skilled presentation of the fly, the latter being meaningless without proper execution of the former. Reading rises, therefore, should be viewed as the epitome of reading water.

It's difficult to speculate how many anglers fail to spot all but the most obvious rises. I suspect, though, that the percentage is greater than widely supposed, so often do fishermen complain that "nothing's doing" on waters appearing to me alive with

21. ISLAND: An area of land surrounded on all sides by the water of a river or stream. Islands are formed by accumulated rock, gravel and silt, frequently held together by the roots of growing plant life.

22. RIFFLE: Water flowing over relatively few rocks or stones.

23. CHANNEL: A rather deep, swift flow of water, frequently found between islands and boulders.

24. DEAD WATER: A spot of slack water protected from the force of flow by the presence of a large mass, such as an island.

25. POCKETS: See number seven.

26. LIP: An accumulation of gravel at the front of a depression.

27. DEPRESSION: A hollowed-out place in a gravel bottom.

28. HUMP: The back side of a depression.

29. SLICK AT TAIL OF POOL: A broad swath of fast-flowing, flat water, usually V-shaped, found at the lower limit of most pools.

30. JABBLE: A slope of uniformly small rocks over which water flows.

31. RUN: Water of uniform depth flowing over rocks large enough to substantially break up the surface picture. A name also given to long stretches of such water.

32. RUSH: A push of water caused by a suddenly increased angle of gradient.

33. SURGES: A series of uniformly broken currents, brought about by swift water pushing over rocks of similar size.

34. TONGUE: A V-shaped, narrow length of flat, swift water, commonly found between stretches of surges or within runs.

35. SIDE EDDIES: A series of small swirls generally encountered at the base of a bank or at the foot of a bedrock ledge.

working trout. While no one can presume powers to make the blind see, it's clear to me that spotting rises is largely an acquired skill, not unlike picking up a fastball at the plate. All that's required is basic knowledge plus lots of practice.

First, you must be savvy to where trout *should* be rising along a stretch. Knowing where to focus attention eliminates distraction, a waste of time and effort. And you must know exactly what you should expect to see, for rises aren't made with cookie cutters. They vary greatly in appearance, depending on water conditions and the types of insects fish are taking (see illustration). In sum, then, spotting rises amounts to focusing and budgeting your attention.

When a trout rises to a fly, its mass displaces water which, in turn, disturbs the surface. To that extent, at least, a trout can be compared to a rock. Surface disturbances created by rising trout are called *rise forms,* the most generally recognized of which is a series of expanding, concentric circles emanating from a central point. (I call that one a *dimple.*) Marks on the surface introduced by rises differ from those resulting from inanimate objects such as rocks, because fish, being living things, add movement to mass which continually varies the consequences when the fish encounter the surface. Movement, in fact, accounts for a surface disturbance in an instant where none existed previously. Further, movement, in the form of *momentum,* determines that a small fish can impart a large rise form, or vice versa. It's fair to say, then, that the nature of a trout's rise form as perceived by an angler is the product of the stream's water velocity as it is impacted by the mass and movement, including momentum, of the fish.

The *Dimple* (**Fig. 1**) is the rise form many anglers associate with trout feeding on the surface, since it is the most common rise form left by fish taking hatching mayfly duns. The *Swirl* (**Fig. 2**), though, is also common during mayfly hatches, particularly on fast-flowing water where trout must move swiftly or chance losing their supper. A swirl, then, may be thought of as an exaggerated dimple. To make a *Splashy Rise* (**Fig. 3**), either some part of or all of a fish's body must clear the surface. The resulting rise form may thus vary greatly from instance to instance, since the exploding trout throws a great deal of water in different directions (1) as the fish leaves the water, and (2) as it returns to the water. Note how difficult it is to perceive the *Sipping Rise* (**Fig. 4**), since the form it leaves behind is nearly imperceptible, particularly on broken water. An angler should train himself to spot these mini-dimple rise forms, however, if he is to take advantage of periods when some trout do much of their feeding.

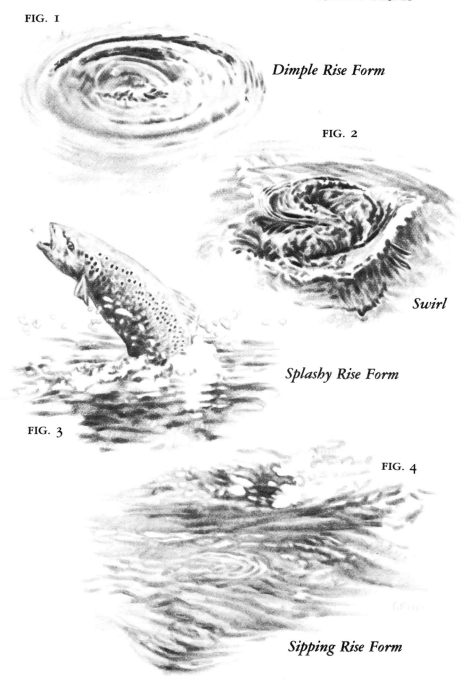

FIG. 1

Dimple Rise Form

FIG. 2

Swirl

Splashy Rise Form

FIG. 3

FIG. 4

Sipping Rise Form

There are as many different rise forms as ways trout can approach the taking of flies. For instance, the mark left by a subtle rise to a spinner or midge won't leave the same mark as one made by a fish breaking water after a fluttering caddis. In cases of subtle or tentative rises, then, it's difficult at best even for experts to accurately gauge the size of fish.

Rises have been given many names—*simple, compound* and *complex,* among others. Memorizing these designations, I'm inclined to feel, serves little purpose. The angler's time is better spent on the water wising up to how rising trout behave under a range of conditions. Splashy rises, for instance, can be expected when substantial energy expenditure becomes the trout's best alternative to losing prey, notably as food is positioned over, rather than on, the surface. Besides fluttering caddis and stoneflies, spinners prior to falls and hovering terrestrials including flying ants, beetles, bees, moths and butterflies are important examples. Splashy rises also result when some mayfly species undergo quick transformations from streambed larvae to airborne duns by propelling themselves to the surface and beyond in frantic runs. The stakes, you see, frequently determine the rise. Ever witness a trout tearing into a large grasshopper as if terrified to blow a one-bite meal? When you have, you won't forget it.

In most cases a feeding trout could teach our best athletes energy conservation. Instinct dictates that it derive maximum nutrition for minimum effort. The splashy rise form, therefore, I view as the result of a *rise of necessity.* The dimple, on the other hand, could be called the consequence of a *rise of luxury.* Trout know, when many insect species float overhead, that flies require time to dry their wings before flight. Most are thus sitting ducks for fish that roll rhythmically to the surface. Dimpling rises are easy to spot because, by traveling from near the bottom, the fish build sufficient momentum to displace considerable water on top. There's also a certain uniformity about the rise forms, to which the average angler can become readily conditioned. Dry fly fishing in my native East centers on periods of these predictable hatches and easily spotted rise forms—a major reason why, I suppose, some eastern anglers fall apart when they don't find dimples on unfamiliar streams.

The sipping rise form is most difficult to spot, particularly on broken water, largely because it represents a trout's *rise of least resistance.* Positioned in a feeding lane just below the surface, the trout arches its body slightly to suck in great numbers of insects, such as the plethora of species we call midges, dead or dying spinners that float spread-eagled, or small terrestrials, including ants incapable of flight. The resulting rise form may amount to nothing more than a pin prick on top, since the rise requires only sufficient momentum to carry the fish's nose a few inches upward through the surface film. Indeed, sometimes trout will inhale insects without entirely breaking surface tension, thus leaving behind only abbreviated wakes or tiny bulges. Yet, it's impossible to be a well-rounded angler without learning to detect even these subtle rise forms, because after years of shortsightedness we now appreciate the importance of minutiae and spent spinners to the trout of many waters. They come about as close to representing a "sure thing" as opportunistic trout ever encounter in the wild. Small wonder, then, that I've seen a fish pass up fine Hendrickson hatches in favor of wee blue quill spinners.

Although experience alone hones the ability to spot rises to maximum sharpness, professional guiding taught me that a valuable short-cut exists in disciplining the eyes to separate the extraordinary from the routine along each stretch surveyed—in other words, to concentrate on things that appear not to fit the natural scheme of water flow. For instance, swirls behind rocks, you'll note, have about them a certain constancy, if only to the degree that they're mechanical responses to diversions over and/or around stationary objects; thus, they inevitably occur downstream of the objects in question. No matter how slight, only momentum from a living thing, a fish, reverses the direction of flow, pushing water upstream against itself. Anytime, therefore, the angler observes water moving counter to its natural course, regardless of how minor the reverse displacement may be, he would do well to make a cast or two, because the odds are good that it's a rise he's spotted—splash, dimple or sip.

~~~~~~

CHAPTER FOUR

You—The Angler

YOU ARE EARTH'S DEADLIEST PREDATOR. Although you lack the grizzly's strength, an eagle's eyesight, the cheetah's speed or a wolf's stamina, nevertheless among all predators you rank the most formidable. You evoke fear in all potent hunters, and those that dare stand to fight are inevitably destroyed, if not by you personally, then by others of you who follow. Trophy rooms testify to your efficiency.

While few contemporary Americans require flesh of prey to survive, fishing with rod and reel, it should be understood, derives from the predatory instinct. What we call *sport,* although symbolic now perhaps, is in fact a manifestation of essential man, predating even the urge to till the soil. It fills a need most of us may never fully fathom, yet to which we are quite correct to assign considerable significance. For each time we cast a fly, flushed with anticipation, we reinvest in our origins. And with each success we reconfirm our place at the head of the world's predatory order, whether or not in the end we kill the catch.

To understand the roots of angling and how those roots anchor our position among predators is, I believe, fundamental to becoming accomplished trout fishermen. In fact, fly fishing may supply the perfect metaphor for man's prosperity despite weakness, because the sport successfully reconciles limited physical strength and dexterity with those unique qualities that separate us from other living things—*intellect and reason.* You, then, the angler—an entity of body and mind, the more homogenized the better—are your own most important piece of fishing gear.

Generations of outdoor writers, I believe, have failed to impress readers with the importance of physical and intellectual conditioning. In particular, during the last twenty years a deceptive notion has been broadcast: that to load up with enough stuff, to spend enough money on tackle, will somehow make a person a better fisherman. While I have no evidence of conspiracy, such thinking has certainly done wonders for the marketplace. However, I feel that its influence has been destructive. *To look the part of an angler isn't to be an angler.* Not that inadequate equipment doesn't inhibit performance—of course it does. But, given the extremes, it is decidedly more desirable to fish poor tackle well than to fish good tackle badly. *There's no way to substitute technology for technique.*

Some years ago a salesman for a major tackle firm visited Roscoe, and during an extended powwow asked that I show him the Willowemoc. Could he ever flawlessly wed the subtleties of aquatic entomology to the principles of engineering? Openly impressed, I couldn't wait to get to the water, hoping to share his expertise. Suited up, he had it all. From poplin hat to felt soles, he was a page from the company catalogue, including the finest rod crafted of Tonkin cane. Beside him I felt like Charlie Chaplin, the little tramp. On the water, though, this guy was something else. To this day I've witnessed nothing to compare with his thrashing around as he beat that poor river to a froth. Needless to say, he didn't raise a fish. I was left awestruck, as much by his apparent immunity to embarrassment as by his incredible performance. Never since have I been dazzled by anybody's mouthwork—not that I don't meet my share of "instant experts" each season who give it their best shot.

Lest a misconception be conveyed, before proceeding further I want to assure the reader that in the overall scheme of things I ascribe no mighty significance to the level of competence each angler attains. Governments don't fall, after all, for want of a trout. That the angler enjoys each outing fully is the substance of the sport, as I view it. However, when an angler decides to step beyond his personal harmless pleasure and presumes to teach others to whom accomplishment may be of ultimate importance, then he'd better know his business thoroughly or be prepared to accept the label "fraud." Unfortunately, there are too many such frauds around.

Because many anglers don't consider, or vastly underrate, the value of mental and physical sharpness, I'm prone to analogies between fly fishing and baseball. Like baseball, fly fishing for trout is *a game of inches.* Presenting a dry a tad off a trout's feeding lane becomes the fly casting equivalent to topping the ball, which usually results in a grounder. Although the fish may chase the fly, perhaps even take it, to hook a trout after a poor cast is like getting a base on an infielder's error. A good ballplayer counts on hits, not errors, to stay in the majors. Similarly, the angler's best hope for consistency is an accurate presentation every time. It's tough, but you must, therefore, summon adequate objectivity to discriminate between good casts and bad ones or suffer the consequence of fewer fish. Another example stems from the compulsion of some dry fly fishermen to strike trout too early or too late, as when infielders blow routine plays by beginning to throw before controlling the ball or letting the ball play them. Striking, just like presenting the fly, requires meticulous timing that only practice—spring training, so to speak—will perfect.

I'm a Pete Rose fan, because he's proven how well a guy of limited natural ability can play the game when he gives it everything. Rose speaks candidly about his athletic deficiencies and how he compensates for them. Self-awareness, then, has carried "Charlie Hustle" to the top of his profession. It's a quality that will never fail a determined angler, either.

Unlike baseball, fly fishing is the ideal lifetime hobby. Barring debilitating illness, retirement should never cross our minds. (I intend to be toted off the water at 106.) To imagine we'll be as chipper after a full day of hard fishing at age eighty as we were at twenty-one, however, is fancy. For better at first, but finally for worse, change is an unalterable fact of life. By the time worse comes to worst, though, canny anglers have learned to cover. It's no miracle that a host of top dry fly fishermen are so-called "old-timers."

It's helpful, I think, to regard the body as a sophisticated fishing machine, every one versatile but unique. Although universally composed of the same parts, nature interprets the specifications differently for each, thus turning out as many potential performance variables as there are anglers. A tiny minority, of course, are near perfect designs—amalgams of physical and psychological characteristics ideal for catching trout. Such specimens make fly fishing look almost too easy, because for them it *is* easier than for the rest of us. Like great writers, actors or athletes, they are unusually talented, possessed of special qualities that cannot be taught. Even their gifts, however, must be enriched with disciplined conditioning, or only the talented underachiever emerges. To master fly fishing, then, requires some work from everyone. Talent alone never carried the superlative angler.

Every angler should be aware of the characteristics that comprise the best "fishing machine," although few of us are lucky enough to enjoy many of them. Finding yourself lacking in several areas, don't despair, since there are virtually none for which you can't satisfactorily compensate. (Nobody knows that better than I: if deficiencies were cause for depression, I'd be an awful mess.)

First, examples of the physical:

Height facilitates deep wading and optimum vantage over long distances. *Agility, good balance* and *weight* assist the wader, particularly in heavy current. *Strength,* notably of forearm and wrist, sustains the caster, while *stamina* facilitates full days of fishing. A sense of *rhythm* and *timing* is also basic to casting. *Keen eyes* that aren't easily strained by glare are of obvious benefit; but more crucial still are acute *depth perception* for precise fly presentation and *accurate peripheral vision* to spot rising trout over broad ranges of water. *Nimble fingers* and good *hand–eye coordination* for tying knots are helpful, too.

Now, some examples of intellectual attributes to which I attach far more value than I do to physical prowess:

Self-confidence minimizes indecision. *Determination* won't let you quit. *Patience* dwarfs frustration. *Self-discipline* limits distraction. *Stoicism* numbs pain. With *acumen* you don't miss a trick. *Imagination* solidifies impressions into ideas. *Adaptability* encourages innovation. *Memory* pays interest on experience. *Courage* carries you beyond where others are willing to go. Most desirable of all such qualities, however, is probably a *sense of humor,* because it sustains perspective and may preserve sanity when everything else has fallen apart.

The influence of conditioning on the angling process is habitually belittled, particularly by those who could most use it. (There seems to be more status in one's capacity for booze than for exercise.) Yet, the finest fishermen try to stay in pretty fair shape, even though they do their damndest sometimes to hide it. This doesn't say the world's worst physical specimen won't hook trout when he plops in a hot spot, but it seems to me that each angler must ultimately decide what he wants from the sport and how hard he's ready to work for it. To be the best, I believe, takes conditioning at least equal to that of the tournament golfer—more work than to become a professional bowler. Therefore, if you're not getting from fly fishing all you expected, a clue to the trouble may be found in your mirror.

Kris snapped this shot on the sly to be certain not to disturb father and son working to rising trout on the Beaverkill. Papa was a patient teacher. But most important, he allowed the lad to do all the fishing. No kid likes to stand idly by while his elders show him "how it's done."

What's the ideal age to take up fly fishing? I'm frequently asked that question, and my pat reply is *the younger the better.* The notion that an eight-year-old can't master the elements of fly presentation is patent nonsense. I've seen dozens of little kids handle both rod and river with finesse. Many of our nation's foremost fly fishermen first shook hands with a rod at eight or younger. I was six, I think, or was it five?

Adjustment to advancing age is basic to any sport. Remember when you played a triple-header without really working up a sweat? It's been proven, however, that the age at which you take up a sport and the constancy with which you practice it thereafter

54

largely determines how comfortably you adapt to the treachery of time. Veteran fly fishermen, therefore, like veteran pitchers or prize fighters, rely more on brains than brawn. By maintaining their bodies through the years, though, they also minimize those "aches and pains" that eventually send most softies to the rockers. Think of a lifetime exercise program, then, as the best brand of liniment.

Virtually all forms of vigorous exercise are therapeutic for fly fishermen. Since everyone's needs are different, though, an exercise program ought to target those deficits or surpluses you see in or on yourself. (No one beyond age thirty-five, by the way, should initiate strenuous workouts without first consulting a physician.) Work on legs and ankles to increase stamina for wading and the long hikes sometimes required to escape angling pressure. Jogging, bicycling and ice skating, among other activities, fill this bill. Develop strength for casting by building shoulders, arms and wrists. Push-ups, lifting weights, wood-chopping and grip exercises do the job. Agility and balance can be improved by skiing and tennis, reflexes by action games such as squash or handball. For rhythm and timing try softball, golf or basketball, sports which also sharpen depth perception and hand–eye coordination. To tie better knots, fool around with macrame or fly tying, the latter, of course, being the most practical for the angler.

Although heavyweights have a decided advantage when wading fast water, that doesn't rationalize flabbiness. Remember, muscle weighs more than fat per unit of mass. A solid two-hundred-pounder, therefore, is likely to wade better than a dumpy one, because he should boast greater strength to haul himself around. Since pounds of equipment as well as body weight help ground you in a riff (I don't wear a fifteen-pound fishing vest for the joy of it), it's best to ascertain your ideal weight and try to maintain it.

Some physical traits, of course, are impossible to fix. You can't make yourself taller, for instance. (Maybe someday somebody will come up with elevator waders.) Short anglers can learn to take

Hat, eyeglasses, neck scarf, heavy vest, wading staff—every item the author wears or carries with him on the water is there for a purpose. Several, including the glasses, vest and staff, compensate for physical deficiencies discovered over the years that would otherwise compromise angling skills. Each angler must become sufficiently self-aware to come up with tricks of his own to minimize shortcomings.

advantage of their height, however, by wearing the longest waders and shortest fishing vests available.

Poor eyesight is another angler's curse about which nothing can be done, except with corrective lenses. I favor wire-rimmed glasses that fasten securely behind the ears. Having discovered my handicap rather by accident (I missed three cock pheasants one afternoon and rushed to an ophthalmologist, the jeers of my hunting partners still ringing in my ears), I'll testify that you can't take good vision for granted. Any doubts you may have about eyesight, underscored perhaps by buddies who spot fish you don't, should send you straight to a physician's office. For those of us who already wear glasses, annual checkups and new prescriptions to bring our vision to 20-20 should be automatic, like replacing worn guides on our favorite rods.

Sensitive eyes can be a terrible burden, sure to tire or tear when we need them most. Headaches occasioned by blinding glare inhibit effectiveness and sap the pleasure from the angling experience. Polaroid sunglasses, ground to prescription when needed, help plenty, particularly when worn beneath the long, black bill of a cap generally associated with saltwater fishing and African safaris. So often have I been photographed wearing such a cap, some friends insist it's an affectation, a "trademark," if you will. While I'll concede ready recognition never hurt a person in my business, it should be pointed out that only a fool would sacrifice performance for image. There's too much at stake to be a dandy. Therefore, each article in my angling wardrobe, every item of equipment I carry, is chosen to somehow enhance my chances on the water. As the reader will see in an upcoming chapter, good angling takes good planning.

Cultivating intellectual traits of service in angling depends largely on character, personality and temperament, which are individual qualities more constructively probed, certainly, by psychologists than by professional fishermen. Yet, although I won't maintain that determination, patience or self-confidence can be absorbed off the pages of a book, I'm convinced that these attributes, like skills, are acquired to some degree; when one flourishes others come along, as if when someone is determined to master a subject it follows he becomes increasingly self-disciplined and patient in pursuit of the goal. As a writer, at least, I'd like to think so.

It's safe to assume, then, that there must be exercises to condition the mind, just as push-ups or jogging strengthen the body. Perhaps most fundamental is to establish drills directed toward assuaging those shortcomings perceived in yourself—laziness,

doubt, impatience, disorganization, rigidity or fear, for instance—
and to stick to the drills scrupulously. Such drills, I guess, can be
as basic as practice-casting an hour a day, or, for that matter, dili-
gently following your physical exercise program. I'm not certain,
though, that more abstract grooming doesn't prove more fulfill-
ing and glean greater long-term benefit. Will tackling Russian
novels, doing difficult crossword puzzles, playing bridge or chess,
or learning second languages make a better fisherman? You'd be
surprised.

The fisherman is at his best, I think, when he pushes himself.
By nature, few skilled anglers are easily satisfied. Self-satisfaction
may be, in fact, the foremost manifestation of mediocre minds.
Through critical eyes you should see little you accomplish that
couldn't be improved upon, no matter how long you've been
fishing. Like skiers who probably stop learning when they stop
falling, I fear that anglers who aren't skunked occasionally lose
the most powerful catalyst for improvement. Similarly, show me a
fisherman who says he has nothing more to learn, and I'll show
you one who knows very little. No angler could untangle everything about even one trout fishing technique in a dozen lifetimes.
If I weren't convinced of that, I'd give up the sport tomorrow.

Digesting every word published on the sport and conditioning
the body and mind to precision are absolutely useless, though,
unless you put it all to work. The water is the realm in which
theories sink or swim. Ultimately, therefore, *fishing dry flies is
the only way to learn to fish dry flies.* And therein, of course, lies the
fun.

It takes experience, which is the product of practice, to develop
skills that maximize strength and minimize weakness. With experience evolves the wisdom to garner the most from difficult situations, to discriminate between alternatives. Experience guides you
to fisheries best suited to your style. It trains you to use the elements, such as sun and wind, instead of fighting them, and to
adapt equipment to changeable conditions. It teaches you to keep
stream notes upon which to rely year after year (see photograph).

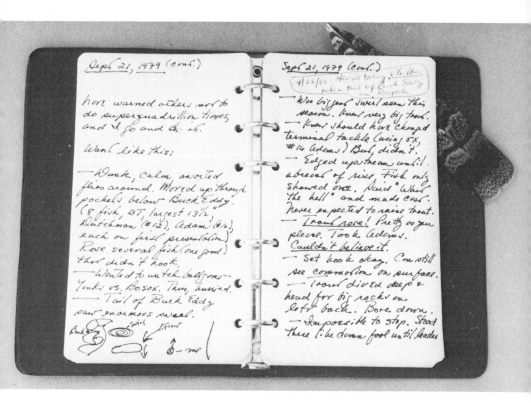

They may read like jabberwocky to anyone else, but stream notes, such as these, have proven invaluable to the author. Over the years they become a diary to be gone over on cold winter nights in search of potential magazine articles. Most important, though, the material jotted on the stream during each outing is transferred nightly from this notebook to a more concise form, shown in chapter eight, to be referred to season after season as the need arises.

Perhaps most rewarding, however, is that experience prepares you to accept the fact that while some aspects of angling become almost automatic, others eternally defy all logic or reason. That knowledge alone, acquired with time, should instill immeasurable love in each fisherman for every minute on the water—not simply for the catch, although it may keep faith with our predatory instinct, but for the spiritual fulfillment of growing with the sport, the doing of it for its own sake.

CHAPTER FIVE

~~~~~~

Getting Warm, Keeping Cool and Staying Dry

NOTHING FOULS FISHING like inadequate dress. Yet it's surprising how many anglers try to get by wearing any old clothes. No wonder they freeze or fry. Not this boy. Long ago I learned that for fishing to be fun great care must be taken to insure comfort and freedom of movement from one's underwear outward.

The amount and type of clothing worn is dictated by air and water temperatures. Since sustained periods may be spent wading waist-deep in water much colder than the surrounding air, comprehensive evaluation of conditions is essential to profit from apparel. When exposed to extremes of hot and cold simultaneously, the body tends to be more sensitive to the cold, explaining why some anglers find themselves hopelessly chilled on balmy afternoons. This is an unpleasant, debilitating and even physically harmful paradox that no properly dressed angler will have to face. Similarly, correct attire guarantees you against becoming overheated during "dog day" outings.

The key to comfort is to start with a foundation of clothes consistent with region and season—underwear, socks, shirt and trousers—and to add loose layers outside for warmth. Then, to cool off, it's necessary only to subtract from the outer layers. It is also essential that clothing be adjusted or changed with ease, since, if it's awkward, most of us opt for expedient discomfort, a silly sacrifice. To this end, I advise against furnishings reached only by digging beneath the foundation, including turtlenecks and quilted longjohns. There are practical outer-garment alternatives for each, the reader will note further along. All dressing decisions must be tempered with common sense, of course. Given frigid weather unlikely to change—a subarctic climate, for instance—then goose-down underwear and a wool turtleneck may well be proper components of foundation clothing.

THE FOUNDATION:

—I'm not about to mess with people's underwear, except to mention that, since sweat is a by-product of exertion, some sort of T-shirt should be worn by men and women to protect against perspiration damage to other clothing.

—I favor all-cotton fishing shirts, available in tropical materials and medium- and heavyweight flannels, including chamois cloth. Manufactured in several weights, chamois cloth, which is soft, moisture-absorbent and durable, makes an ideal shirt for the sport except during hot weather. Most anglers are thrilled to find that these fleecy shirts become more comfortable with age. Whereas cotton shirts are warm in cold weather and cool in hot weather, the reverse seems to be true of those made of permanent press or artificial fibers. Perhaps because they are full of chemicals, I've yet to wear one that hasn't irritated my skin or caused me to perspire profusely.

Regardless of fabrics chosen, consider the design. Shirts should be loose-fitting for freedom and have long tails to prevent untucking when you stretch. I purchase only long-sleeve models (sleeves can be rolled when required to stay cool) as a hedge against sunburn and insects. Breast pockets should have button flaps to minimize inconvenient or costly losses. Corraling a pair of glasses that might otherwise fall in the drink more than offsets any additional cost.

—There are a variety of trousers, including styles tailored specifically for fishing, to serve you on the water. I consider only one kind absolutely wrong for the sport, although hordes of anglers seem willing to suffer them. I refer to form-fitting jeans, which are no better than waist-to-ankle straight jackets, inhibiting movement. Inadequate in cold or heat, wearing jeans inside waders constitutes a sure way to become chilled or fatigued. Those who wear them would be better off b.a.

Although not prone to promoting retailers, I'd be remiss not to mention Ballard cloth woodsmen's pants offered by L. L. Bean, Inc., of Freeport, Me. Weighing about 2½ pounds, I've found nothing comparable for cold-water wading. (Similar trousers, called Herringbone Twills, are available for women.) Those aside, I wear washable corduroys in all but midsummer conditions because they offer warmth, absorb condensation and are incredibly comfortable. During hot spells I choose khakis of the sort worn by construction workers. They wear like iron. Only rarely would I spring for tropical chinos, which while delightful, especially when fashioned of Egyptian cotton, are now priced to doubtful advantage, since trout, being coldwater fish, aren't given to environments likely to punish you with excessive heat, except perhaps between river and car.

Trousers, like shirts, should fit loosely to hold maximum body heat when wading cold water, permit air circulation in warm water, and allow unrestricted activity under all conditions. Because a belt may cause discomfort, try sewing suspender buttons into trousers, making sure, though, that your suspenders are long enough to avoid trading a sore tummy for sore shoulders. Nothing, anglers learn, is more annoying than trouser legs that crawl up the calfs in waders or hip boots because they're not adequately tucked inside socks. Eliminate this problem with cuffless trousers about an inch longer than those you normally wear. There are trousers specially designed for wear in waders that generally come with small tabs to fasten pant legs at the ankles. Although handy, each fisherman must decide whether or not this convenience is worth extra money.

—By the time people take up fishing, they know what socks suit everyday use. For wear under waders, however, socks should be nappy to absorb perspiration. Sweat or tennis socks, knitted primarily of natural fibers, fill this bill best. Fishing socks should also have elastic tops to prevent slippage down into boots, a cause of cramped toes and heel blisters.

OUTER CLOTHING:

Because outer clothes worn from the waist upward—sweaters, down jackets, wind-breakers, hats, and the like—remain above water unless you take a bath, some fishermen are convinced they aren't spotted by nearby trout, regardless of color. Alert fly fishermen know better. For those not schooled, however, a few words about color are long overdue.

Although reticent to bite the hands that feed me, I must blame outdoor magazine editors and art directors for promulgating an illusion that brightly colored clothing is right for trout fishing. Competititon among publications is intense and, in the scramble, slick "art," as it's called, plays a significant role. Too often accuracy is waived for flair. Models decked out in red or orange make snappier subjects than fishermen in tan or olive drab. However, nobody bothers to reflect about the impact of published photos on audiences. "If orange is okay for pros," readers reason, I suppose, "it must be fine for us." What they don't realize, however, is that good photographic strategy frequently runs counter to that for productive angling.

It's crucial, therefore, that fishermen be informed that trout are *extremely sensitive to color intensity,* if not to color *per se.* Were this not so, we might sport bright yellow waders or fish only one fly pattern without regard to shade. Thus each compromise for vanity can cost big trout, especially for the dry fly fisherman who enhances his chances in proportion to his ability to approach the quarry closely. My advice, then, is to leave beauty to "beautiful people" and stick to tans, olives, grays and browns, colors that blend into most natural surroundings.

Seldom a day hands out what we expect. Where I'm from, for instance, you may fish in shirt sleeves in March and hit snow in May. Climates of other regions are even more unpredictable. "If you don't like our weather," chortles Wyoming rancher Hank Snow, "wait a minute." In view of this potential for inconsistency, I don't trust to luck. A suitcase full of extra paraphernalia is stowed in my car's trunk before opening day and remains there all season.

—From fishing sweaters I demand warmth, comfort and durability. In lighter weights those criteria are met by loose-fitting wool V-necks in neutral colors. With reasonable care they last years, particularly since the V-neck design permits access to shirt pockets without stretching the collarband. Access and easy-on, easy-off are attributes too of my favorite heavy sweater, the cardigan. The finest cardigans for fishing, in my opinion, are those knitted in Iceland and exported for sale around the world. Unique Icelandic wool, fashioned into patterns of earthy tones, makes the warmest sweater I've worn; plus, they're virtually impervious to rain.

—Over many years I've experimented with heaps of outer clothing, trying to approach a perfect melange for each situation. It has proven dicey, as I've never found a suitable jacket, for example, to satisfy my "medium weight" requirements. The most practical alternative to jackets for every occasion until it gets really cold has proven to be a putty-colored poplin Eisenhower jacket, worn when necessary over sweaters of varied weights. Then, for moderate cold, I switch to a waist-length nylon jacket insulated with goose down. My favorite model is beige for camouflage, has an insulated collar, Teflon zipper and sleeves that fit snugly at the wrists. With an Icelandic sweater worn underneath and a hooded nylon shell outside, I've encountered no climate, including the far north, too cold to stay toasty.

Because down jackets and nylon shells are frequently worn over several layers of clothes, it's important that they be large enough not to constrict movement. I buy a *large* size in down jackets, *extra large* in nylon shells, for instance, although at almost six feet tall I weigh only about 160 pounds.

—All the above is worthless, of course, if you get drenched every time it drizzles. Therefore, a dependable rain jacket is indispensable. Have one always at hand, preferably as close as the rear compartment of your fishing vest. Don't scrimp on this item, either, since leaky rainwear subjects everything from the vest inward to destructive soaking. I like a drab-colored rubberized model with zipper front, a subjective choice, granted, but based on having remained dry when wearing such a garment for a dozen years. Regardless of material, however, a jacket must be ample to protect what's inside without restricting movement. Never buy one without a hood that tightens at the neck and elastic cuffs to prevent water running up the arms. Jacket length should suit prevailing conditions, that is, *regular* for shallow water and *short* for wading above the waist.

—Having rejected quilted longjohns, how do I ward off chilled legs when wading? Ten years ago I discovered insulated overpants and have suffered no discomfort since. Manufactured, it's my guess, by one firm but available under several brand names, the overpants are made of two-ply cotton and nylon, lined with quilted polyester, which, in turn, is stuffed with nylon taffeta. For convenient dressing and undressing, they feature Teflon zippers from waist to ankle, and as the legs are cuffless, they tuck beautifully into socks. Because overpants are worn outside regular trousers, I suggest buying them two sizes larger than your belt measurement.

—Keeping hands and feet warm can be a real challenge. Hands

constitute a dilemma, because without nimble fingers, routine jobs such as changing flies represent terrible chores, and dexterity may be diminished equally by exposing hands to chilly air and water or wearing bulky gloves. On balance, though, I advise against gloves unless absolutely unavoidable, and then a compromise only to the extent that they don't enclose the fingertips. Millarmits, sold by most angling retailers, are adequate, but not nearly so effective, I've discovered, as those knitted of eighty-five percent virgin wool and fifteen percent nylon.

—Although wader socks present fewer problems, maximum warmth from minimum bulk should set the standard by which to buy them. There's no substitute for wool socks, which retain body heat well yet permit the feet to breathe. Socks should also be sufficiently long to insure trouser legs remain securely tucked inside them.

—Some anglers regard hats only as "part of the uniform," unaware, I guess, that they perform useful functions such as saving the eyes from glare, as noted some pages back. A practical fishing hat also protects the head from undue shots of sun, rain and cold, not to mention flies gone astray on windy days. A swordfish-bill or safari cap, as described earlier, is, I'm convinced, the best all-around fishing hat money can buy, since it satisfies all the above needs except perhaps for warmth, while (unlike a cowboy hat, for instance) staying on your head even in a gale. If warmth becomes a problem, the safari hat's skull-cap design ideally accommodates a Scottish tam or knitted watch cap over it, as shown in the accompanying illustration.

—For years I've worn a cotton bandanna as a neck scarf, despite ribbing from cronies who believe it's just for show. Let 'em joke. Secured with a loose square knot for convenient removal, the bandanna serves a dozen purposes, including—you guessed it— spiking a runny nose. With no fumbling around inside waders, the scarf is handy to wipe my eyes, clean glasses, remove grit from reels or dress fly lines. In a shake it becomes a streambank marker to guide me back to a certain spot. I've even been known to wrap pan-size trout in it since I don't carry a creel.

The swordfish-bill or safari cap is illustrated here with the Scottish tam the author wears over the cap for warmth. The skull-cap design without the tam is shown in numerous photographs and illustrations throughout the text.

WADERS AND HIP BOOTS:

Anglers who'd spend months agonizing about rods would, you'd think, reflect a moment before leaping into waders. What could be worth more attention than staying dry? Yet it's ironic how many fishermen know less about waders than waterbeds, although waders are among their most costly purchases. No wonder they complain about wader performance.

As an outdoor writer, the question I'm asked most is: "What waders do *you* wear?" I wear Hodgman Brighton waders and hip boots, imported from the Far East. They are, incidentally, appreciably less expensive than Hodgman Wadewells, for years standard among American fly fishermen. Although thoroughly content with these, my experience shouldn't be interpreted as an unqualified endorsement. Until you fish everywhere, you can't presume omniscience about such things. Given the waters I do fish both at home and abroad, however, no one has shown me more dependable equipment.

Anyone seeking to exclude water from a place it's trying to go tastes the essential frustration of the wader business. Ultimately, anglers either remain dry or get wet, and since they can get as wet through little flaws as big ones, quality control is paramount from manufacturer to distributor to retailer to consumer. Consumers—anglers—who assume otherwise are patently irresponsible, for without their enlightened purchasing and meticulous care, everything that comes before is wasted. Oh, it's human to blame manufacturers, I guess, but anglers with leaky waders really deserve no sympathy unless it's certain they bought the correct products for their needs and treated them responsibly thereafter. Wet feet, then, may signal our own incompetence.

The two wader styles—boot-foots, to which outer footwear is directly connected, and stocking-foots, over which brogues or sneakers must be worn—each have advantages and disadvantages for everyday use. Boot-foots, for instance, are easy to put on and take off, while stocking-foots with brogues deliver great support for walking and wading. Boot-foots are warm; stocking-foots aren't. Wading shoes over stocking-foots, however, can be changed to adapt to conditions. Because quality brogues are expensive, boot-foots are probably more economical. So it goes. Before investing in waders, therefore, consult several anglers familiar with your region, deriving from their thoughts and your inclinations a consensus as to which style will best fill your needs.

The accompanying illustration shows what to look for in waders. It should be helpful to remember the following. Waders don't fit unless you can: (1) walk naturally without material inside one leg rubbing against that of the other, (2) raise each foot high enough to rest it on the arm of a chair, (3) do deep knee bends, (4) sit and cross your legs, and (5) wiggle your toes inside the boots. Consider, too: (1) rocky streams usually require felt soles; (2) felt soles are useless on mud or clay; (3) gum rubber tears easily in brushy terrain; (4) fine sand is murder on stocking-foot waders; (5) dark colors get hotter than light ones.

Once the right waders are chosen
according to the criteria outlined in
the text, the angler should set about
choosing those wader accessories—
suspenders, a wader belt, stream
cleats, for instance—that will best
suit him for the waters he's likely
to fish.

By following guidelines that apply to waders, choosing hip boots should present no problem. Also be sure, however, that leggings don't bind at the crotch, and that the straps that fasten to the belt are long enough to prevent downward tension at the waist.

Which to wear on favorite streams—waders or hip boots—puzzles some anglers perhaps, although one good soaking should help the future decision-making process. When in doubt wear waders, I say. Since hip boots are limiting on all but small waters, you can't go wrong that way. However, well-equipped anglers budget to own both, and when possible, decide which to wear on a given day only after careful study of stream conditions.

Many anglers plagued by leaky waders boast of being "hard on clothes." Waders are only as good as you treat them but, given a modicum of care, they should last several seasons. In practice wader care translates into keeping part of your mind on them at all times, just as you do to protect rods when negotiating brush-lined paths. Most accidents to waders can be viewed as fines for jaywalking, easily avoided by self-discipline. Nor will wader materials tolerate sloppy short- or long-term storage. After each outing, therefore, permit waders to dry thoroughly, roll them loosely and put them in a cool, dry place. Don't fold or hang them, particularly for protracted periods, since in the former instance the fabric wears at the folds, while in the latter, a chemist warns, prolonged stretching decomposes fabrics from which waders are constructed.

Occasional accidents are inevitable, of course, and anglers must be prepared with suitable patch kits to make immediate repairs. Ask dealers from whom waders are purchased for recommended procedures to mend the brand purchased, since any old patch won't do on many fabrics. Often a hunk of material like that from which your waders were made does the job nicely when affixed with Barge cement; thus large pieces of it cut from old waders destined for the dump should be squirreled away for later service. Salvaged suspender buttons, draw strings, belt loops, pouches, and even an old pair of wader boots may come in handy sooner or later.

In emergencies nothing doctors waders like Magic Patch, an inexpensive stick that's gooey when heated, rubbery when cooled. For best results: (1) using a cigarette lighter, heat an end of the stick and a butter knife blade; (2) cover the area over and around the hole with an ample amount of melted patch material; (3) before it cools, quickly spread the goo with the heated knife until the patch has no rough spots around the edges. This method is also ideal for preventing holes before they happen. To find worn spots, shine a light into your waders while in a dark room.

CHAPTER SIX

~~~~~~

Gearing Up

ONLY DOCTORS, who seem to fall prey to any investment scheme, are bigger "fish" than trout fishermen in the market for tackle. I oughta know; for years I was a "lunker." It's so easy to believe the latest do-da will make you a better angler. Fact is, we dry fly fishermen are "tackle addicts"—so many advanced cases of the nose-pressed-against-the-toy-store-window syndrome—for whom there's no "crisis line," not even an "anonymous." Ultimately, only huge doses of expensive experience may help us kick the habit.

Thirty years back, my dad told me, a rodmaker friend was asked by a sawbones (curiously enough) to construct a bamboo rod. Because the doctor was a buddy, the rodmaker chose his finest cane and built "my best rod ever," a practical fishing instrument, too, not one for show. The charge: $75.

The customer blew his top. "I ordered your best," he stormed, "and will settle for nothing less."

The rodmaker, realizing that reasoning was futile, agreed to re-place the rod. What he did, however, was dress up the first one and, returning it to the customer, anticipated his question with the statement: "Three hundred bucks."

"Now *that's* a fishing rod," the customer said with reproach, but not apparently regarding the tab. "This one has the proper ac-tion . . . Difference of night and day."

"Yeah," sighed the rodmaker. "You get what you pay for." Later, however, he confided, "That day I was introduced to the 'King's New Suit' school of design," adding that he'd lived com-fortably ever after.

Dry fly fishermen thirty years ago had little tackle to choose from, at least by today's standards. It's been during the past de-cade that the tackle business has really taken off, as one extension of the nationwide awakening to the outdoor experience. A target market ready to scap up everything in sight has proven too good to pass up. The resulting glut of tackle and accessories ranges, therefore, from the sublime to the ridiculous. If Izaak Walton were around today, I bet he'd title his classic *The Compleat Angler—Being a Discourse on Wading into Abject Poverty.* To which I'd recommend an epilogue: *Caveat Emptor.*

Quality tackle is as important to anglers as clubs are to golfers. Just as the level of play on the links has improved with advances in club design, so too are average fly fishermen able to accomplish feats once reserved for *bona fide* experts. Graphite rods, for in-stance, draw seventy-five- to ninety-foot casts into range, while monofilament, strong at tiny diameters, makes practical leader tippets for size-28 flies. From the perspective of tackle, therefore, it's probably fair to assume the "good old days" were nothing to write home about. The first casualty of reflection is often truth. It may be, in fact, that dry fly fishing labors under an unfortunate reputation for being tougher than it is precisely because during the so-called "golden age" of cumbersome bamboo and greenheart rods, heavy brass reels, sticky silk lines and fragile gut leaders, not to mention snelled flies, it was just that: *very* tough.

American anglers spent $15.2 billion on the sport in 1975, according to a U.S. government report. While it's impossible to judge what hunk went into fly fishing, it was surely considerable. The clutter of catalogs around my workroom sufficiently illustrates the broad choice available to fly fishermen. Many anglers, particularly novices, complain they're intimidated, even paralyzed, by so many alternatives, each portrayed with appropriate hype. It's enough to make you wonder, "Can't there be too much of a good thing?" Probably there is.

The ideal amount of equipment unquestionably enhances the angling experience. Difficult as it is, therefore, fishermen must learn to outfit themselves without going broke. The key is not to get carried away. Ask yourself, *"Why* do I need this?" If the answer is unclear, don't buy it. Too much equipment, I learned the hard way, works against you by forcing decisions there's no time to make on the water. Each decision, no matter how minor, takes seconds, minutes, away from fishing. And a trout, after all, can't take a fly it doesn't get to see.

Given waters of endless variety, plus infinite potential for physical and psychological differences among people, seeking to represent a perfect potpourri of equipment from afar is an exercise in futility. Nothing, in fact, offends me more than cavalier attempts to do so. Anglers who poke around little brooks have vastly different needs, obviously, than those who challenge brawling rivers, and advertising to the contrary aside, I've handled no outfit that will properly cover all fishing situations, certainly not without creating handicaps. One thing is certain, however: somewhere within the store of tackle offered is everything each angler requires. The task, then, becomes to sort it out.

No one must be more disciplined in purchasing habits than professional anglers, since equipment cost is our major overhead. (It's a myth that manufacturers visit truckloads of free gear upon us.) Speaking for myself, every dollar counts, and, therefore, I want efficient and durable items, knowing my finds are in for rugged tests. I've made plenty of mistakes, but in the course of trial and error have developed, I think, a pretty accurate sense of worthwhile investment. Perhaps my views can help the reader.

Rule one is to bear in mind a cliché: "One man's meat is another man's poison." Unfortunately, many anglers choose gear solely by its reputation or on recommendation of friends. Too much "follow the leader" is played among fishermen, I'm afraid, particularly where "status" items are concerned, until frequently image outweighs efficiency. Diminished skill is the inevitable consequence of those caught up in this game. Without looking over your shoulder, try to stick with tackle that suits you, regardless of label, and to dispose of that which doesn't. Sell unwanted items to someone whose requirements they fill and reinvest the cash in gear you can use.

FISHING VESTS

Readers who wonder why vests (fishing jackets are but vests with sleeves) weren't considered while on the subject of apparel fail to appreciate that this package of pockets and pouches represents the critical piece of equipment, out of which the best conceived campaigns are mobilized. Here is the encampment where reserves are billeted, your major source of supply and reinforcement. Winning or losing each battle with the trout and, ultimately, the war, depends to great measure upon an angler's capacity to administer his gear. Without a proper fishing vest it's a futile mission.

A practical vest carries what you may need where it's readily available, even in failing light. Selecting the right vest, therefore, requires analysis of your needs and preferences before accommodating a garment to them. Doing the opposite—that is, buying a vest first and seeking to reconcile what you'll carry to its capacity without regard to your potential demands—limits the scope of fishing technique to the patterns of tailors. Unfortunately, many anglers make this mistake.

Two fundamental notions about applying vests to dry fly fishing predominate today. The first emphasizes keeping the vest "light" by toting in it only gear, including flies, likely to be required during a single outing. Other stuff, particularly fly patterns representing hatches either past or not anticipated for considerable time to come, is stored elsewhere until needed. The major advantages of this view are, of course, that the angler is free from (1) a substantial physical burden, and (2) the need to scramble through a mess just to make minor tackle adjustments. It's probably the best way to go for most novices who have yet to develop a feel for equipment—as well as for some marvels who, although experienced, just never could learn to pair up their socks. The second option, to which I subscribe more or less, is to stock the vest liberally for every eventuality, no matter how unlikely, that may be encountered on waters most frequently fished. Only unmistakably surplus gear is laid away, while everything carried in the vest is rotated among compartments by preconceived plan to guarantee accessibility at opportune times. This principle, of course, necessitates spacious and somewhat heavy vests. Thus outfitted, however, not only are lightweights like me given extra ballast against heavy currents, but our chances of being caught short by unexpected or unusual conditions are virtually polished off. I recommend this course, therefore, for anglers well organized and in good physical condition.

Tackle quartered in a vest, of course, relates directly to the water to be fished. Streams inhabited by jaded browns naturally call for more equipment than those bursting with unsophisticated brookies. At very least, though, the well-outfitted dry fly fisherman provides room for: several fly boxes, a "fly saver" box, extra reel or spare spool, a leader wallet, spools of tippet material from 1X through 8X, stream thermometer, dry fly flotant, absorbent powder for treating flies, clippers, tweezers, a piece of leather or rubber to straighten leaders, a rain jacket, and a net affixed to a sliding keeper. The accompanying photograph shows how much gear I'm able to allocate to my shorty dry fly fishing vest with room to spare. All wets, nymphs and streamers, by the way, are filed in foam plastic in the three-tray Fye-Box outside the vest, also illustrated in the photo.

The vest is an Orvis shorty model, customized by friend Elsie Darbee so that two stock vertical, zipper pockets became two horizontal pockets with button flaps. This modification made room to add an exterior bellows pocket, an exterior slit pocket and two additional interior pockets. In the vest the author carries: eight dry fly boxes, a leader wallet, dry fly flotant, leader sinking liquid, line grease, fly drying powder (not shown), a stream thermometer, a night light, a small seine, two fly reels, his stream notes, a fly-saver box and a rain jacket. Pinned to the front of the vest is a sliding keeper that holds clippers, tweezers and a square of rubber for straightening leaders. Attached to a keeper on the back of the vest is a wood frame landing net. Also shown (at left) is the Fye-Box in which the author totes his nymphs, wets and streamers. Spools of tippet material are stored in the ammunition case glued to the front of the Fye-Box.

So helpful is the right vest that I've tested at least a dozen models and continue to use several, leaving gear earmarked for specific fisheries in them between trips. A vest hung in your closet makes a more convenient and economical cache than those expensive bags of leather-trimmed duck sold expressly for the purpose, particularly since storage represents only a secondary function of the vest. When keeping flies for long periods in a vest, however, it's important to protect them against bugs with moth flakes.

While some angling technologists have distinguished themselves with recent innovations nothing less than brilliant, those responsible for vest design are, in my view, turning out numbers that could lead you to believe they've never fished one day in their collective lifetimes. They won't acknowledge, for instance, that *zippers are absolutely worthless guardians of fishing vest pockets,* or that the pockets they contrive for many current models are too small for two standard fly boxes and too large to hold a single box securely. Even when treated gingerly, zippers break and stick, and they're damned expensive to replace, although less expensive, certainly, than full fly boxes lost by anglers trucking around with open vest pockets. Less than ideal but preferable to zippers, Velcro adhesive on flap pockets appears the most reliable alternative today. It performs reasonably well and gives ample warning before wearing out. When Velcro goes, or even before for that matter, get a seamstress to adapt the pockets of your vest to buttons. The button, among man's truly brilliant inventions, is the perfect lock on an angler's precious gear, even though many modern manufacturing wizards can't seem to see it.

Anglers who haunt both big and small waters require a pair of vests, a regular model for shallow wading, and a so-called "shorty" for venturing in above the waist. Although the design of short vests limits their capacity, making advance planning essential to effectively utilize their space, they remain a wise investment to spare flies from persistent soaking. Water standing in boxes, even for a few hours, is one of the most malignant influences inflicted

Saddlebags, as worn by the author in this photograph taken on a river in northern Iceland, make either a nifty alternative to a vest or, as in this instance, an ideal place for supplemental storage when fishing a remote region. The model shown was manufactured as saddlebags for a motor scooter. However, even better ones, made expressly for fishing, are marketed by both Thomas & Thomas of Turners Falls, Mass., and L. L. Bean, Inc. of Freeport, Me.

on dry flies, rusting hooks and weakening hackle fibers often beyond repair. The most practical alternative to short vests is a pair of angler's saddle bags that rest fore and aft, connected by shoulder straps (see photograph). If the weight is equally distributed they're quite comfortable, the only notable disadvantages being that they provide neither room for a rain jacket nor a handy spot to attach a net.

When buying a vest, take the equipment you'll put in and on it to the store. While merchants probably won't abide sticking their vests full of pin-holes, be certain that there is convenient space to attach clippers, leader stretchers and other essential accessories. No salesman, however, should deter customers from trying fly boxes in vest pockets (if they do, go elsewhere). When fly boxes and other gear fit a vest with room to spare for additions later, you're in clover. If they don't, the question becomes whether to opt for another vest or to purchase more suitable tackle, a matter of personal priorities. Should problems arise due only to fly boxes, before writing a vest off, consider that plastic boxes (the only kind I endorse for dry flies) represent a minor expense.

Never try on a fishing vest with its pockets empty. It's best, in fact, to stuff the pockets to capacity before donning the vest over several outfits, from a light summer shirt to bulky sweater and down jacket. If one vest must serve you season-long, it's better that it be a mite large for freedom of movement than too small. Because vest designers seem oblivious to standardized sizing, comfort is a more reliable measure of fit than labels sewn inside.

Following are some further criteria of a quality vest: (1) Is it made of substantial, water-resistant material? (2) Is the color neutral, such as putty or olive? (3) Are seams double-stitched? (4) Is there an inside bellows throughout the garment? (5) Do pockets for tippet spools have flaps? (6) How about a tab and ring in back to hold a net keeper?

Most anglers, including novices, are aware that wading can be tricky, and even dangerous, under certain conditions. Some rivers are tough at any time of year. Last season, for instance, I snatched one frightened fellow from the Beaverkill, reputed a relatively easy stream to wade. Taking a swim can happen to anyone, and frequently does. Each fisherman, therefore, must assess his ability to cope with spills. Poor swimmers should shun high water and powerful currents unless outfitted with flotation devices, the most reliable of which are built into several models of angling vests (costs are comparable to regular models). Nor can parents in good conscience permit youngsters access to sizable streams unprotected, for doing so is like encouraging them to play in traffic. It's no disgrace to wear a flotation vest. Rather, it proves that future fishing is important enough to you to invest in assurance you'll be around to enjoy it.

RODS FOR DRY FLY FISHING

If a perfect all-around fly rod is on the market, I've never been lucky enough to buy one. Despite highfalutin claims by a minority of makers, it is generally accepted for obvious reasons that ideal rods for search and destroy missions on turbulent rivers will be reduced to clumsy impedimenta in the game of inches played by trout sipping minutiae on glassy spring creeks. At issue isn't whether rods get flies from one point to another. In skilled hands *any* rod accomplishes that. Rather, the issue is the measure of influence an angler possesses over his fly as he delivers it to its appointed destination. Or, put another way, when assessing the virtues of fly rods, casting represents but one of many elements in the comprehensive business known as *presentation*.

Through the years I've fished with hundreds of anglers from novice to expert, including many well-known pros. Observing them all, however, I have yet to encounter two with identical techniques for presenting a fly. I've reached the unshakeable conclusion, therefore, that no fly casting standard exists, and, further, that to advocate one would contradict common sense by denying the margin for natural inclination brought to the exercise by individual casters. To illustrate the point, consider what would have happened to the late Charles Ritz, a man of modest stature, had it

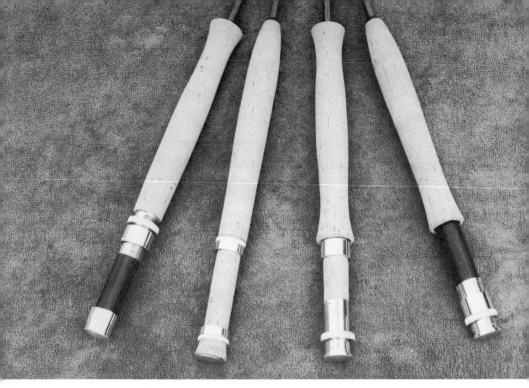

More beautiful examples of cork grips and reel seats couldn't be turned out than these by friend Ted Simroe of the Rodon Manufacturing Co., Newark, N.J. They are, from left, the half Wells grip with screw-lock reel seat, the cigar grip with sliding rings, the full Wells grip with reverse screw-lock reel seat, and the western grip with reverse screw-lock seat.

been dictated that he adopt the style of, for instance, a bruiser like Lefty Kreh, or vice versa. The prospect is unthinkable, although both men have epitomized the fly-casting art as refined to near perfection. To that end, though, each had to assert prerogatives when it came to reconciling the tools of the trade to his talents. And so it goes with us all. A rod functions only as efficiently as the angler does, not the other way around.

Rods constitute a subject about which it is easy to get bogged down in a heap more technical compost than anybody needs or should really want. Were I willing to put up with it, few days would go by when I'd be spared a lecture by some parrot on "flex," "recovery" or, my pet peeve, "parabolic action," an authoritative definition of which I've yet to unearth. (I have a hunch it doesn't exist, or at least not outside some dusty old engineering manual.) To become mired in such trivia represents, in my opinion, the ultimate obsession to which anglers can fall prey—a fate worse than drought.

In simple terms, a good fly rod has fluid and uniform action from tip to butt, regardless of whether it's fast (stiff) or slow (limber). One characteristic fault of many inferior two-piece models, for instance, is a stiff butt and whippy tip which, by causing contradictory action, thwarts a caster's essential senses of rhythm and timing. Guides on good fly rods are sized and spaced to minimize sag, drag, wobble and coil as line passes through them. Clicks, slapping sounds and, of course, resistance when false casting or shooting line can often be diagnosed as rod guide problems. Nor do properly outfitted rods require ceramic stripping guides, also called speed-guides, although these do compensate somewhat for other deficiencies in mediocre models.

A variety of cork grip designs are featured for quality fly rods, as shown in the accompanying photograph. To promote control and/or power when presenting flies—by maximizing continuity between forearm and thumb (this being, in effect, an extension of the rod)—the standard cigar grip and the so-called western grip suit me best. However, fine casters with different techniques argue persuasively, and quite correctly I'm sure, in favor of other shapes that better satisfy their needs. Therefore, to endorse one shape on the basis of my experience alone would represent an irresponsible generality. Discretion dictates, instead, that I offer the following bits of useful advice:

—Don't buy a fly rod unless you've put it, or one exactly like it, through its paces, even if you have to do so in a parking lot. And, if the rod is available with several alternative grips, try each, comparing your performance for control and accuracy over short, moderate and long distances.

—If when you shake hands with a rod its grip seems lost in your grasp, save yourself agony by not buying it. The tendency of most anglers is to clasp thin grips too tightly which, in turn, causes the hands to cramp with sustained casting. If, on the other hand, a grip feels too fat, it can be turned down on a lathe by a knowledgeable craftsman.

—Because a proficient caster continually adjusts the position of his hand to modify his technique, cork grips into which permanent indentations have been ground, ostensibly to custom-fit your hand, should be avoided, as impressive as they may appear to the part of the brain that houses the ego.

Like rod grips, reel seats come in a range of styles, the most utilitarian of which is unquestionably the screw-lock design (see the photograph). While it's true that a screw-lock mechanism is heavier than, for instance, cork and rings or butt cap and ring systems (both of which, incidentally, I find aesthetically pleasing), as a practical matter the weight difference is insignificant, particularly in most dry fly fishing situations for which rod weight should be back from the tip. I've actually put lead in reels to redistribute weight when I perceived rigs as tip heavy. Whatever seat is chosen, however, be the priority function or beauty, be sure it's made to accommodate your favorite reels securely.

Before exploring rodmaking materials and features, such as length and action, a few words on *cosmetics* are in order. Over the years Kris and I have seen enough of the world to acquire tastes for things we'll never be able to afford on a regular basis. Our consolation is that, by exercising judgment, we own what we need and enjoy what we love to do most. While pride of ownership is commendable in fly fishermen, it should be indulged, I believe, only to the degree that the ability to put what you buy to work on the water doesn't suffer. Anglers should be warned, therefore, that a substantial percentage of the expense of many fly rods is devoted to costmetics, which, although beautiful, add nothing to rod function or angler performance. So, before purchasing rods for appearance, pause to consider, as I do, that *discretion is the better part of value.*

Most contemporary fly rods are constructed of split bamboo, fiber glass or graphite (also known as carbon fiber). Of these bamboo is the most beautiful, expensive and difficult to care for, fiber glass the most economical, and graphite the most practical in every sense. For many seasons I fished dry flies almost exclusively with bamboo rods (I had little use for fiber glass then and have even less now). As time passed, however, graphite technology improved to the extent that virtually any rod action could be found within the range of models available. So, this lightweight material converted a skeptic into a real evangelist. Indeed, so complete is my conversion to graphite that I've exchanged most of my bamboo rods for it, financing a couple of memorable excursions with the extra cash I pocketed in the deals. Besides being light, graphite is easy to care for and, despite the contrary claims of some critics, is sturdy when handled with the respect due anything six to ten feet long and less than a half-inch in diameter. I've never broken a graphite rod casting or playing fish, although I'm not timid about doing either. An 8½-footer (number 5 line) I've owned several seasons has handled hundreds—nay, probably thousands— of trout of up to ten pounds and is every bit the rod today it was when I bought it. That's more than I'd dare say of the finest bamboo rod I ever owned. Anyone, therefore, who hasn't tried graphite owes it to himself to do so.

The model an angler chooses depends, of course, on many factors, the most important being the water to be fished. Unless a dry fly fisherman devotes all his time to one fishery, or several of strikingly similar composition, he'll want and need more than one rod. The notion that he should have a different one for each location, however, is overkill—the sort of nonsense that discourages people from taking up such an "elitist" (that is, expensive) hobby. One rod with power for larger fisheries abounding in pockets and otherwise broken water, where keeping flies over the trout as much time as possible represents the essential criterion, plus a rod that doubles for small streams and bigger ones where delicate presentations of tiny imitations ahead of fine tippets are called for, should serve for average use nationwide. Only anglers who travel extensively require three, four or more rods. Even we professionals could probably get by with far fewer rods than we somehow feel compelled to own (but seldom use).

To look for more than a practical fishing implement in a fly rod propels anglers into the hazardous precinct of *specialty,* or in the extreme, of *gimmickry.* While creating handicaps or unique challenges to intensify the angling adventure—for example, tackling ten-pounders using five-foot rods weighing only half-ounces—is entirely acceptable, even admirable, as practiced by seasoned sportsmen, such tests of skill must be recognized by the angling public for what they are and nothing more. Certainly to purvey them as fundamental or even recommended procedures manifests a cynical and dangerous point of view typified, I believe, by the "midge" rod craze that swept the country several years ago, during which a multitude of unsophisticated fishermen were sold a "bull of goods" by retailers I'd like to think were also dragged into the fad with the best of intentions. Couldn't these merchants see, I wondered then and do today, that the majority of patrons would be bewildered by the toys represented as essential? Perhaps not. That being the case, however, I'm compelled to warn fellow anglers to *beware of fads* that by their nature may constitute vehicles of abuse and exploitation. Don't be fooled by yourself or anybody else into compromising countless hours of pleasure by saddling yourself with tools of ignorance.

For 99.9 percent of the situations I've encountered, including wee brooks, no rod shorter than seven-and-a-half feet is required or recommended. I sold my last short rod a year or so ago. It's preferable, for instance, when tackling brushy little streams for which short rods have been touted, to use a rod long enough to keep backcasts high over obstacles than to try to pick openings between branches behind you, an exacting job that demands considerable skill and patience. Covering big waters with small rods is a hopeless cause unless you're Lee Wulff or one of those lucky enough to have studied under this true master of miniatures.

To complement most surface-water rivers and streams, I suggest graphite rods with rather fast actions, handling the AFTMA line sizes shown in parentheses: 7½-foot (numbers 5 or 6); 8-foot (number 6); 8½-foot (numbers 6 or 7); 9-foot (numbers 7 or 8), this size applying only for the biggest rivers or, perhaps, extraordinarily large trout. My choice among these rods for the widest range of conditions is the 8½-footer (number 6 line). In bamboo for similar waters try: 7½-foot (number 6); 8-foot (numbers 6 or 7). In fiber glass consider: 7½-foot (numbers 5 or 6); 8-foot (numbers 6 or 7). Among bamboo rods the ideal for a broad variety of situations is the 7½-foot (number 6), while in fiber glass the best all-around choice is probably the 8-foot (number 6). Anglers with experience sufficient to refine technique to precision might also investigate odd-length rods, such as 7-foot 9-inch models for number 6 lines. They are available from several reputable manufacturers in graphite, bamboo and fiber glass. On all but the best fishermen, however, these fine distinctions in length are generally lost and may be a waste of money, particularly if rods must be custom-built, a costly process.

To insure delicate presentation of small flies—or large ones for that matter—cast to glassy surfaces of the sort encountered along fisheries of subterranean origin, the idea is to wed rod taper and action to line size so that fly control is optimized over short or long distances. Until recently, bamboo was the only answer— models like the 7½-foot (number 4); 8-foot (numbers 4 or 5); and 8½-foot (numbers 5 or 6). Revolutionary developments in graphite are such, however, that at least a dozen current models compare favorably to the finest bamboo rods ever made, certainly functionally if not aesthetically. I suggest the following: 7½-foot (number 4); 8-foot (numbers 4 or 5); 8½-foot (number 5); 9-foot (number 5); 9½-foot (number 6). Of those, my favorite is the 8½-foot (number 5).

The essence of a dry fly rod—whether it be for use with traditional fly patterns on broken water where trout tend to be relatively undiscriminating, or with midges to fool finicky fish stationed beneath smooth surfaces—is built into its action.

Requirements to present dry flies to an infinite array of feeding and holding stations guarded by endless combinations of currents that govern each float over the fish dictate character of rod design unlike that found, for instance, in models associated with nymph, streamer or wet fly fishing. This character, perceived by the angler in the action, is a product of taper, or the composition and amount of material and how it's distributed in the rod. Rather than become painfully technical about all this, it's enough to say, I think, that no matter how light the line a dry fly rod is designed to accommodate, it must possess the capacity throughout its full length to enable the caster to open and close his loop at will, thus providing potential to introduce either dramatic or subtle changes in line speed with minimum rhythm adjustment. Immediate reponse by the rod to a caster's manipulations is therefore paramount. Such quick responses are, of course, impossible to ask of extremely slow rods, commonly referred to as "buggy whips" or "wet noodles." Unless you anticipate doing a lot of roll-casting, avoid tip-heavy rods of the ilk favored by many European rodmakers. Look, instead, for rods with fine tips and gradual but pronounced weight emphasis back into the butt. Most important, never judge weight distribution until you've rigged a rod with a reel, line, leader and a bit of fluff to represent a fly, and, thus prepared, have put the outfit through a rigorous series of tests to simulate a host of angling situations.

REELS

Once it was believed that fly reels accounted for no more than line storage, and anglers were urged to make do with the cheapest models they could buy. Where the notion originated I can't imagine, but it was nonsense then, is now, and will be as long as trout fishing exists. To hold line is but one of many functions performed by the reel, not the least significant of which is to balance the angler's entire rig. The fly reel gives line and takes it back, and in skilled hands becomes the *most important* piece of equipment for playing fish—much more important, in fact, than the rod. For a dry fly fisherman to determine what reel best complements each rod he owns, therefore, is basic to outfitting himself for peak effectiveness.

Fly reels can be divided into two categories: *single-action* and *multiplying* models. *Single-action* refers to the principle that one revolution of the reel handle retrieves one turn of line onto the spool, while *multiplying* means that 1½, 2, 2½, or more, revolutions of the spool result from only one turn of the reel handle. Although extreme cases—such as, perhaps, a few raging rivers abroad that hold gigantic trout—call for multipliers, the majority of trout fishing situations around the world can be managed nicely with single-action reels.

Reels for dry fly fishing should be milled from lightweight, rustproof material, such as aluminum alloy, which is anodized after milling for additional protection. To minimize malfunctions, the finest reels contain the fewest moving parts possible without compromising operation. Internal works are best tooled (not stamped) from metal. I've found reels with nylon or plastic innards, for instance, singularly unreliable. I like reels with perforated spools for lightness. Weight, sometimes required to balance an outfit, can be added by opting for a larger-size reel of otherwise identical design, which, in turn, allows for extra fly line backing. Since skilled anglers learn to interpret every move hooked trout make by listening to the pitch of their reels, I won't use one without a click built in. Beyond its fish-fighting role, a click provides the resistance, even without drag added, to prevent overspin when line is drawn from the reel as in casting.

When it comes to mass-producing fly reels, no manufacturer holds a candle to Hardy Bros., of Alnwick, England. With meticulous concern for quality, Hardy doesn't stop at making its own models, the Flyweight, Featherweight, LRH Lightweight, Princess, St. Aiden, Zenith, Husky, St. George, Perfect, Marquis and, most recently, the Sunbeam. The firm also manufactures the Bat-

For the author's money the Marquis reel by Hardy Bros., of Alnwick, England, is the finest mass-produced fly reel for trout fishing made in the world. Note the polished spool rim which is just the right touch to keep running fish in check.

tenkill, C.F.O., Magnalite Multiplier and Lord series for the Orvis Co. of Manchester, Vermont, as well as several models for Pezon et Michel, famous French rodmakers. It's common to see fifty-year-old Hardy reels still in use, and old Hardies in mint condition fetch astronomical prices from collectors and traditionalist anglers. When deciding on a fly reel, therefore, it's hard to go wrong with a Hardy. Nor should you have to look farther than a nearby quality tackle shop to find one, because no company boasts a better wholesale reel distribution network.

Among Hardy reels, the Perfect carries most snob appeal. Heavy for its size and line capacity, though, I like the Perfect less than, for instance, the Princess, a model of similar dimensions, retailing for about two-thirds the price. Hardy's best effort, however, in my opinion, is represented in the Marquis series, which many American fly fishermen won't recognize by name because it was distributed here for many years wearing the moniker "Scientific Anglers System" (see photograph). Slightly less expensive than even the Princess-type reel, the Marquis (or System) nevertheless is equally well-made, weighs about the same, and has similar line capacity. Like most Hardies, it's easily modified for left- or righthand wind. And it's good looking. But most significant to me is that, in addition to the reliable Hardy drag mechanism, a polished spool rim overlapping the frame is engineered to function as a further check against running fish by pressing the heel of the hand against it. Eight Marquis models are available in the U.S., five of which, measuring from 2¾ to 3⅝-inches in diameter, are used widely to balance the gamut of rods and lines dry fly fishermen require for our nation's varied trout waters.

After years spent wedging lines, leaders, or both, between spools and frame cages on dozens of reels, I vowed several seasons back to abandon interchangeable spare spools forever, regardless of the financial impact. Only the Orvis C.F.O. series, I found, is constructed to minimize the trouble, thanks to the brilliance of reelmaker Stanley Bogdan, who designed it. So, had not a bit of elementary math revealed a fascinating economic fact, I might have recommended the C.F.O. as the smartest way to go, particularly for novices starting from scratch. However, I discovered that an Orvis catalog advertised the C.F.O. III, for instance, at $81.50, with a spare spool at $32.50, for a total of $114, while the Hackle & Tackle Co. offered the System-5 reel, my favorite, for $44.25. Thus, two System-5 reels cost $88.50, or $25.50 less than one C.F.O. III and a spare spool. The C.F.O. is a fine reel, certainly, but whether it's worth the substantial investment is a question of personal priority. To buy one for every line is surely not for me.

About two matters concerning reels and their use, in my view there's no effective margin for compromise: (1) Never purchase a reel too small to accommodate at least fifty yards of backing, even if that means lopping off a piece of fly line to make room. Every angler, including he who fishes mostly small waters, must *always be prepared for extraordinary situations,* a sterling example of which is a magnificent trout that grabs your fly and hightails it for the next county. The bigger the water, the more backing reels should carry. On broad rivers, for example, I'm not comfortable with less than 150 to 200 yards of fifteen-pound test braided nylon, just in case. More than once I've needed every inch. (2) An entirely proficient fly fisherman, despite what Granddad might have believed, doesn't pass his rod from one hand to the other after hooking a trout in order to crank the reel with his casting hand. Changing hands is awkward and inefficient and will eventually cost big fish. (No angler of skill or experience, by the way, plays trout by stripping line. *All trout should be played off the reel.*) The righthanded caster, therefore, should learn to reel with his left hand, and vice versa. Most novices, uncorrupted by bad habits, will have little trouble with the technique, while the best bet for veterans might be to think of themselves as old slogs learning a new trick.

LINES FOR DRY FLY FISHING

The dynamics of fly casting are unique among fishing techniques in that the weight to maintain the lure's momentum is distributed through the line instead of concentrated within the lure itself. Principles that govern catapulting a heavy object, such as a plug, to a fish are simple. However, when the weight that carries the lure must be distributed along a thirty-yard fly line because the lure has virtually no weight of its own, the capacity to mobilize and sustain flight becomes a matter of precise balance between the medium of weight distribution (the line) and the lever that launches and keeps the line in the air (the rod). In virtually all fly lines used by skilled anglers, weight is distributed by tapering formulas. Proper balance for presenting a fly, then, is achieved by matching a line's weight and taper to a suitable rod.

There are three orders of fly lines: the *floating line* (F), the *sinking line* (S), and a line of which the fore end sinks and the aft end floats, called the *sinking-tip line* (F/S). Only floating lines, however, are serviceable with dry flies. Among floaters, two taper styles concern us—the *double-taper* (DT) and *weight-forward taper* (WF). (*Level* lines [L], those with no taper, are virtually useless in my opinion, even for tiny streams.) Fortunately, almost two decades ago the American Fishing Tackle Manufacturers' Association (AFTMA) unraveled an involved procedure for line weight and taper recognition by establishing a standard by which the approximate weight of fly lines, measured in grains over the first thirty feet of line, is translated into a simple number code (1, 2, 3, 4, 5, 6, etc.). The number code, then, coupled with a line's taper and how it rides when introduced to water, both shown as abbreviations in parentheses above, easily identifies the crucial characteristics of concern to prospective buyers. A weight-forward floating line, weighing approximately 140 grains over its first thirty feet, for example, is known simply as a WF5F. The accompanying diagram and chart illustrate typical fly line tapers and AFTMA designations, including weight in grains for each size commonly used for dry fly fishing for trout. (See page 94.)

For convenience, many rod manufacturers print the line weights they recommend for their models just above the cork grip on the butt section of each rod. This good intention, however, I view as a mixed blessing, because, although helpful in some cases, to mention only line weight can lull inexperienced anglers into believing there's no consequential difference between, for instance, DT6F and WF6F lines, when in fact they have little in common beyond approximate 160-grain weight. The information supplied says nothing of how line weight should be distributed to suit a rod—that is, the desired taper. This is a conspicuous omission because many rods that handle DT5F lines beautifully, for example, behave like they're being asked to cast soupy Jell-O when rigged with WF5F's. It's common, in fact, for rods to function most efficiently when outfitted with weight-forward lines one size heavier than double-tapers that complement them, such as a

FLY LINE TAPERS

FIG. 1 DOUBLE-TAPER (DT)

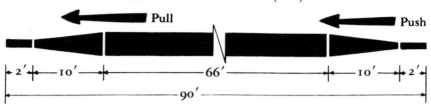

FIG. 2 WEIGHT-FORWARD (WF)

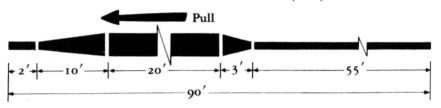

FLY LINES GENERALLY APPROPRIATE TO DRY FLY FISHING
Double-taper (DT) Floating (F) Lines

Designation	Weight*
DT3F	100 grains
DT4F	120 grains
DT5F	140 grains
DT6F	160 grains
DT7F	185 grains
DT8F	210 grains

Weight-forward (WF) Floating (F) Lines

Designation	Weight*
WF3F	100 grains
WF4F	120 grains
WF5F	140 grains
WF6F	160 grains
WF7F	185 grains
WF8F	210 grains

* 437½ grains = 1 ounce. AFTMA standards permit a margin of variation of plus or minus six grains for lines numbered three through five, plus or minus eight grains for those numbered six through eight. Thus, a DT6F line might weigh as little as 152 grains or as much as 168 grains over the first thirty feet of its length, depending on the manufacturer.

WF6F on a rod also balanced by a DT5F. Even that formula, though, constitutes no reliable rule of thumb. Walt Dette, legendary Catskill fly tyer, likes DT5F lines on rods calling for DT7F's. This is a rare case perhaps, but it's not really so far out because, ultimately, harmony between rod and line must be determined by individual casting styles. Before purchasing a rod, therefore, try several lines of various weights and tapers on it, casting over short, moderate and long distances to see which fares best.

Double-taper and weight-forward lines are intended to serve decidedly different purposes. As the illustration indicates, double-tapers perform in a *push-pull* fashion, while weight-forwards are limited by design to *pull only*. Relative to rod momentum the weight-forward is a fast line and the double-taper is slow, a principle which dictates, for instance, that double-tapers optimize line control but curtail distance. The contrary is true of weight-forwards. Double-tapers ideally suit small- to medium-size waters where casting curves, making delicate presentations, and mending line are frequently necessary. Weight-forwards, by contrast, work to peak efficiency on big waters where presentation is, perhaps, secondary to casting distance. They're also effective for battling head winds and presenting bushy flies. Anglers, I believe, should own both tapers, but because polishing presentation represents the cornerstone of my dry fly fishing technique, as the reader will recognize a little further along, I urge that double-tapers be used to the limits of their practicality, even when sticking with them may limit the angler's range a bit.

It's a rare occasion when trout are so skittish that line color makes the difference between success and failure. Yet, from the angler's perspective, monitoring the behavior of every inch of line put on the water from rod tip outward is fundamental to proper dry fly presentation. Undisciplined line is the prime cause of fly drag, which, in turn, becomes the basic reason most trout reject our offerings. Therefore, I advise lines in colors easily seen even in failing light, of which peach, as found in Cortland 444 lines, is my favorite. The 444's, by the way, are manufactured by Cortland in

Kinks and coils are guaranteed to reduce the efficiency of even the best fly caster. Straighten your fly line by stretching it carefully around a stump or tree and then applying constant, even tension for about ten seconds.

every DT and WF weight dry fly fishermen require and are available at hundreds of shops, both in the U.S. and abroad.

Following is a shopping list of additional tips concerning lines for dry fly fishing:

1. Lines stored on reels may become kinky. Always pull them off reels and straighten them by stretching before starting to fish. (see photo)
2. Unless you make an awful lot of ninety-foot casts, a double-taper line that appears worn out at one end can usually be reversed on the reel to extend its usefulness.

3. A fly line that sinks makes it virtually impossible to get a good dry fly drift. Try cleaning and dressing it. If that doesn't help, throw the line away and buy a new one.
4. Keep dry fly dressing and insect repellent away from fly lines. Some brands destroy fly line finishes.
5. Clean fly lines shoot much better than dirty or gummy ones. Use the line cleaner supplied by the manufacturers several times during each season.
6. Check rods for worn guides that may fray your fly line's finish.
7. Fly lines not in use should be stored in cool, dry places.
8. When traveling to remote areas, always carry an extra fly line. Many a big trout has taken an angler's line, leaving him all dressed up with no way to fish.

~~~~~~

CHAPTER SEVEN

The End of the Line

FOR A QUARTER CENTURY dry fly fishing in North America (and to a lesser extent abroad) has been dominated by the technique called *matching the hatch*. In theory it involves identifying insects upon which trout feed on local or regional bases and developing fly patterns to imitate those insects. However, the technique, as it has evolved from theory to practice, has come to amount to much more than that.

My living room has seen many a battle royal as to who should get credit for originating the concept, each probably a colossal waste of time and creative energy, since it's doubtful anybody really knows. It's safe enough, however, to credit Ernest Schwiebert, then a mid-western college student, with popularizing the phrase after he came up with it to title a book, published in 1955, that really got the whole thing rolling. Since then *matching the hatch* and *dry fly fishing* have become virtually synonymous terms to many anglers. Whether the sport, or those practitioners of it who have embraced the concept with unquestioning faith, have benefited accordingly, however, is a question of growing concern to me.

It's important to understand that from the earliest days most skilled dry fly fishermen have matched the hatch to some degree; that is, they've tried to offer trout flies perceived as appealing to the fish's feeding impulses. When there are lots of insects on the water, as during hatches or spinner falls, for instance, you'll see experienced anglers opt for patterns somewhat resembling those flies in size, color and configuration. Thus, whether or not they call what they're doing by a catchy name, they are, in fact, making a stab at matching the hatch. Common sense dictates that to do otherwise in most cases would constitute poor angling technique. Where such dry fly fishermen part company with those married to matching the hatch, however, is the point at which some anglers feel obliged to abandon common sense in favor of obsessively locking themselves into *precise representation,* as if failure to do so would erase all chance of success.

Most production resulting from overenthusiastic hatch-matching, as I view it, is the consequence of artistry at the fly tying vise, not artistry on the water. There's no way to state it without raising hackles, so I'll say it flat out. I've met few people preoccupied with precise representation whom I believe are truly skilled fishermen, however expert they may be at manufacturing bugs so realistic you'd expect them to fly away on their own. Nor have I encountered many waters where practiced anglers will be stumped if they know how to present flies with proficiency. I have witnessed, though, many anglers who attempt to rationalize deficiencies in technique by spending countless hours memorizing insect species by Latin names and then concocting replicas of them, hours that would be more wisely used mastering the elements of fly presentation. I'm compelled to question whether this fixation with technology (for that's what fly tying really comes down to) over technique isn't a matter of priorities run amok. Certainly it tends to make fishing dry flies appear more difficult than it is.

The most outspoken critic of compulsive matching the hatch I know is Catskill angler Ed Van Put who fishes only three dry fly patterns the season through—the Adams, the Royal Wulff and the Pheasant Tail midge. Ed, a fisheries technician with the New York State Department of Environmental Conservation, spends much of his time around trout water—"Too much time," he says, "to take matching the hatch very seriously." Ed's knack for bringing trout to the fly has prompted numerous magazine articles and newspaper columns about him, creating a sort of Van Put mystique, based more on romantic license, I'm afraid, than on sound observation. For it doesn't require many days with Van Put to perceive that his secret is no more involved than a practiced eye for making each trout an offer its opportunistic nature won't let it refuse.

A sterling example occurred recently when we fished a stretch of flat water in the tail of Cairns Eddy on the Beaverkill. It was toward evening, and the water was clear and low. Although few sizable flies could be seen, scores of trout were sipping at the surface, as if to midges.

"What are you going to use?" I asked. He held up a size 14 Adams. I should have known.

Most of the next two hours I spent watching Ed moving from trout to trout, casting once, twice, occasionally three or four times, hooking each fish in turn, playing it quickly but expertly, netting and releasing it to fight another day. To anybody unfamiliar with Ed Van Put this performance might have seemed uncanny, but I accepted it for a characteristic outing, like many others we'd had together—a matter of him placing his Adams right on each trout's feeding lane, not an inch one way or the other, of knowing before he made each cast there would be no drag to disrupt the fly's float, and of allowing enough drag-free float astern of each trout to permit the fish to follow the fly downstream several feet before deciding whether to suck it in or reject it.

Clichéd though the phrase may be, Ed Van Put's dry fly fishing technique is "poetry in motion." Note the perfect loop of leader and line, the angle of the rod over the water, the position of Ed's hand and arm, forming an extension of the rod, as well as that of his head with his eyes staring intently over the rod tip to the precise spot he knows his fly will light. It is this practiced technique that makes Ed Van Put a great dry fly fisherman, not his choice of fly patterns.

Finally, just before sundown I saw that Ed had taken on a fish he couldn't seem to attract, despite what looked to be a dozen or so letter-perfect presentations. That trout actually got Ed sputtering out loud. "Take it, you blankety-blank," he grumbled. "Come up. Where the hell are you." Ed stayed with the fish almost fifteen minutes, unaware, or so it seemed, that I'd edged downstream for a closer look. Then I saw him set the hook, and he crowed, "There you are, you blankety-blank." He turned to me. "Calling a trout a blankety-blank seems to work when nothing else will," he said. "It gets 'em every time."

"I don't know why that fish wouldn't take," Ed told me later, "but it obviously wasn't the fly that was wrong. Betcha, though, a hatch-matcher would have changed patterns a dozen times and then trotted around telling everybody the trout in Cairns are 'ultraselective.' What a lot of crap.

"Art, I don't care what fly you use within reason. If you put that fly over a trout the way the trout wants to see it, that trout is going to take. But if your presentation is wrong, if you show a fish leader (regardless of diameter), if you slap the fly onto the water, if the fly drags, even though the drag may be invisible to you, the trout won't take. If you want to say trout are selective, okay, *say they're selective about presentation.* But, about fly pattern, no way."

The dozen or so nice fish Ed hooked that evening would have converted, I'm sure, even the most skeptical. I just wish every dry fly fisherman in America could have been there to see it.

There's no question that matching the hatch will work if an angler feels inclined to bother with it. Experience teaches, however, that the more practiced the angler the less apt he will be to rely on the technique, especially as it's carried to extremes.

Before proceeding, there are two propositions promoted by hatch-matching's most zealous advocates with which I wish to take particular exception. The first supposes that to be other than a hatch-matcher somehow assigns you second-class status among fellow fishermen. What self-serving snobbery and patent nonsense. Quite the contrary, in fact, would probably follow were we to ponder that an angler able to present a fly, regardless of pattern, with sufficient finesse to lure a trout becomes, in essence, that trout's nemesis, while he who feels compelled to offer the trout only lifelike imitations relegates himself to the role of a butler. The second proposition that troubles me is the notion that without becoming hatch-matchers, anglers can expect little success on the stream. That bit of blarney has represented an effective sales pitch for some books recently, although a more credible argument could likely be made for the opposite point of view. Matching the hatch, which requires substantial investments of both time and money, actually distorts the essential criteria for competent dry fly fishing by creating a canon of procedure which paradoxically renders the technique the narrowest approach to fishing imaginable. Ultimately, then, a sound hypothesis, as it was originally conceived, now seems determined with its inflexibility to discourage initiative and innovation, each a cornerstone of angling expertise, while its obsession with fly pattern rather than fly presentation wastes hours of fishing time, as devotees change flies every twenty seconds to find the "right pattern" at the "right time" for the "right fish." Just thinking about it should wear a good man down. Trout, after all, can't rise to flies they don't get to see, and anglers, no matter how nimble their fingers, are certain to have the devil's own time keeping flies on the water when a third of each outing is spent lopping off tippets and tying knots. Thus, if readers glean anything from this volume, let it be that *no fly is "right" unless it's fished correctly.*

I wouldn't venture to guess how many dry fly patterns are dressed by amateur and professional tyers today. Considering all sorts of liberties taken with materials that give birth to countless variations of traditional patterns, the number probably is in the tens of thousands. Out the window forever, I'm certain, is a custom dictating that fly patterns be specific and unalterable compositions of furs, feathers, etc. Were this not so I wouldn't have dared refer to Ed Van Put's favorite as an Adams, since the original called for a golden pheasant tippet tail, while the variation Ed prefers (the one, incidentally, favored by most contemporary anglers) wears mixed brown and grizzly hackle fibers behind it. This license, of course, can be interpreted as a mixed blessing, since on one hand it encourages latitude among tyers to adapt flies to local conditions, while on the other it makes purchasers of flies uncertain at times about what's in store when they order. One fact is clear, however: there are more dry fly patterns available now than any angler, including the most traveled professional, should either need or want.

Professional anglers are frequently asked, "What constitutes a good fly?" Only a dunderhead would presume to have an authoritative answer. Consider the following: a deadly pattern may be fragile as angel's lace, while another, perhaps not quite so effective, lasts like Churchill. . . . A fantastic fly isn't widely known and, thus, is dressed by few tyers. . . . A dry that floats perfectly on placid water goes down like a rock when it encounters turbulence. Another fly floats like a cork through pockets but lacks the qualities to fool finicky fish on flats. . . . Materials for one pattern are expensive, but those for a reasonable facsimile aren't. . . . Your fishing experience has been exclusively in the Rockies, and you're about to make your first Eastern trip. Can you rely on your regional favorites? . . . A pattern picks up eight-inchers like a vacuum cleaner, but it bombs when shown to three-pounders. All this, I think, illustrates that there's really no such thing as a "good fly" by definition, but rather that a pattern's worth exists only when all aspects of design and performance are measured against the requirements and priorities of its owner.

In light of the foregoing and anticipating what follows, a comment about the state of fly tying is essential. Unfortunately, fly tying hasn't remained immune to contemporary society's consuming naiveté that leads it to embrace self-proclaimed and instant experts. Volume tying of quality flies isn't mastered overnight. Indeed, among the nation's thousands of commercial tyers, there are few Dettes, Darbees or Poul Jorgensens, although many individuals sell flies who, I'm convinced, are sufficiently deluded by an abundance of self-confidence and a dearth of expert instruction to believe they're in the same class. Furthermore, since the demand for flies is growing at a rate faster than skilled tyers can be self-taught or trained, a decidedly inferior product is finding its way to the market and is gaining acceptance—indeed, is even being touted at times as the standard for the business.

There is a lifetime of pride and experience wedded to each hook when Walt Dette dresses a dry fly. Despite increasing difficulties obtaining materials, Walt and his wife, Winnie, of Roscoe, N.Y., have refused to compromise one iota the quality of their creations. No one knows the secret process Walt uses to pre-wax the fine silk thread he still insists upon using, for instance, or the countless hours spent sorting through feathers most tyers would love to have just to find the few he deems worthy of winding on a hook. Nor is it widely appreciated—because he is a modest man who assiduously shuns publicity— that Walt Dette is probably the greatest tyer of classic dry flies of all time.

Walt Dette, perhaps the world's premier dresser of traditional dry flies for sale, shocked me recently when he asserted, "You can teach someone the rudiments of tying flies in a few hours." Anticipating my response, he added, though, "Then all he needs is forty or fifty years to learn materials and to put the mechanics and the materials together, and he may have it—if he has a good sense of proportions and his eyes don't go bad." Asked whether he believes that people are capable of taking some lessons through an adult education course or Trout Unlimited chapter, for instance, and then turning out flies that should be accepted by the public, Walt's answer was, "No. If it were that easy, I wouldn't still be learning after fifty years."

Walt, among other fine tyers, has shared many of his secrets with me. (Although I dress serviceable flies for my own use, I wouldn't presume myself capable of producing flies for sale. Speed without compromising quality is a hallmark of solid commercial tyers, and were I to speed up to make minimum wage, my flies would look like chickens struck by lightning.) Friendships such as that with Walt have also fostered the rare opportunity to field-test a wide range of creations and, thus, to evolve a personal viewpoint regarding fly quality which, although thoroughly subjective, may prove helpful to fellow anglers, especially those relatively new to the sport.

Among the several characteristics I consider essential in dry flies are *availability, durability, floatability, proportion* and *uniformity.* Because I fish so much and tie so little, I generally opt for patterns I know I can get as I need them. Similarly, considering the passel of flies I go through, I want flies to withstand a lot of fishing and, if I may say so without seeming immodest, a lot of fish. To that end, I buy flies of sturdy construction or, when fragile materials, such as peacock herl, must be used, flies dressed by tyers with the knowledge and inclination to re-enforce those materials. Peacock herl, by the way, is re-enforced by counter-winding silk thread through it.

Believe me, there's nothing glib in writing that *I want dry flies to float,* for, unless tyers bring to bear abundant knowledge of materials, including how the properties of each accommodate the use of others, they're likely to tie a lot of rocks. Consider, for example, two patterns, the Adams and the Royal Wulff. The former can be effectively dressed sparsely on standard wire hooks because it calls for a buoyant muskrat body and lightweight hackle-tip wings. The latter pattern, by contrast, with its body of peacock herl and tightly-wound floss, plus its wings of heavy kip (calf tail), requires a stiff tail and ample hackle to keep it up, particularly on turbulent water, unless the tyer opts for light wire hooks or chooses to put his Royal Wulffs of size 12 dimensions, for instance, on size 14 hooks, 2X long, to minimize weight.

Proper *proportions,* of course, make flies look nice, and beyond that they indicate whether a tyer knows his job. Even more significant, though, is that *proportion*—the way one material is applied relative to another—largely dictates how reliably an angler can present a fly, as well as whether or not the quarry views the angler's offering as a reasonable rendering of something it wants to eat.

The accompanying illustration shows two mayfly imitations dressed in traditional style. The fly on the left is overdressed. It

wears too much material, particularly hackle, for its hook size, a flaw often encountered when unskilled tyers try to turn out midges, flies in sizes 20 through 28. Anglers in the market for tiny patterns must beware, therefore, of flies labeled, for instance, size 22 when, in fact, they're size 18's ineptly dressed on size 22 hooks.

Now examine the tails, and you'll discover that of the improperly dressed fly to be too short, which, besides making the fly appear unnatural, would render an angler powerless to insure that the fly rides correctly. Inadequate tails make flies list astern, which, in turn, causes tail fibers to break the water's surface tension, making the flies semi-float tail downward.

Next, compare bodies. The body of the poor fly is both too short and too bulky for the hook size. Oversized bodies make flies difficult to float, especially when they've been fished awhile. All dubbing materials absorb some water that increases a fly's overall weight. A fly, therefore, is best dressed with its body tapered gradually forward to where the hackle begins from just in front of the tail, or a point slightly ahead of the slope of the bend of the hook. For dubbed bodies, incidentally, I prefer natural materials, especially fur, to the synthetic fibers popular today. Despite contrary claims, my experimentation indicates that virtually all synthetics are more prone to take on and hold water than those of fur-bearers, and particularly those fur-bearers that spend considerable time around water, such as the muskrat.

Carelessly set wings seem to be the singular trademark of incompetent tyers. Notice that the wings of the poor fly are situated too far forward on the hook and are decidedly tilted. Dry fly wings should be placed on the fore one-third of the hook in a position that permits two turns of hackle behind and two ahead of them. Tilted wings, of course, cause flies to list on the water, no matter how able the caster. A fly floating on its side appears unnatural to trout, except, perhaps, in a rare instance when it's taken for a deformed dun, incapable of swimming upright to dry its wings before takeoff, or a spinner fallen to the surface with enough life in it after mating to kick up a fuss.

The hackle on the improperly tied fly, besides being too large, is wound incorrectly with several turns behind the wings and only one turn in front. The hackle is of poor quality, that is, soft and hinged near the tip of each fiber. Sloppy hackling is a common cause of imbalanced float, while poor quality hackle frequently collapses, causing flies to sink with use.

(Obtaining quality dry fly hackle at reasonable cost is the bane of every commercial tyer's existence. There are means to compensate for poor hackle, however, although few tyers seem to use them. Some mediocre hackle improves with age, for instance, and thus if stored from several months to several years stiffens up beautifully. The process, incidentally, can be speeded up by placing necks in a warm oven to dry. Probably the best way to improve hackle quality, though, is to clip it, either square across the bottom of each fly or around the collar. In this way excellent hackle for, for instance, size 6 or 8 flies, which are in little demand, can be utilized in popular sizes, including sizes 10, 12 and even 14, without inhibiting whatsoever the potential performance of the flies. Were more tyers to clip hackle, particularly across the bottom which actually *enhances* float, a trick many ignore only for fear of customer resistance, the general run of flies reaching shops could be substantially improved overnight.)

Finally, note the heads of both flies. The poor fly has a bulky, uneven head that obscures part of the hook eye, while the good one has virtually no head. Because each turn of tying thread adds weight, I like almost headless flies, such as those traditional with the Catskill school. Skilled tyers, such as Walt and Winnie Dette and Harry Darbee, require just a couple of turns of thread to secure their hackle and three or four to perform a whip finish. Good penetrating cement then secures their flies against wear and tear. I understand and accept, however, that many anglers and tyers prefer headed flies. To keep their flies lightweight, I'd suggest the minimum turns of thread essential to satisfy their criteria for a head. They should also insist heads be completed well behind hook eyes to insure room (1) to pass tippet material through, and (2) to tie proper knots.

Since no two insects in nature are identical, *uniformity* of fly dressing becomes more the product of concern for a tyer's ability to perform an exacting task consistently than of whether or not trout give a damn if all flies of a pattern and size look exactly alike (trout couldn't care less). When ordering flies, however, it's reasonable to desire the fewest possible surprises; thus, given typical alternatives of rigid conformity and whimsy, I'll take flies of which each of a pattern in a size might have come from a cookie cutter. Symmetry has a magical way of signaling quality.

It's fine to assign dry flies to categories, as long as you don't get carried away. To simplify things, therefore, I've chosen the following classifications, shown with my choices of patterns, sizes and dressings for each in the next chapter: *mayfly duns, mayfly spinners, caddis imitations, midges, terrestrials* and *attractors* (including stoneflies). I hasten to add, though, that the designations are *very loosely drawn,* since it's altogether practical to adapt a fly from one group for use in another under a host of conditions, including several that readers will note in upcoming chapters. The Adams, for instance, which is listed as a mayfly dun primarily because of its silhouette, is sufficiently versatile to be deadly fished as an insect from any of the other groups, the reason Ed Van Put refers to it as, "My matching-the-hatch fly. Represents nothing—looks like everything." Similarly, the Pheasant Tail midge makes a dandy small caddis; and a large attractor, such as the White Wulff, looks suspiciously like the mayfly dun from which my neighbor and friend, Lee Wulff, originally drew the concept.

Recommending patterns is the part of this job about which I feel least comfortable, because surely scores of other experienced fishermen could compile lists of equally effective flies without repeating a single name. But I guess such exercises would serve only to punctuate my conclusion that fly pattern is less critical than the skill of the person fishing. Ultimately, I'm convinced that the condition that makes one fly better than another rests with the angler's faith in the fly, which, in turn, translates into making a better fisherman of him each time he ties it on. Could anglers with sufficient faith and skill, then, fish only *one* pattern the season through? Might Ed Van Put abandon his Pheasant Tail midge and Royal Wulff and use only the Adams? Under most stream and river situations across the United States, probably so. Yet, there are worlds of difference between what anglers can do, should do and will do; and so, bearing in mind that most of us are at once practical and romantic, disciplined and chaotic, rational and superstitious, I'm obliged to offer in the next chapter an adequate shopping list for tastes between modest and imposing. I've used each pattern cited with success on a range of waters, and while I have little doubt readers will revise my list with gems of their own sooner or later, newcomers to the sport can rest assured that, with these patterns in recommended sizes, there's virtually no dry fly fishery at home or abroad they'll be ill-equipped to tackle, at least not among those I know anything about.

When a natural or artificial fly floats over a trout, how is it perceived by the fish? Enough conflicting theories exist among scientists to prove that nobody is really sure. The scientific community can't even agree on whether or not trout see color. Because measuring perceptions of sophisticated life forms is a function not only of interpreting the workings of the eye but also of the processes that occur between the eye and the brain, I doubt that we'll ever reliably define the images trout depend upon to discriminate between what they want and what they don't; or that were we able to do so electronically, for instance, by means of some complex device, that a reliable facsimile of what the trout see could be projected on a screen or printed in a book without risk of further misunderstanding when the image became caught up in the circuitry involved in our human powers of observation and interpretation.

It's a safe assumption, though, that when trout see dry flies the impact triggers the same processes used by the fish to (1) satisfy the need for nourishment by feeding on floating insects, or (2) respond to external stimuli out of excitation or irritation. It's also evident that trout are able to differentiate at least between color intensities, although maybe not between colors as we define them.

During Hendrickson hatches, for example, I've experienced equal success fishing the traditional Hendrickson pattern (dun tail, tannish body, dun hackle and gold, mottled wings) and the Adams (grizzly and brown tail, gray body, brown and grizzly hackle, and grizzly hackle-tip wings), although the flies really don't look a bit alike, except that they are of neutral or "earthy" hues. However, I've also tried to lure trout to dries of red, yellow and blue, primary colors not found in nature, with absolutely no score.

I like to think my most effective dry fly patterns are those that evoke in trout a *sense* or *impression* of insects they expect to see and accept, although to the human eye the resemblance to those insects may be suspect. To that end, I prefer dressings into which life is breathed by their designers to those attempts at precise imitation which, I can only speculate, trout view as we might wooden beefsteaks. Size is important, yes, and silhouette, as well as color shade to a lesser degree. The critical ingredient, however, I'm convinced, lies in a gift for animation, even though, as in the instance of spent spinners, the insects suggested may well be dead. Thus flies should be supple, not stiff—concocted of materials to indicate life as a "plain, plump fact," in the words of Browning. Such materials include soft furs, feathers segmented and mottled as only nature can yield them, sheeny synthetics, and hackle prepared to dance to the rhythms of flowing water. Why do trout prefer such flies to our most strenuous tries at precise imitation? I can't say for certain. Perhaps the answer exists somewhere in the space reserved for words like "soul."

Dry fly fishing is unalterably entwined with the life-cycles of insects. Varying with each fishery, of course, this relationship prevails to the degree fish depend on insects for sustenance. This dependence can account for eighty-five to ninety percent of trout feeding, according to scientists, although some of it occurs beneath the surface. Therefore, dry fly fishermen must know something about insect behavior. However, it's neither crucial, nor even desirable in my opinion, for us to become entomologists. Imagining such a need diverts attention from fundamental angling to extraneous biology. Anglers so inclined are sometimes tagged "fly swatters."

Bugs of interest to trout are divided into two groups: *aquatic insects*—those that spend some portion of their lives in water—and *terrestrials,* or land-based insects. Of principal concern to dry fly fishermen among species of the former group are *mayflies, caddis* and *stoneflies,* although there are others, including dragonflies, mosquitoes, dobsonflies and a plethora of wee real flies, such as gnats and diptera, of only incidental importance in many regions. The terrestrial category is composed of such trout delicacies as hoppers, crickets, beetles, ants, spiders, moths and butterflies, all in a seemingly endless array of sizes and colors.

Aquatic insects naturally constitute standard fare for most surface-feeding trout, since their life-cycles put them in the wrong places at the right times, thus making them easy pickings. Much dry fly fishing lore, in fact, has sprung from mayfly "hatches," although angling techniques of late have been refined to cash in too on mating flights and falls of spinners. Similarly, dry fly fishermen are only gradually recognizing and adapting to the role of caddis, some eight hundred species able to survive, if not flourish, amid pollution problems more damaging to mayflies and stoneflies. Where water quality remains good stoneflies still represent a notable food source for trout, however, although the degree varies by region. On some Western rivers, for example, seasons are chronicled in terms of the annual appearances of juicy stones some four inches long, just as in the Catskills of the East anglers define prime periods by plotting mayfly emergences.

The drawings on pages 115 and 116 illustrate typical life-cycles of mayflies and caddis. The periods of urgent concern to dry fly fishermen are obviously those when the insects are on or near the surface. That's not to say, of course, that trout can't be "pounded up" to dries during other periods. But because particularly active feeding may occur underneath at such times, it would be an irresponsible author, even one writing exclusively of fishing dry flies, who failed to point out that subsurface techniques, including the use of nymphs, wet flies or emergers, frequently prove most productive during those periods. Note, too, that caddis, depending on species, are vulnerable to surface feeders either when they deposit eggs on the water by touching down and taking off, or when they land on the surface, dive to the bottom, deposit their eggs and swim to the top again, where they ride the flows several seconds before take-off. Observers of the latter group, incidentally, frequently mistake these adults for hatching caddis, an understandable error since they differ from emerging adults only in behavior, not looks.

For the reader's sake it might be nice to declare that the illustrations portray the essential story of aquatic insects, at least for purposes of accomplished angling. Unfortunately, that isn't the case. For years I've wrestled with the problem of how to impart missing information about some 1,700 species of flies as it would apply to all angling situations without resorting to extraneous or plain bum scoop. The scope of trout fisheries and the insect populations that inhabit them, however, have led me finally to the conclusion that any such exercise must deteriorate into the sort of vain generalities I'm so quick to condemn in contemporary American angling literature as boring and useless, if not downright destructive.

All sports make demands on practitioners. Dry fly fishing is no exception. Angling's foremost demand is *observation,* which must then be translated into enlightened action. Pertinent information about insects gleaned with experience on one river or stream may prove insignificant elsewhere, as numerous factors, including climate, structure and fertility, can be expected to prompt considerable variations in both the insect species present and the size, appearance and behavior of those species. Such variation from fishery to fishery is what makes the most determined tries at cataloging insects hopelessly irrelevant to practical angling. To observe, interpret and utilize, then, is the province of the fisherman, to which he's well advised to give his best shot.

Observation, of course, is greatly simplified when anglers have pretty good ideas of what they should look for. To that end it's

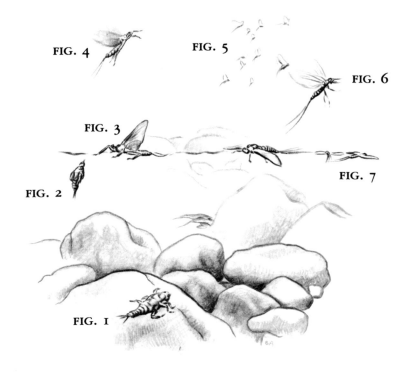

FIG. 4   FIG. 5

FIG. 6

FIG. 3

FIG. 7

FIG. 2

FIG. 1

MAYFLY LIFE CYCLE

After spending most of its life underwater as a *nymph* (Fig. 1), a
mayfly swims to the surface to hatch. During the swim-up stage
(Fig. 2), it is known to fly fishermen as an *emerger*. The emerger
hatches into a *dun* (Fig. 3) which, while it is on the surface, is a
primary source of food for trout. The dun then flies off the water
(Fig. 4), usually to nearby foliage where it will undergo yet
another transformation. When it has become a *spinner* (Fig. 5), it
will join others and be seen swarming over the surface in mating
flights. Some spinners simply drop their fertilized eggs, but
others will touch down on the surface to deposit them (Fig. 6).
Then, finally, the act of renewing the species completed, the
spinners fall to the surface (Fig. 7) where they drift along with
the flow either totally helpless or dead and are eaten in great
numbers by awaiting fish.

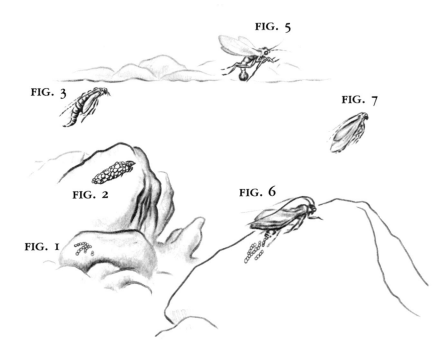

FIG. 4

FIG. 5

FIG. 3

FIG. 7

FIG. 2

FIG. 6

FIG. 1

CADDIS LIFE CYCLE

Like the mayfly, the caddis fly begins its life in an *egg* (Fig. 1).
After the egg stage, the caddis spends most of its life as a
larva, encased in a protective shell it manufactures either of
small sticks or bits of gravel (Fig. 2). When it is ready to
hatch, the caddis swims up as a *pupa* (Fig. 3) and often rides
with the flow on the surface where it may be taken by trout if
it doesn't escape to a nearby shore as an *adult* (Fig. 4). When
adults have mated, some deposit their eggs on the surface of
the stream (Fig. 5), while others swim to the bottom (Fig. 6),
deposit them and then swim up again (Fig. 7). It is these
diving ovipositers that anglers frequently confuse with
hatching caddis, because both are usually spotted after
swimming up from the bottom.

116

tough to beat experienced partners for each spot to be fished. (Joe Brooks, legendary angling editor of *Outdoor Life* magazine, once confided he seldom tackled strange waters without guides, professional or otherwise.) For those times you must go it alone, however, here is the kind of thing your powers of observation must be keyed to.

1. Most fisheries have sequential mayfly, caddis and stonefly hatches, although external conditions are liable to influence their precise timetables. Note emergence dates as encountered, as well as the size of flies, their coloration and, most important, their behavior during the intervals when they are vulnerable to trout. Pay particular attention to water and air temperatures, for they are apt to affect both insect hatching and trout feeding.

2. Observe where various species of flies come off. Some, you'll note, emerge exclusively from pocket water where there's plenty of rock, while others favor flats with silt, sand or gravel bottoms.

3. As each season progresses, be mindful that the timing of hatches will probably change, too, from late morning through mid-afternoon when air and water temperatures are cool to early morning and evening as heat and low water stress both fish and fisheries. Also be aware that the earliest hatches each season tend to be small dark flies that are followed in succession by larger dark ones, then light large ones, then light small ones, then darker small ones, then dark large ones and, finally, small dark ones.

4. Watch for dovetailing hatches, that is, emergences of more than one insect species simultaneously. They can appear either for brief periods as overlapping hatches or as parallel hatches of similar duration. Trout, you'll find, sometimes prefer one species to another during multiple hatches. Therefore, the angler should concentrate on fishing his flies to behave like the species his quarry favors. Also, be ready for hatches and spinner falls that occur concurrently, because trout frequently pass up larger duns that must be chased for smaller spinners that constitute a sure thing.

5. Try to fix in your memory the time lapses between emergences of insect species and their return as spinners or ovipositing caddis or stoneflies. Having done so, you can anticipate likely periods for exciting action before they're on you.

6. Observe rise forms intently, as they can tip you off to the kinds of insects on which trout are feeding. The *simple rise,* for instance, may indicate trout coming for duns riding on the surface (see illustrations on pages 120–122). The *head-and-tail rise* is standard practice among trout working on midges or spent spinners. The *splashy rise* is common with trout chasing caddis, whether the flies are hatching, ovipositing or simply fluttering over the water. The *splashy rise* may also signify trout chasing emerging mayfly species that swim rapidly from streambed to surface and leave the water without pausing to dry their wings. The *leaping rise* may be a trout's only means of capturing stoneflies or mating spinners over the water.

7. Estimate how plentiful flies are during each emergence. When trout must choose your imitation from among multitudes, sometimes you'll find too many flies can be worse than too few.

8. Pinpoint feeding rituals of trout during hatches and spinner falls. Note that some fish hold to precise feeding stations, while others tend to cruise, thus making the angler present his fly not where a trout was but where it's next likely to be.

9. *Keep notes.* I like the log form shown on page 123, although any concise format will do. Before hitting the water refer to your log, for with passing seasons you'll perceive standards of behavior to assist you in targeting in on the most effective angling techniques.

The role terrestrials play in trout feeding habits is less easily defined than that of aquatic insects. Their availability varies markedly by region, even by fishery. When terrestrials end up floating over trout, you can be sure the bugs didn't plan it that way. Many terrestrials, it seems, are simply victims of accidents of birth, hatched too close to rivers or streams. One thing is certain, though: when trout can get terrestrials, they'll gobble them up.

With the exception of occasional clouds of flying ants in the East and mobs of hoppers typical in some parts of the West, I've never encountered full-blown terrestrial "hatches." Thus, to discern imitations most appealing to fish for particular outings becomes a matter of both *observation* and *experimentation*. Following are some thoughts about land-based insects the reader should find helpful.

1. Because the appearance of terrestrials on the water is largely incidental, trout generally seem willing to accept a number of patterns during a given day. Experience teaches, for instance, that trout like ants regardless of season. Similarly, large hopper imitations appeal to the instinct dictating that trout endeavor to get the most food for the least energy expended.

2. Vegetation along rivers and streams in great measure prescribes the availability of terrestrial insects. Grassy areas such as meadows, for example, are ideal habitat for hoppers, crickets and beetles, particularly when grasses lean over the water. Likewise, stream-bank trees make perfect homes for terrestrials, including ants, some of which are bound to fall into the drink.

3. Most terrestrial species are seasonal. A walk along a stream bank should clue you in to what species are most plentiful at any time of year.

4. Sudden spates represent the terrestrial insect's worst environmental foe. Remember, exposed streambeds are "land" to terrestrials that are frequently caught napping when waters rise. This phenomenon is especially influential along tailwater fisheries where releases below dams may yo-yo water levels daily.

SIMPLE RISE

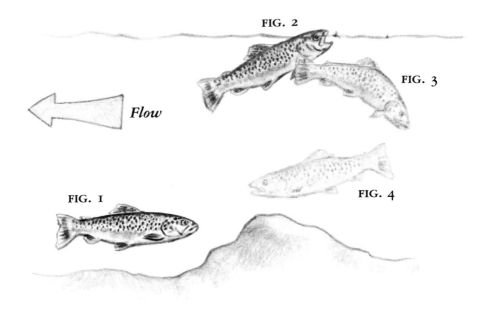

FIG. 2

FIG. 3

Flow

FIG. 1

FIG. 4

The *simple rise* begins with the trout facing into the flow near the bottom of the river or stream (Fig. 1). Having spotted a morsel floating on the surface, the trout swims slowly but deliberately all the way to the top, where it butts its head through the surface just in time to intercept the bug it is after (Fig. 2). The trout then arches its body downward (Fig. 3) and, turning (Fig. 4), returns to its regular lie near the bottom. This cycle may be repeated scores, or even hundreds, of times during a single hatch.

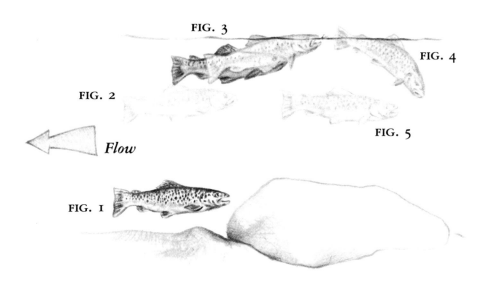

FIG. 3

FIG. 4

FIG. 2

FIG. 5

Flow

FIG. 1

The *head and tail rise,* like the simple rise, begins with the trout lying near the bottom, facing into the flow (Fig. 1). In this case, however, having seen a copious supply of food floating overhead, the trout swims up very slowly and takes a new position only inches below the surface (Fig. 2). Thus stationed, the trout turns upward just enough to sip a fly (Fig. 3), before rotating downward again, usually showing us the tip of his tail (Fig. 4). Once below the surface after taking the fly (Fig. 5), the trout doesn't swim to the bottom. Rather, it simply drifts with the flow back to the position just under the surface from which it began its leisurely rise. The rhythm of the head and tail rise is generally steady and may be repeated many hundreds of times during a single feeding period.

SPLASHY OR LEAPING RISE

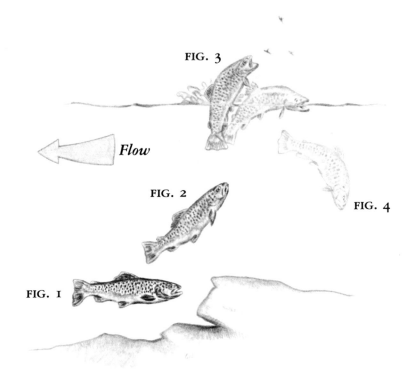

FIG. 3

FIG. 4

Flow

FIG. 2

FIG. 1

When a trout is about to make a *splashy* or *leaping rise*, you would seldom guess it, since the fish generally seems to be resting unconcerned near the bottom, facing into the flow (Fig. 1). Then, suddenly, the trout will shoot almost straight up (Fig. 2), as if shot from a gun. Nor is the trout apt to stop at the surface (Fig. 3), as its momentum will usually carry it upward into the air. Upon falling or diving back through the surface (Fig. 4), the trout can be expected to beat it to the bottom again, swimming downward almost as fast as it did to the top. Anglers frequently say that a splashy rise is made by a fish that doesn't entirely clear the water, while a leaping rise is made by the fish when its entire body comes out of the water.

LOG FORM

DATE: _____   PLACE: _____

TIME: A.M. 5 6 7 8 9 10 11 12 1 2 3 4 5 6 7 8 9 P.M.

AIR TEMP: 25 30 35 40 45 50 55 60 65 70 75 80 85 90 95

WATER TEMP: 35   40   45   50   55   60   65   70   75

WEATHER:	_____ Sunny	_____ Cloudy
	_____ Showers	_____ H. Rain
	_____ Overcast	_____ Drizzle
	_____ Rain	_____ Snow

HUMIDITY:	_____ Low	_____ High
	_____ Moderate	

WIND:	_____ None	_____ Moderate
	_____ Light	_____ High

BAROMETER:	_____ Low	_____ Falling
	_____ Rising	_____ High
	_____ Moderate	_____ Steady

WATER:	_____ Very Low	_____ Normal
	_____ Low	_____ High
	_____ Very high	_____ Cloudy
	_____ Clear	

FEEDING ACTIVITY:	_____ Very slow	_____ Slow
	_____ Moderate	
	_____ Active	_____ Very active

HATCHES:	_____ None	_____ Light
	_____ Sporadic	_____ Heavy

SPECIES/STRETCH/TIME _____

_____

_____

NOTES: _____

_____

_____

TIME	NUMBER	SIZE	SPECIES	SIZE FLY	STRETCH
	TOTAL				

~~~~~~

CHAPTER EIGHT

Do-It-Yourself

IT WOULD BE IMPOSSIBLE to gauge the number of American anglers who tie their own flies, but it's certain the percentage of those who do increases every season. It's a great thrill, of course, to hook a trout on any dry fly. To bring a trout to one you've dressed yourself, however, is the ultimate thrill. So, while all flies featured in this volume were chosen in part for their ready availability from commercial tyers, for the convenience of those who will want to go it alone, including those who would have it no other way, here are the dressings for the twenty-nine patterns shown in the color plates:

MAYFLY DUNS

ADAMS
Hook: 10–18
Thread: Black

Wings: Grizzly hackle-tips, preferably those of medium-dark saddles (wings can be tied in either upright or spent)
Tail: Brown and grizzly hackle fibers
Body: Muskrat
Hackle: Mixed brown and grizzly

BLUE-WINGED OLIVE

Hook: 12–20 (size 20 should be straight-eyed hook)
Thread: Black or rusty-brown
Wings: None
Tail: Rusty-dun hackle fibers
Body: Blend of olive yarn and muskrat dubbing
Hackle: Rusty-dun

CREAM VARIANT

Hook: 10–16
Thread: Yellow
Wings: None
Tail: Cream hackle fibers
Body: Center quill from stripped cream saddle hackle (lacquer body when fly is completed)
Hackle: Stiff cream

GRAY FOX VARIANT

Hook: 10–16
Thread: Primrose
Wings: None
Tail: Ginger hackle fibers
Body: Center quill from stripped cream hackle (lacquer body when fly is completed)
Hackle: Ginger, cree and grizzly

LIGHT CAHILL
Hook: 12–18
Thread: Pale yellow
Wings: Wood duck fibers from flank feathers
Tail: Light ginger
Body: Cream fox fur dubbing
Hackle: Light ginger

MAYFLY SPINNERS

CREAM SPINNER
Hooks: 14–22 (sizes 20 and 22 should be straight-eyed hooks)
Thread: White
Wings: White poly yarn
Tail: Cream hackle fibers
Body: Cream fox fur dubbing
Hackle: None

OLIVE SPINNER
Hook: 14–22 (sizes 20 and 22 should be straight-eyed hooks)
Thread: Rusty-brown, tan or primrose
Wings: White or pale gray poly yarn
Tail: Medium dun hackle fibers
Body: Olive wool fluffed for dubbing
Hackle: None

RED QUILL SPINNER
Hook: 12–24 (sizes 20–24 should be straight-eyed hooks)
Thread: Brown
Wings: White or pale gray poly yarn
Tail: Pale dun hackle fibers
Body: Rusty-colored wool or synthetic yarn fluffed for dubbing

Hackle: None, except for sizes 12–14 when a couple of turns of pale dun, clipped across the bottom, will enhance float.

TRICO SPINNER
Hook: 20–28 straight-eyed
Thread: Black
Wings: White poly yarn
Tail: Pale dun hackle fibers
Body: Rear one-third, white moose mane; fore two-thirds, black fur dubbing
Hackle: None

CADDIS

CREAM CADDIS
Hook: 12–20 (size 20 should be straight-eyed hook)
Thread: Pale yellow
Wing: Bleached deer body hair
Tail: None
Body: Pale yellow wool fluffed for dubbing
Hackle: Light badger

GRAY CADDIS
Hook: 12–22 (sizes 20–22 should be straight-eyed hooks)
Thread: Black
Wing: Photo-dyed, dark dun, deer body hair
Tail: None
Body: Muskrat fur dubbing
Hackle: Dark dun or brown and grizzly

HENRYVILLE SPECIAL
Hook: 12–18
Thread: Black or brown

Wings: Mallard primary quill over wisps of wood duck flank feather
Tail: None
Body: Green floss under palmered grizzly hackle
Hackle: Brown

MIDGES

BLACK GNAT
Hook: 18-24 (sizes 20-24 should be straight-eyed hooks)
Thread: Black
Wings: Fibers from dun hen body feathers
Tail: Dark dun hackle fibers
Body: Black fur dubbing
Hackle: Dark dun

CREAM MIDGE
Hook: 20-28 straight-eyed
Thread: White or pale yellow
Wings: None
Tail: Cream hackle fibers
Body: Stripped center quill of small cream hackle (lacquer body when fly is completed)
Hackle: Cream

MAHOGANY MIDGE
Hook: 20-22 straight-eyed
Thread: Black
Wings: None
Tail: Dun hackle fibers
Body: Stripped center quill of small brown hackle (lacquer body when fly is completed)
Hackle: Rusty-dun

DRY FLY PATTERNS

color photo #1   MAYFLY DUNS:
(below—left to right from top)
Gray Fox Varient, Adams, Blue-winged Olive, Cream Varient, Light Cahill

color photo #2   ATTRACTORS:
(next page—left to right from top)
Dutchman, Katterman, Royal Wulff, Brown and Grizzly Spider, Brown
and Grizzly Bivisible, White Wulff, Ausable Wulff, Clipped-Hackle Egg Sac, Hornberg

color photo #3   CADDIS:
(third page, top—left to right from top)
Henryville Special, Cream Caddis, Gray Caddis

color photo #4   MAYFLY SPINNERS:
(third page, bottom—left to right from top)
Trico Spinner, Cream Spinner, Rusty Spinner, Olive Spinner

color photo #5   MIDGES:
(last page, top—left to right from top)
Pheasant Tail, Cream Midge, Black Gnat, Mahogany Midge

color photo #6   TERRESTRIALS:
(last page, bottom—left to right from top)
Letort Hopper, Black Cricket, Black Beetle, McMurray Ant

Flies dressed by Ed Van Put

1

3

4

5

6

PHEASANT TAIL
   Hook: 20–28 straight-eyed
   Thread: Black or rusty-brown
   Wings: None
   Tail: Two fibers from a cock ringneck pheasant tail
   Body: Extension of tail wound up the hook shank
   Hackle: Medium dun

TERRESTRIALS

BLACK BEETLE
   Hook: 10–14
   Thread: Black
   Tail: None
   Body: Peacock herl re-enforced with counterwound silk thread; black hackle palmered from rear to front of hook and clipped across the bottom
   Wing: Dyed black duck quill or dyed black deer hair, tied in at the bend of the hook and brought forward as a hood over the body (several coats of lacquer are applied when the fly is completed)
   Hackle: None
   Head: Wing material flared and clipped short

BLACK CRICKET
   Hook: 12–16
   Thread: Black
   Tail: None
   Body: Black fur dubbing
   Wings: Dyed black deer body hair over dyed black duck quill
   Hackle: None
   Head: Dyed black deer hair, flared and clipped short

LETORT HOPPER
Hook: 10–14
Thread: Rusty-brown
Tail: None
Body: Pale yellow wool fluffed for dubbing
Wings: Deer body hair over mottled turkey wing quill
Hackle: None
Head: Deer body hair flared and clipped short

MC MURRAY ANT
Hook: 14–22 (sizes 20–22 should be straight-eyed hooks)
Thread: Black
Wings: None
Tail: None
Body: Two small cylinders of balsa wood affixed to a strand
of monofilament and lacquered black
Hackle: Black, clipped top and bottom

ATTRACTORS

AUSABLE WULFF
Hook: 8–18
Thread: Hot orange
Wings: White kip (calf-tail)
Tail: Woodchuck guard-hairs
Body: Australian opossum with a decided orange cast
Hackle: Brown and grizzly

BROWN AND GRIZZLY BIVISIBLE
Hook: 8–14
Thread: Black
Wings: None
Tail: Brown and grizzly hackle-tips
Body: Brown and grizzly palmered hackle (very thick)
Hackle: A few turns of white near the hook eye

BROWN AND GRIZZLY SPIDER
Hook: 12–22 short shank with upturned eye
Thread: Black
Wings: None
Tail: None
Body: None
Hackle: Brown and grizzly tied convex toward rear and front of hook

CLIPPED-HACKLE EGG SAC
Hook: 12–14
Thread: Black
Wings: Dun hackle-tips tied spent
Tail: Dun hackle fibers
Body: Rear one-eighth, yellow hackle with fibers clipped close to center quill; fore seven-eighths, brown hackle with fibers clipped close to center quill
Hackle: Light dun

DUTCHMAN
Hook: 8–14
Thread: Black
Wings: White kip (calf-tail), tilted forward and oversized for hook
Tail: Brown and grizzly hackle fibers
Body: Peacock herl re-enforced with counter-wound silk thread
Hackle: Brown and grizzly

HORNBERG
Hook: 8–14 (2X or 3X long)
Thread: Black
Wings: Gray mallard breast feathers over yellow hackle tips
Tail: None
Body: Flat silver tinsel
Cheeks: Jungle cock eyes (long)
Hackle: Grizzly

KATTERMAN
Hook: 12–18
Thread: Brown
Wings: None
Tail: Light ginger hackle tips
Body: Peacock herl ribbed with fine gold wire, and dark brown palmered hackle
Hackle: A few turns of white behind the hook eye

ROYAL WULFF
Hook: 8–18
Thread: Black
Wings: White kip (calf-tail)
Tail: Brown bucktail
Body: Peacock herl and scarlet floss
Hackle: Brown (Note: I mix brown and grizzly)

WHITE WULFF
Hook: 8–14
Thread: Black
Wings: White kip (calf-tail)
Tail: White kip (calf-tail)
Body: Cream wool and white seal blended for dubbing
Hackle: Badger

CHAPTER NINE

~~~~~~

Care of Flies

ANYONE WHO TIES FLIES, or has been lucky enough to peek over the shoulder of a master at work, knows that to produce a quality product is exacting and time-consuming. Although fly tyers don't get rich, prices have increased substantially of late, and there's no immediate end in sight. (Dressers of flies have to eat, too.) According to an unscientific survey of mine, dry fly prices have risen by about one-third over the last four or five seasons, largely the result of climbing material costs and general inflation. Yet, because flies are generally small in size and are usually purchased in twos and threes, I suspect few anglers, except perhaps for professionals at tax time, fully appreciate that flies, or the materials to tie them, represent their largest financial interest in the sport over a lifetime on the water.

Most skillful fly fishermen try to be careful with equipment. Indeed, it's frequently claimed that for some "pride of ownership" exceeds catching fish in importance. It's not uncommon, however, to see an experienced angler—the sort who wouldn't dream of putting his bamboo rod away without wiping it clean, for instance—abusing fine trout flies into uselessness in a single outing, although to do so is both needless and wasteful, not to mention contradictory to the essence of fly fishing. The fly, after all, represents the only item of tackle you want a trout to admire.

When quality flies as described in chapter seven are acquired, the tyer has done all he can to hedge the angler's bets. Care of the flies is the angler's responsibility—a matter of some organizational know-how, plus a little discipline that will pay off in countless trout over the course of a season.

Flies if fished won't last forever, regardless of the tyer, but their longevity can be prolonged by extending to them attention equal to that commonly afforded the finest rods and precision reels.

Because dries in particular tend to be damaged easily, they should be quartered in containers where they are well protected against crushing and have sufficient room to breathe. My choice is clear, unbreakable plastic boxes with compartments to file flies according to pattern and size. Compartment dimensions, of course, must vary with the sizes of your flies, but it's crucial that there be enough space in each one to accommodate several flies of a pattern and size without overcrowding. The best model I know is inexpensive, has metal hinges and a double clasp to secure the lid, and is available at most fly fishing tackle outlets. Almost air-tight when purchased, I modify mine by drilling tiny holes through lids in line with each compartment to insure air circulation, since standing moisture, even in the form of seemingly microscopic droplets caused by condensation, rusts hooks, breaks down feather fibers and fades colors. Ironic though it may seem, water can be a fly's worst enemy.

If moisture is a persistent problem, another perpetual foe is wind. What angler can swear he's never opened a fly box only to lose a half-dozen of his favorites to an unexpected gust? While the only surefire means to prevent blowaways is to quit changing flies,

A standard plastic dry fly box slit as shown makes an excellent hedge against losing flies to wind. Note, too, the tiny holes drilled in the lid to permit air to circulate inside the box.

a good way to cut your losses is to slit box lids in half as shown in the accompanying photograph. A picture framer's mat cutter does the job nicely. Be certain, however, that your cross-cut follows the line of a compartment separator to support each half of the lid, and that a clasp is situated on each side of the finished cut to secure the modified lid, or you'll end up losing more flies to spillage than would be taken by the teeth of a gale.

One pocket in my fishing vest is reserved for a "fly saver" box. Exactly like the others I carry, this one begins each day empty, although by evening it's usually well stocked with the physical history of the outing—all the flies rejected by the fish or by me, as well as those that have served me well but were in need of R&R after spending too much time locked in the jaws of trout. Turning around a temporary lull in the action, I've found, is frequently as simple as putting on a fresh fly of the same pattern and size I've been using, probably the result of its better float. It's also important to note, I think, that when changing flies, dries in particular should never be stuck into those squares of fleece some manufacturers pin to their vests. Losing nymphs, wets or streamers from them is bad enough, but to see your dries with matted hackles and bent tails after spending just an hour squashed into the nap can be considered nothing short of sacrilegious.

On the water I've developed a fly care ritual that's easy, takes little time, and has saved me plenty of dough over the years. Before cinching a fly to a tippet, first check to be sure that the hook eye is tightly closed and that all excess head cement was removed from the eye by the tyer. An open eye or lacquer chip will cut monofilament tippet material, especially as the angler sets the hook, thus costing him not only a fly but a trout too. Tweezers that are handy for disgorging hooks from fish are also ideal for closing hook eyes, while a heavy sewing needle carried in a small cork is the perfect tool to clear hook eyes of lacquer.

Next, dress the fly to keep it afloat. My favorite commercial dry fly dressing is Gehrke's Gink, although I've found that unscented Albolene cream works equally well and is far less expensive when purchased in pint jars at the neighborhood pharmacy. (I have no proof, but I'd guess Gink and Albolene are the same stuff in different packages.) As a rule I prefer paste dressings to spray flotants that must be used more frequently and are difficult to keep off leader tippets that you want, of course, to sink. Despite some claims to the contrary I've seen no evidence that any brand of dressing or flotant damages flies, although one, Mucilin, a British-made cream, I suspect is tough on fly lines.

When the time comes to change flies, first inspect the one you've been fishing to be certain the hook barb is intact and the head isn't unraveling. Then swish the fly in the flowing water for about five seconds and blow on it several times. Next, squeeze a small quantity of fly drying powder into the palm of your hand and rub the fly in it until the fly is generously coated with the granules. Wait ten seconds, give a few more hearty bursts of air, deposit the fly in the "fly saver" box for closer inspection after the day's fishing, and the job is done.

Fly drying powder, by the way (manufactured, I believe, by one firm but distributed wearing numerous labels), is the greatest fly care innovation to come along in many years. Even veteran ama-dou users are coming around to acknowledging that their infernal fungus, treasured by earlier generations of anglers, is now as out-dated as the gut leader or the silk line. The new magic granules go a long, long way, a single container lasting several seasons, especially if you dump the excess back into the bottle each time for use again.

My system for fly care after taking trout is substantially the same as when I change flies. Flies must be checked for damage, cleaned of fish slime, dried and re-dressed. Should a fly be damaged beyond repair, incidentally, I put it in my "fly saver" box anyway as a reminder that it must be replaced.

After each outing, inspect all fly boxes for moisture and if any is suspected or found leave the boxes open in a safe, dry place over-night. The contents of your "fly saver" box should be studied meticulously and any needed fly repairs made before returning the flies to permanent quarters. The flies held in the "fly saver" box, you'll find, will prove an invaluable aid to maintaining reliable stream notes, since by segregating them from the bulk of your patterns you can reconstruct each day's fishing in far more accu-rate detail than you could by relying on unaided memory. Com-piling my notes, incidentally, I've discovered it's altogether as im-portant to record patterns that didn't work as those that did, if only to keep me from making the same mistakes twice.

Even with the best of care, the time arrives when flies will be all but done for. Here's a trick to give them a little more lease on life, although it should be used only as a last resort. Place flies you feel are in rough shape in a colander and shake them over a pan or kettle of boiling water for a couple of minutes. Even terminal flies should look almost new. It's important to note, though, that steaming dry flies weakens the stiffest hackle fibers, meaning the most you can expect from a steam-restored fly is an additional trout or two before the fly will be ready for permanent retirement.

Savvy anglers also consider carefully the problem of out-of-season fly storage. I like almost airtight plastic boxes into which flies are sorted by pattern and size, keeping those I expect to use during similar periods or on similar waters as close together as possible. Airtight boxes are important, I feel, because I have a pesty prejudice (or superstition, perhaps) against subjecting anything I anticipate will come in contact with trout to smelly moth flakes. My fear may be groundless, but trout have highly developed olfactory senses and I'm not about to take chances. When flies are kept in tightly closed containers, however, it's wise to air them out a couple of times each winter.

~~~~~~

CHAPTER TEN

Leader-Words

THINK OF DRY FLIES AS PROMISES—political promises, perhaps—the angler hopes will be eaten up. Like the politician, the fly fisherman seeks to soften up his target with a flannel-smooth approach or presentation. If he pulls it off, the quarry will be hooked; but should any element of his delivery system be out of whack, all he will get is disdain.

Different politicians, like different anglers, make the same offerings with uneven success. The promise to lower taxes coming from one guy is swallowed by the constituents, while the same pledge from another is snubbed. And so it goes, for instance, with anglers plying the Adams on a piece of water. One cleans up; the other is skunked. Why?

At issue certainly isn't substance, for an Adams is an Adams, just as lower taxes are lower taxes. In fact, were one able to disconnect all of the promises and all of the dry flies from their purveyors, and yet manage to cast them through all the wards and upon all the waters, it's fair to assume their appeal would be virtually uniform, if acutely boring to a monitor. Thus it's safe to say that a fly or a promise is seldom the root of its own rejection, but that rejection of the fly or promise instead represents a product of the flaws to be found in the mechanics of its delivery.

The delivery system for political promises is well known and will suck no more ink out of me. (Nor will I give in to an urge to dally with how it might be improved, although I could scarcely do less to affect it for the better than can the hive of political bees, most of whom, it seems, must have been born with broken stingers.) As for dry fly delivery systems, however, it's crucial that every angler understand that between the human body on one end and the fly on the other, everything must harmonize flawlessly, because each flaw, no matter how minor, diminishes the odds for consistency. Remember, a dry fly lives to a trout only to the extent it's imbued with life by the technique of the angler, as if the fly were music akin to the old song, *Dem Bones*—the arm bone's connected to the rod bone . . . the rod bone's connected to the reel bone . . . the reel bone's connected to the line bone . . . the line bone's connected to the leader bone . . . the leader bone's connected to the tippet bone. . . . Drop one phrase, interrupt the balance, and the music stops; it dies, and so, therefore, dies the dramatic tension that had riveted the audience to it.

Accomplished dry fly tactics must personify *balance*. Without balance, including tackle able to respond fluidly to varying amounts of energy generated by the angler, the culmination of each presentation—that is, the precise attitude in which the fly greets the trout—is relegated to chance. Most competent fishermen are familiar with the need for balance, of course, but it's puzzling how frequently their appreciation stalls at the splice between fly line and leader. To my way of thinking dry fly presentation leaves no margin for compromise, but were such a margin to exist I would certainly want it from the fly line back, not from the leader butt out.

The importance of a leader—that seemingly simple article of terminal gear situated closest to the dry fly—is, perhaps, the most frequently disregarded feature of tackle dynamics. A leader of the correct length, weight, taper and flexibility is critical to balancing a dry fly outfit. To attempt to present a dry fly without one is a nightmare. So, when difficulties with presentation arise, check your leader first. More often than not, you'll need look no further.

A leader's essential objective is to provide a nearly invisible link between line and fly of sufficient length to insure the quarry isn't spooked by the bulk of the fly line. Yet, were deception the only point, wouldn't it make sense to simply attach a length of fine untapered monofilament to the line and have at it? Try doing so sometime and you'll quickly discover the additional benefits of a proper leader by finding out just how difficult presenting a fly can be.

A leader should be viewed as an extension of the line, spliced in such a way as to minimize disturbance to the rhythm of fly presentation. Like the line, it should be tapered. However, to guarantee continuity to the flow of inertia set in motion by the angler with his rod, the leader has to be a single taper outward from butt to tippet that, in effect, prolongs the forward slope of the line. The line, then, pushes the leader butt which in turn pushes the tippet. Since just minor irregularities along the way can disrupt the smoothness of a presentation, the taper should always be gradual through the length of a leader. Even one abrupt change in diameter or weight anywhere between the splice and the fly is likely to undermine the evenness with which everything may be propelled to the trout.

There are two types of tapered dry fly leaders: (1) the *compound leader,* constructed by knotting together sections of monofilament in decreasing lengths and diameters; and (2) the *knotless leader,* commercially manufactured by stretching a single strand of monofilament to a desired length and taper. Both can be purchased at fly fishing shops, generally in 7½-, 9-foot and 12-foot lengths. Some knotless leaders are packaged with extra tippet sections enclosed. Handy spools of tippet material from 0X (diameter .011 inch) to 8X (diameter .0035 inch) are also available at those outlets.

Finding the right leader to do the right job is much like finding a sportcoat that fits. One lucky guy can walk into a haberdashery, amble to a rack, choose a coat and wear it home without a lick of tailoring. Another requires a tuck here or some cutting and refitting there to make his choice sit well. Similarly, some anglers are able to buy leaders off the rack without compromising fly presentation, while others learn to adjust slightly to compensate for commercial leaders that aren't, perhaps, quite right for them. By all means you should purchase commercially-packaged leaders to satisfy the bulk of your needs, assuming, of course, the waters you fish don't dictate otherwise. For many of us, though, standard leaders won't perform, usually because of individual casting eccentricities, and thus we have no alternative but to sit down each time the need arises and build our own.

For most fishing situations I prefer compound leaders to knotless ones, a major exception occurring on rivers and streams that carry floating weed (few such waters exist in the U.S.). Compound leaders encourage more critical tapering, I believe, at least to the extent that an angler can discern (if the leader is commercially tied) or decide (if he's tying the leader himself) where one diameter is best absorbed by another. The compound leader also accommodates varying monofilament stiffness and elasticity as the tyer proceeds from butt to mid-section to tippet, while the knotless kind must, by definition, be made from one strand that can't be hardened or softened along the way. Another deficiency I've perceived in most knotless leaders is inadequate butt diameters that promote troublesome hinging near where they are spliced to fly lines.

The accompanying drawing illustrates how a *blood knot,* the best knot for building leaders, should be tied. Although some anglers complain that it's tough to master, it must be learned to fish dry flies effectively. Having once produced custom leaders by the gross for sale, I can attest that the primary qualification is practice. Practicing knots is an ideal pastime for cold winter nights.

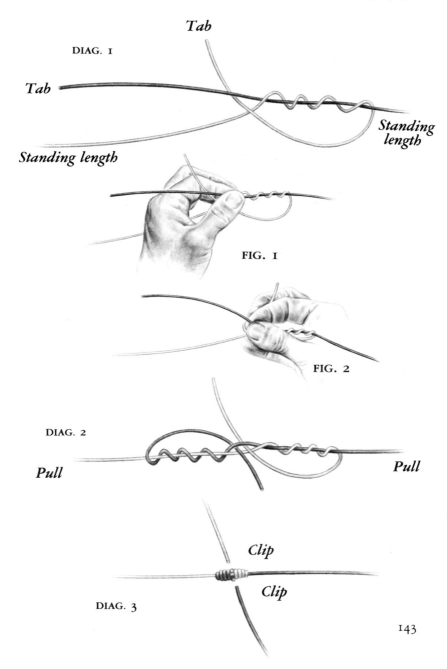

DIAG. I

Tab

Tab

Standing length

Standing length

FIG. I

FIG. 2

DIAG. 2

Pull

Pull

Clip

Clip

DIAG. 3

1. Assuming you are right-handed, make an "X" with two lengths of monofilament you wish to connect, clasping them between the thumb and forefinger of your left hand precisely where the two bisect. Be sure the two tabs of monofilament are five or six inches long to insure enough material to work with later.

2. Now, using the thumb and forefinger of your right hand, plus the middle finger of your left as a guide, pass the tab of monofilament on the right four or five times around the standing length of monofilament on the right, as shown in Diag. 1.

3. Take the tab you have wrapped and guide it upward into the "V" made by the other tab and the standing length of monofilament which should be positioned below the tab, as also shown in Diag. 1.

4. Once you've passed the first tab through the "V", you should have something that looks like Fig. 1.

5. Next, switch the partial knot from your left hand to your right hand, clasping it now between the pads of the thumb and forefinger of your right hand (Fig. 2). Once you are confident the knot is securely in your right hand, use either the forefinger or middle finger of your left hand to guide the tab in the center of the "V" back over the fingernail of the forefinger of the right hand (Fig. 2). Remove the forefinger of your left hand carefully and replace it with the pad of the middle finger of your right hand, as shown in Fig. 2.

6. At this point, the partial knot should look like Fig. 2.

7. Now, using the thumb, forefinger and middle finger of your left hand, twirl the second tab of monofilament around the remaining standing length of monofilament, the one on your left, four or five times, as shown in Diag. 2. (As you proceed with this step, you should note that the way you are holding the first half of the knot in your right hand has left a nice wide opening into which the second tab can be inserted when the time comes.)

8. Using the thumb and forefinger of your left hand, guide the second tab downward into that opening, as shown in Diag. 2.

9. Next, gingerly let go of the knot itself and clasp the two

standing lengths of monofilament, one with your left hand, the other with your right.

10. **Bring the knot to your mouth and wet it liberally with saliva.**

11. **When the knot is lubricated, snug up the knot by pulling on the two standing lengths of monofilament, drawing the right length to the right, the left length to the left.** (Before pulling, I usually use my teeth to adjust the two tabs of monofilament to be sure they are straight and that they won't slip out as I tighten the knot. In fact, one tab may be held between my teeth when the knot is being tightened.)

12. **When the knot is tight, it should look like the one in Diag. 3.**

13. **Finally, clip the excess material of the tabs flush to the knot, as shown in Diag. 3, and your blood knot is completed.**

Following are several hints to simplify tying blood knots:

—Always start with adequate lengths of material, so that the tabs aren't too short when the knots are pulled tight.

—Each time a tab of monofilament is passed around a section to be spliced, the tab twists. If twists are retained, the strength of a finished knot is diminished. It's important, therefore, that tabs be released after each turn to permit twists to unwind.

—Leaving an opening wide enough to accommodate the second tab after the first is wrapped is one of the frustrations experienced by anglers tying blood knots. To eliminate the problem, after wrapping the first tab around a section to be spliced, guide the tab carefully into the "V" left by the other section and the tab still to be wrapped. Then compress the first tab back between the fingernail of the forefinger and the pad of the middle finger of the right hand (assuming you're right handed) as shown in Figures 1 and 2. The tension created by one tab wedged in the "V" while the other is being wrapped insures an adequate opening to aim at with the point of the second tab.

—To avoid crimping, wet knots with saliva before drawing them tight.

Other knots, of course, are touted for building compound leaders. The *improved surgeon's knot* (see illustration), for example, is sometimes recommended because it's strong and easy to tie. For adding tippets when you're in a hurry, the improved surgeon's knot is a dandy, although in my opinion it's unsatisfactory for building entire leaders. Its major flaw is that the knot emerges offset, a minor drawback when only one is used, as in affixing a tippet, but a troublesome inconvenience when the flaw is manifested many times in 7½ to 12 feet, as along the length of a compound leader. The relatively new *uni-knot* (see page 158), by contrast, makes strong, straight leaders, but is unfortunately bulky and as difficult to learn as the blood knot.

SURGEON'S KNOT

Three Overhand Knots

To Reel

Pull Both

Pull Both

1. Assuming you are right-handed, place two lengths of monofilament you want to join parallel to each other with the longest section, such as that which might eventually go to the reel, facing to your left. Clasp the two parallel lengths of monofilament between the pads of the thumb and forefinger of your left hand and be sure the tab facing to your right is four to six inches long.

2. Now, using the thumb and forefinger of the right hand, make one loop with both strands of monofilament, either downward, as shown in the illustration, or upward, if you prefer.

(The direction the loop faces is entirely optional.) Either way, however, the loop should then be clasped between the thumb and forefinger of the left hand precisely where the strands of monofilament cross each other.

3. Next I like to clasp the tab and standing length of monofilament to my right between the thumb and forefinger of my right hand and pass them around the tip of my left pinky in order to form a tiny loop. I then clasp this tiny loop between the thumb and forefinger of my right hand. (The little loop is made only to help me guide the monofilament to my right as a unit through the larger loop I continue to hold in my left hand.)

4. Now the tiny loop in the right hand is passed through the large loop in the left hand, and all the monofilament to the right of the large loop is pulled gently through that loop. What you have done, then, is to have tied a simple overhand knot around the large loop.

5. Still clasping the large loop between the thumb and forefinger of the left hand, the identical procedure for making overhand knots around it is repeated twice more, until you have three such knots around the loop, as shown in the illustration.

6. When the three overhand knots have been completed, release the loop and clasp the tab and standing length of monofilament to your left between the thumb and forefinger of your left hand, the tab and standing length of monofilament to your right between the thumb and forefinger of your right hand.

7. Now bring the knot to your mouth and wet it liberally with saliva.

8. When it is lubricated, draw the knot tight by simultaneously pulling the material you are holding in your right hand to the right and that you are holding in your left hand to the left.

9. Finally, when the knot is good and tight, clip the excess material from the two tabs, and your improved surgeon's knot is completed.

The singular advantage of tying leaders is the option to choose materials. For instance, I like a stiff butt, a soft tip and something between the two in the mid-section. Gradual limbering of mono-filament through a leader unquestionably optimizes its perform-ance, whether the leader be six or fifteen feet long. Stiff monofila-ment, as its name implies, is hard material with plenty of muscle to sustain the authority punched into each cast, while soft mono-filament is very supple and thus is responsive to the most delicate maneuvers telegraphed to it.

Several firms manufacture leader-making kits but, since the con-sistency of material tends to be uniform throughout every size provided by each kit, I don't use them. Assembling your own kits, of course, is more work, but over the long haul I feel it's worth-while.

Dividing leaders into thirds—the butt-third, the mid-section and the tip-third—the nicest material I've found for butts is Max-ima, made in West Germany and sold here by numerous tackle outlets. A stiff monofilament, it is available on spools clearly marked by diameter and pounds of breaking strength. The Glad-ding Company of South Otselic, New York, also makes a good monofilament for stiff leader butts. For mid-sections, I favor Mason material, manufactured by the Mason Tackle Company, of Otisville, Michigan, or, when I intend to dye leaders, Stren mon-ofilament spinning line, a product of DuPont. Stren is available on large spools but, because it's labeled only according to break-ing strength, each size must be subjected to a micrometer test to ascertain its diameter. For tip sections, including tippets, I'm con-vinced one material is in a class by itself—Nylorfi, a French-made soft monofilament marketed in the U.S. by the Cortland Line Company, of Cortland, New York. Available at tackle shops across America and abroad, it's by far the strongest (you could hang yourself from 6X) and most responsive material per unit of diameter I've tested. I hear occasional complaints, however, that Nylorfi is prone to kink when drawn through knots, particularly in fine sizes, such as 6X, 7X and 8X. I've asked several friends who experienced difficulty to demonstrate their knot-tying techniques and discovered in most instances that the predicament emanated not from any property of the material itself, but from the heavy hands trying to use it. Whether the material be Nylorfi or any other soft monofilament, remember that a light touch and plenty of lubricating saliva are essential for tying all knots.

Standard leader lengths, that is 7½-, 9- and 12-footers, are ideal for normal conditions found along most trout waters. Use 7½-footers tapered to 4X or 5X, for small to medium-size streams, and 9-footers for bigger ones. Unless fisheries are low and clear, 12-footers are necessary only on big rivers when you want extra reach. For low water, 12-footers with fine 5X–8X tippets are generally adequate to keep fly lines far enough back from the eyes of wary trout to prove effective.

Special situations, however, require special leaders. Small brooks, for instance, may prove impossible to handle with leaders longer than five or six feet. Such fisheries present particular challenges when they're low, clear and inhabited by wary trout; in such cases leaders must be at once extremely short and tapered to the finest diameters—7X or 8X. Conversely, on broad rivers or streams where waters are low or characteristically very clear, leaders fully fifteen feet long with fragile tippets can represent the angler's only alternative to getting skunked. In the main, though, I advise the shortest leaders feasible for prevailing conditions, since most anglers find *the shorter the leader, the better the control.*

The following chart provides tapering formulas for the dry fly leaders I use most frequently, although I can't guarantee, of course, that they'll complement the casting styles of every reader. Also included is the type of fishery for which each formula is earmarked. Unlike formulas recommended by most leader manufacturers, note that mine require more knots, thus more tapers, over given lengths for the fine tippet leaders than for heavy ones, since I'm determined to maintain undisrupted gradual tapers along the full lengths of all my leaders.

Dry Fly Leader Tapers*

1. 6 feet—4X**

Diameter (inches)	length (inches)
.020″	13″
.017″	10″
.015″	8″
.013″	7″
.011″	5″
.010″	4″
.009″	3″
.008″	2″
.007″	20″ (4X)

2. 6 feet—7X**

Diameter (inches)	length (inches)
.020″	12″
.017″	9″
.015″	7″
.013″	6″
.011″	5″
.010″	4″
.009″	3″
.008″	2″
.007″	2″
.006″	1″
.005″	1″
.004″	20″ (7X)

3. 7½ feet—3X**

Diameter	length
.022″	18″
.020″	12″
.017″	10″
.015″	8″
.013″	7″
.011″	6″
.010″	5″
.009″	4″
.008″	20″ (3X)

4. 7½ feet—5X**

Diameter	length
.022″	15″
.020″	11″
.017″	9″
.015″	8″
.013″	7″
.011″	6″
.010″	5″
.009″	4″
.008″	3″
.007″	2″
.006″	20″ (5X)

* Each leader length found in the chart is exclusive of the length of a loop at the end of the butt section, as well as sufficient material at the point of the tippet to affix one dry fly by using the Tweed Clinch Knot (See page 161).

** My finished leaders may be slightly longer, as when tying them, I sometimes add between four inches and twelve inches of extra tippet material in anticipation of prevailing conditions.

Dry Fly Leader Tapers*

5. 9 feet—4X**

Diameter	length
.022″	22″
.020″	15″
.017″	10″
.015″	9″
.013″	8″
.011″	7″
.010″	6″
.009″	5″
.008″	4″
.007″	22″ (4X)

6. 9 feet—5X**

Diameter	length
.022″	23″
.020″	15″
.017″	11″
.015″	9″
.013″	7″
.011″	6″
.010″	5″
.009″	4″
.008″	3″
.007″	2″
.006″	23″ (5X)

7. 9 feet—7X**

Diameter	length
.022″	19″
.020″	12″
.017″	10″
.015″	9″
.013″	8″
.011″	7″
.010″	6″
.009″	5″
.008″	4″
.007″	3″
.006″	3″
.005″	2″
.004″	20″ (7X)

8. 10 feet—6X**

Diameter	length
.022″	21″
.020″	15″
.017″	11″
.015″	10″
.013″	9″
.011″	8″
.010″	7″
.009″	6″
.008″	5″
.007″	4″
.006″	3″
.005″	21″ (6X)

Dry Fly Leader Tapers*

9. 10 feet—8X**

Diameter	length
.022″	19″
.020″	12″
.017″	11″
.015″	10″
.013″	9″
.011″	8″
.010″	7″
.009″	6″
.008″	5″
.007″	4″
.006″	3″
.005″	3″
.004″	2″
.003″	21″ (8X)

10. 12 feet—5X

Diameter	length
.022″	28″
.020″	20″
.017″	14″
.015″	12″
.013″	10″
.011″	8″
.010″	7″
.009″	6″
.008″	5″
.007″	4″
.006″	30″ (5X)

11. 12 feet—7X**

Diameter	length
.022″	24″
.020″	16″
.017″	13″
.015″	12″
.013″	11″
.011″	9″
.010″	8″
.009″	7″
.008″	6″
.007″	5″
.006″	4″
.005″	3″
.004″	26″ (7X)

12. 15 feet—4X

Diameter	length
.022″	36″
.020″	24″
.017″	18″
.015″	15″
.013″	13″
.011″	12″
.010″	11″
.009″	10″
.008″	9″
.007″	32″ (4X)

Dry Fly Leader Tapers*

13. 15 feet—7X**

Diameter	length
.022″	32″
.020″	24″
.017″	16″
.015″	14″
.013″	12″
.011″	11″
.010″	10″
.009″	9″
.008″	8″
.007″	7″
.006″	6″
.005″	5″
.004″	26″ (7X)

14. 17 feet—5X

Diameter	length
.022″	36″
.020″	28″
.017″	20″
.015″	18″
.013″	16″
.011″	14″
.010″	12″
.009″	11″
.008″	10″
.007″	9″
.006″	30″ (5X)

15. 20 feet—7X

Diameter	length
.022″	38″
.020″	28″
.017″	22″
.015″	19″
.013″	17″
.011″	15″
.010″	13″
.009″	12″
.008″	11″
.007″	10″
.006″	9″
.005″	8″
.004″	38″ (7X)

Dry Fly Leader Tapers*

1. 6 feet—4X: For work on smallest streams where trout don't tend to be leader shy. Especially good for broken water on surface water streams. Ideal for larger flies.

2. 6 feet—7X: For use on small waters when tiny flies are a must. Perfect for small streams of subterranean origin or the glassy-smooth stretches of small surface water streams where trout tend to feed on midges.

3. 7½ feet—3X: An excellent general purpose leader where trout are large and not leader shy. Especially useful when large flies must be fished to large trout.

4. 7½ feet—5X: A fine everyday leader for use on all sizes of water for anglers relatively new to dry fly fishing. Also excellent for smaller waters during hatches of dries, sizes 12-16.

5. 9 feet—4X: A good all-round leader with flies, sizes 10-16. Appropriate to waters of moderate to large size where trout run large but aren't leader shy. Excellent for use with big terrestrials and attractors, including skaters.

6. 9 feet—5X: This is the leader I use most frequently on eastern surface water streams during traditional mayfly hatches and spinner falls. A good bet when fishing moderate to large size flies to spooky trout on surface water streams. However, 5X is considered a large tippet diameter for fishing most streams of subterranean origin where trout are shy.

7. 9 feet—7X: This is the standard midging leader, used on moderate to big waters, including most rivers and streams of subterranean origin and the flat, clear stretches of surface water rivers and streams.

8. 10 feet—6X: A compromise leader utilized when extra length and some strength are needed on clear waters holding spooky trout. A good choice for weedy waters, as well as when you fish small flies to large trout that aren't so wary that 7X or 8X are indicated.

9. 10 feet—8X: Its tippet strength requires a subtle touch, but sometimes the only recourse when after extremely shy trout on clear waters with tiny flies. Most useful on moderate to large rivers and streams.

10. 12 feet—5X: My far-and-away favorite for big water and medium-size flies. The key to a bit of extra reach when the trout always seem to stay a couple of feet out of casting range.

11. 12 feet—7X: The best big water-shy fish leader. On most rivers and streams it will keep the fly line far enough back from wary trout to keep from spooking them. Generally used with midges.

12. 15 feet—4X: A specialized leader used for working big flies on big waters or large flies on waters such as flats where neither the angler nor his line can approach the quarry closely without risk of spooking it. Ideal for large trout.

13. 15 feet—7X: The perfect leader to fool extremely spooky trout on big water. Especially effective for use with the Stop and Drop presentation (see page 199) when fishing small flies.

14. 18 feet—5X: Not necessarily used for extra reach but for specialized presentation techniques, including the Mend-and-Twitch (see page 206) and Stop and Drop (see page 200). Best used on big water.

15. 20 feet—7X: A fine leader but also a test of skill. Generally too much leader for inexperienced fly fishermen. Used when presenting small flies to finicky trout on very large waters, notably those of subterranean origin.

Anglers who tint monofilament leaders, expecting them to be less conspicuous to feeding trout than undyed ones, should know that the upshot of their pain is probably more cosmetic than utilitarian. I've dyed leaders for years—gray for local Catskill waters, olive for the limestoners of Pennsylvania's Cumberland Valley, brown for brandy-colored rivers and streams of Maine and eastern Canada—but must admit I have *absolutely no reason to believe* all the work has improved my trout production one iota. Still, I continue to dye leaders just because I like their looks, which is good enough for me. There is, after all, a difference between self-deception and self-indulgence, a prudent amount of the latter being all to the good.

For those with similar inclinations it's helpful to learn that popular fabric dyes, such a Tintex or Rit, do the job beautifully. Silver nitrate can also be used to achieve burnished tones, but at more than $100 per ounce (compared to 30 cents or so for a package of Rit), "developing" leaders like they were photographs for exhibition represents a plateau of self-indulgence too rich for my blood. To tint leaders with fabric dyes, you should (1) dissolve a package of dye in about a pint of water; (2) simmer it several minutes, but don't permit the solution to boil; (3) strain the solution through a piece of tightly woven material; (4) allow the solution to cool to about 170 degrees (F) (Caution: if it's too hot, the coiled monofilament will pucker); (5) drop coiled leaders into the dye solution and, using cooking tongs, turn the leaders constantly for several minutes while the dye takes; (6) when the color looks right, remove the leaders and rinse them in lukewarm water; (7) place the leaders on paper towels to dry thoroughly before packaging. All surplus leaders, by the way, as well as leader-making monofilament and tippet material, should be stored in the refrigerator.

Are there rules anglers can follow to decide the leaders to use? Considering the range of angling situations the answer is no, probably not. There are, though, some guidelines worthy of consideration: (1) practicality dictates the shortest leader reasonable for the water to be fished; (2) if a certain leader formula works, stick with it until conditions warrant a change; (3) experimenting with formulas for the sake of it can wreak havoc with timing; (4) broken waters hide tippets better than flat waters do. For the fewest spooked fish, however, the finest tippet diameter feasible is normally best.

The ideal leader will perform badly when improperly spliced to the fly line. I've tested a dozen splicing methods, the majority of which proved either inefficient or too darned much trouble to bother with. The loop-to-loop method? Worthless. The Krazy Glue splice? Risky. Leader Links? Unreliable. The epoxy splice? *Give me a break.* Until recently I was resigned to the nail knot as the most effective splice, although, like many anglers who tie it, I'd prejudiced my chances for eternal bliss with every change of leaders. But then an angel of mercy revealed the *uni-knot splice,* a single simple operation that can be accomplished with cold hands right on the riverbank. The following illustration shows how to tie it, and, for the sake of your soul, I'd heed it well.

UNI-KNOT SPLICE

1. Assuming you are right-handed, place your fly line with its tip facing to your left, directly over and parallel to the butt of the leader you wish to splice to the line. The leader butt should be facing from left to right with the standing length of it to your left, as shown in Fig. 1. Allow a full six inches of fly line tip tab and leader butt tab to be sure you have plenty of material to complete the job.

2. While clasping the fly line and leader butt between the thumb and forefinger to make an overhand loop (Fig. 2). Then clasp the loop between the thumb and forefinger of your left hand, use your right thumb and forefinger of your left hand at the precise spot where the materials forming the loop intersect.

3. Next, clasp the leader butt tab at your right between the thumb and forefinger of your right hand and pass it through the

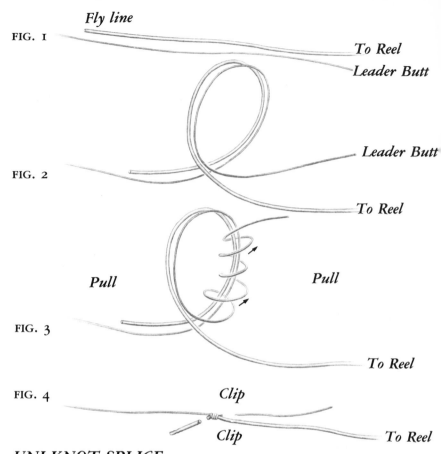

FIG. I

Fly line

To Reel

Leader Butt

Leader Butt

FIG. 2

To Reel

Pull

Pull

FIG. 3

To Reel

FIG. 4

Clip

Clip

To Reel

UNI-KNOT SPLICE

loop from back to front as few as four or as many as eight times
(Fig. 3).

4. After winding the leader butt tab around the loop a sufficient number of times, and while continuing to clasp it as before,
that is, between your right thumb and forefinger, reach down
with the middle finger, ring finger and pinky of your right hand
and catch hold of the standing length of fly line which should be
found directly beneath the leader butt tab, as in Fig. 3. At the
same time, while continuing to grip the loop with the thumb and
forefinger of your left hand, squeeze the middle finger, ring finger and pinky of your left hand around the fly line tip tab and

158

standing length of the leader butt, both of which will be conveniently nearby if you're tying the knot correctly.

5. Now release your grip on the loop and pull simultaneously on the leader butt tab and the standing length of the fly line to the right and the fly line tip tab and the standing length of the leader butt to the left (Fig. 3). This will straighten the line and leader, removing the loop, and will tighten the knot sufficiently for you to do the fine work that comes next.

6. To complete the knot, first bring it to your mouth and wet it. Then alternately tug gently, first on the standing length of the leader butt with your left hand while firmly clasping both the standing length of the fly line and the leader butt tab in your right hand, then on the leader butt tab with your right hand while holding the fly line tip tab and the standing length of the leader butt with your left hand. Repeat this step as many times as necessary. (Sometimes the monofilament coils around the fly line will require a bit of additional persuasion which can be accomplished easily by adjusting them with either one or both of your thumbnails.)

7. When the knot appears secure, one last powerful tug should be exerted on the standing length of the leader butt to the left and the standing length of the fly line to the right. This tug insures that the knot digs into the fly line coating sufficiently to prevent slippage.

8. Finally, the leader butt tab and the fly line tip tab should be clipped flush to the knot to insure against snagging rod guides (Fig. 4), and your uni-knot splice is completed.

〰〰〰〰〰〰〰〰〰〰〰〰〰〰〰〰〰〰〰〰〰〰〰

CHAPTER ELEVEN

What Knot to Tie

NO TROUT ARE CAUGHT on dry flies that don't light on the water; so, to be effective, every angler must become a part-time efficiency analyst, whether or not the notion appeals to his sense of romance. Among the chores we inevitably must do every time out, changing flies probably imposes the biggest strain on this time–efficiency relationship. Since the skilled angler decides what pattern he wants before he begins each change, lost fishing time really becomes a product of cinching the chosen fly to the leader.

There are many knots that can be employed to attach dries to monofilament tippets, but the one in most common use is surely the clinch knot or one of its variations, such as the improved clinch (see accompanying illustration). Boasting ninety to ninety-five percent breaking strength, the clinch is quick and easy to tie and would seem, therefore, to appeal to the time–efficiency analyst in most of us. However, few anglers apparently consider that, except when midges tied on straight-eyed hooks are required, the clinch is among the poorest knots ever conceived from the standpoint of fly presentation, because it demands almost continuous attention if the angler is to be certain trout see his fly the way he wants them to.

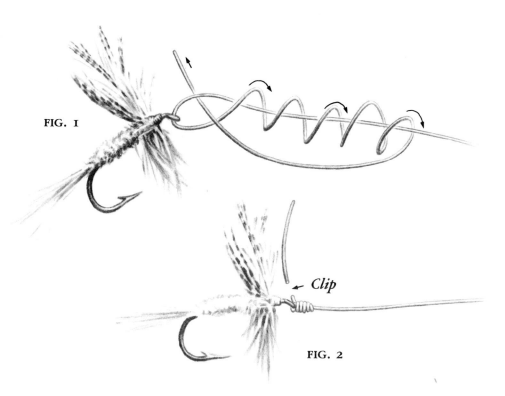

FIG. I

Clip

FIG. 2

THE CLINCH KNOT

1. Assuming you are right-handed, clasp the fly between the thumb and forefinger of your left hand, making certain you don't damage the fly. Clasp the leader tippet between the thumb and forefinger of your right hand with the tippet tab facing to the left.

2. Now pass the tippet tab upward through the hook eye until you have about four inches of this material to complete the knot.

3. When the tippet tab is through the eye, release the fly so it dangles straight down. This should position the fly directly below your left forefinger.

4. Next, raise the standing length of tippet so it intersects the tippet tab and hold it there with the pad of your left thumb. The resulting loop should be around the tip of your left forefinger, held firmly against the upper side of that finger by the pad of the thumb.

5. Now, gripping the standing length of tippet with the middle finger, ring finger and pinky of your right hand, use your right thumb and forefinger, plus the middle finger of your left hand (as a guide), to make about a half-dozen overhand loops of the tippet tab around the standing length of tippet, as shown in Fig. 1.

6. Remove your left forefinger from the loop, and you will find it becomes practical to pass the tippet tab up through the open loop (Fig. 1). (To tie an improved clinch knot, the tippet tab, after being passed upward through the loop, is then passed back downward again through the second loop that is formed by the wrapped standing length of tippet and the tippet tab.)

7. When the tippet tab is through the loop, it should be clasped between the thumb and forefinger of your left hand, while the position of your right thumb and forefinger is adjusted so they can clasp the standing length of tippet just behind the unfinished knot.

8. Now bring the knot to your mouth and wet it. After lubricating the knot, tighten it by pulling gently but firmly on the standing length of tippet while continuing to hold the tippet tab between your left thumb and forefinger.

9. Finally, clip excess tippet tab material flush to the knot, and your clinch knot should look like the one in Fig. 2.

Prove it yourself. Take a dry fly and clinch-knot a piece of tippet material to it. Be certain to draw the knot up as tight as possible. Note that the knot's bulk is ahead of the hook eye and that only one loop of monofilament is attached to it, the result of passing the tippet through the eye from above or below as you began to tie the knot. Now, holding the fly in a stationary horizontal position, clasp the tippet about six inches ahead of the knot and move it from side to side on a level plane. In most instances you'll see the loop through the eye and the knot ahead of it can slide almost ninety degrees, or about one-quarter of the 360 degrees of a hook eye, regardless of how tight you've drawn it. Think of this happening as you fish the fly on a stretch of productive pocket water. Consider how a sliding knot might affect the fly's drift over a big trout. If such images don't make you a tock nervous, well, they should.

Some experienced fly fishermen, of course, have been aware of the problem for a long time but have accepted it as one of those things you live with, unless, for instance, you're willing to wrestle with the tricky and comparatively weak turle knot.

"I'd quit fishing before I'd tie a turle every time I wanted to change flies," a friend told me recently. I had to sympathize.

Then, however, it gave me a real kick to make his day by showing him a knot that had made mine when it was shown to me several seasons back by a veteran gillie on the River Tweed in Scotland. Every angler with whom you fish teaches you something, I've found, but never has anyone passed along a trick so simple that so profoundly enhanced my angling technique. Reflecting on it now, I can't believe I never thought of it myself. For lack of another name, I call Gordon Lesinger's knot the *Tweed clinch*.

Here, as shown in the following illustration, is how to tie it:

TWEED CLINCH

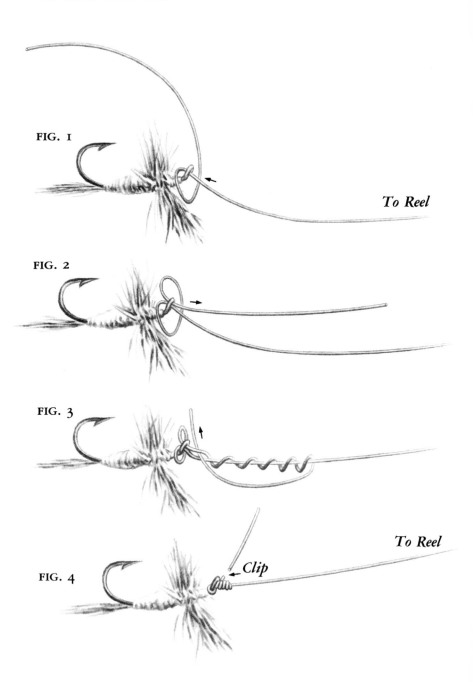

FIG. 1

To Reel

FIG. 2

FIG. 3

To Reel

FIG. 4

Clip

1. Before beginning the knot, clasp the fly between the thumb and forefinger as if the hook had an upturned eye (this is accomplished by holding downturned-eye flies upside down) (Fig. 1).

2. Pass the tippet material upward through the eye, allowing yourself between 2½ and 3 inches of surplus material to work with. Then take the working material and pass it under the head of the fly, keeping it as close as possible to the point at which the head meets the eye of the hook (Fig. 1). (Note that flies with small heads somewhat back from the hook eye make this procedure easiest to perform.)

3. Push the end of the tippet material through the eye of the hook again, this time in a downward direction (Fig. 2). By so doing, a collar of monofilament is formed between the head of the fly and the eye of the hook, just as when you complete a turle knot.

4. Finally, using the ample monofilament remaining, tie a clinch knot, drawing it up as far as it will go into the eye of the hook (Fig. 3). To facilitate drawing up the clinch knot and to avoid a kinky tippet, be sure to wet the clinch before tightening. When tying the Tweed clinch, you'll often find that the clinch can be drawn right into the hook eye, which is all the better since no flies in nature have big bunches of material at their heads.

5. Clip the excess material (Fig. 4), and you're ready to fish.

After tying your first Tweed clinch, it's good to use it to repeat the experiment mentioned earlier for the standard clinch. The Tweed clinch's collar of monofilament that replaces the standard clinch's single loop over the hook eye, you'll discover, eliminates cocking and other undesirable consequences of uneven pull on a fly. No matter how suddenly the angler or the current alters the direction of drift, the Tweed clinch guarantees the straight pull without which proper fly presentation is impossible.

The Tweed clinch has served me for years, with interesting results beyond hooking more trout. While the knot has never been officially tested for breaking strength efficiency, I've noticed fewer breakoffs when striking fish, even when using dries on tight lines directly downstream. While hooking many hundreds of trout during this period I've lost none I could attribute to a fault in the knot. In fact, I've found I can now use lighter leader tippets with substantially less worry of them breaking off at the shock of heavy strikes. And not once have I lost a fish because the knot pulled out or unraveled.

In sum, then, the Tweed clinch represents yet another example of the virtue of Scottish thrift. After trying it, I believe most anglers will agree it covers the important bases with minimum hassle, kind of like a kilt.

CHAPTER TWELVE

~~~~~~~~~~~~~~~~~~~~~~~~~~~~~~~~

Presenting the Fly

WHEN A PERSON STANDS, say, on a lawn or a platform overlooking a pond barren of fish and uses the long rod to propel his line, leader and fly somewhere in front of him, that person can be said to be *fly casting*. However, when a person stands waist-deep in a river or stream or picks his way along a brook or spring creek, the object being to use his rod to propel a fly to a spot in such a way as to attract a trout, it should be understood that he's *presenting the fly*. Differentiating between fly casting and fly presentation is *not* nitpicking, nor is the distinction largely semantic. Becoming an accomplished fly caster doesn't make a person an accomplished fly fisherman, essential though casting may be to that end. To become an accomplished fly fisherman, the angler *must* master all the elements of fly presentation, of which fly casting should be perceived as just one.

Several seasons ago I guided a fellow who had "Done a lot of fly fishing," although all of it had been in saltwater along the Florida Keys. For his first assault on moving trout water, therefore, I suggested three-quartering wet flies or streamers downstream through a cordial stretch of the Willowemoc. I might as well have been pushing worms. Trout fishing meant dry fly fishing, I was informed in no uncertain terms. On the spot I bet myself a new rod we were in for a long three days.

The first ten minutes were enough to assure me that Cheryl Tiegs would look like a prune before my sport hooked a trout on a dry—unless, that is, he'd take some friendly advice. Figuring he might appreciate that the time I spend trout fishing teaches me something worth passing along, I tried my darndest to help the guy out. But he was convinced that fly fishing is fly fishing, and that any criticism, constructive or otherwise, would best be directed by him toward the river, the fish, or, most of all, me. Suffice it to say that the Catskill trout population remained stable as a consequence of his visit, and in less than a week I owned a new rod.

Here are but a few of problems for which this angler was unable or unwilling to adjust: (1) Having never encountered moving water before, his depth perception was confounded by its action; (2) Since he didn't know how to compensate for the effects of the flow on his fly, he couldn't get a decent drift; (3) Unaccustomed to approaching fish closely, he was incapable of making a presentation, even an inaccurate one, of less than forty feet; (4) His presentations of more than forty feet were "heavy handed," that is, he had no line speed control and, thus, no control over how violently his fly, leader and line struck the water at the limit of each presentation.

The essence of dry fly presentation is control. An angler can be said to control a presentation only when he's able to place his fly exactly where he wants it, when he wants it there. Once that's accomplished, he must also make the fly behave as a trout would see it. Unlike horseshoes, "close" doesn't count in the game of fly presentation. Fly presentation is a game of *instants* and *inches,* not unlike hitting a baseball. And, to use the baseball analogy just once more, it's certain that an angler's batting average—the ratio of fish hooked to presentations made—depends entirely on the degree of precision with which he controls each presentation.

Aptitude varies among anglers, of course, but for most it's apparent that the shorter our presentations, the greater our measure of control over them. Or, put another way, increasing the distance between angler and quarry generally introduces pressures that make precise presentations proportionately more difficult, even for the most versatile practitioner. For so-called "casting" instructors to instill in their students an obsession with distance, therefore, does the students immeasurable injury by subverting one of dry fly fishing's fundamental principles: *Never traverse the stream with line when a pair of waders will do just fine.*

The section of illustrations and explanatory text that follows provides what I believe to be a comprehensive instruction manual for effective dry fly presentation. Considered separately, the mechanics highlighted here may constitute nothing more or nothing less than nuts and bolts fundamental to dry fly fishing technique. Taken in the aggregate, however, I doubt if there's a single trout fishery either in the U.S. or abroad so tricky it will undo an angler who has thoroughly mastered this tactical repertoire. For, if my time on trout water has taught me anything, it is that the key to effectiveness anywhere you fish turns on your capacity to adapt a limited number of fundamental presentation principles to a virtually unlimited number of angling situations.

Part I, you'll note, is devoted entirely to the mechanics of fly casting, including grip, stripping line, false-casting, developing line speed, controlling the loop, the power stroke, shooting line, and the pickup and retrieve, among others. Part II, by contrast, demonstrates how to apply the mechanics of casting to a variety of more involved presentation techniques, such as the dead drift float or the skittering caddis. Thus, the section conveys at least in general terms how to, for instance, (1) optimize and maximize drift over trout feeding lanes, (2) overcome climatic handicaps like wind, (3) get flies into tricky places, (4) limit the need to false-cast, (5) present flies when backcasts aren't practical, and (6) hide line, leader and human silhouettes from spooky fish.

PART 1

THE ELEMENTS OF FLY CASTING

Illustration 1 shows the way I believe a fly rod should be gripped, unless, perhaps, some physical problem, such as an arthritic thumb, dictates otherwise. Note that by positioning your thumb along the top of the cork grip, it is in direct line with your wrist. The wrist, then, lines up with your forearm, which serves to make the rod an extension of your arm. Such alignment is critical when you drive line forward and aft, as in false-casting, and punch line ahead to shoot it.

A fly rod should be gripped firmly but not too tight. The object is to have it feel part of you, not to crush it. A too-tight grip tends to cramp your hand with prolonged casting and to overstress those forearm muscles and tendons from which a lot is demanded during a normal day's angling. Nor should the rod be gripped too loosely. A "cold-fish" grip permits chafing, which is the quickest way to build fat blisters.

The position of your grip should be adjusted, depending on the dry fly presentations you want to make. I like the grip shown in Fig. 1 for general use and long work; that shown in Fig. 2 for meticulous in-close work.

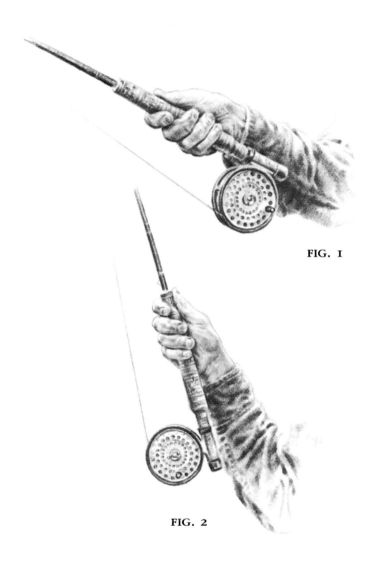

FIG. 1

FIG. 2

2. TAKING LOOPS

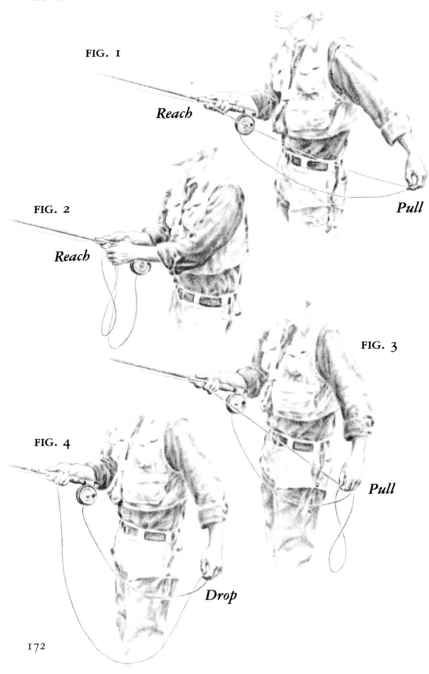

FIG. 1

Reach

Pull

FIG. 2

Reach

FIG. 3

Pull

FIG. 4

Drop

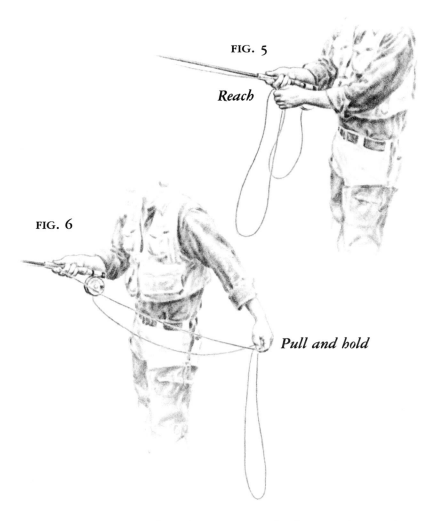

FIG. 5

Reach

FIG. 6

Pull and hold

A fly fisherman is denied the luxury of a free-spooling reel to dish up and collect his working line. Yet to fish flies effectively, this working line must be free of snarls at all times. The novice soon learns that line dumped at his feet or on the water is unmanageable. Thus it is essential that each angler knows how to take and hold loops with his free hand.

Illustration 2 shows the method I employ for collecting loops in my left hand between casts. Incidentally, it is the same method I generally use to retrieve line while fishing. Note that throughout the series of drawings my fly line is compressed between the pad of my right forefinger and the underside of the cork grip of my rod. It is important to apply just enough pressure on the line to insure sufficient tension to maintain control of the line.

Here's how you take loops of line:

1. Assuming you are right-handed, hold your rod with your right arm slightly extended and reach up with your left hand and clasp the line between your left thumb and forefinger where the line emerges from beneath your right forefinger. Then pull an arm-length of line across your body to an imaginary spot off your left hip (Fig. 1). (When wading deep water, your rod will be elevated, and the imaginary spot will be correspondingly higher.)

2. Now, while continuing to hold the line you have taken, reach up again and clasp the line between your left thumb and forefinger, exactly as you did before (Fig. 2).

3. Pull this line to the same imaginary spot off your hip (Fig. 3), except this time, drop the second length of line while continuing to hold the first (Fig. 4).

4. Next, reach up and clasp the line as before (Fig. 5), once again returning to your imaginary spot (Fig. 6). This time you'll find you have made a nice plump loop, which, like the others you'll collect, you will continue to hold throughout the procedure.

5. Remembering this sequence, then—reach, pull, reach, pull, drop, reach, pull and hold—repeat the process as many times as is necessary to collect all the loops of line you will need to make your next cast.

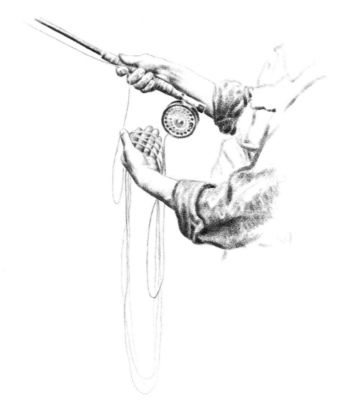

Depending on how much line you are fishing, you may frequently find yourself with a lot of loops in your free hand. After taking the loops, as shown in Illustration 2, it is critical that you be able to release them again without snags when casting. This is accomplished by holding the loops across the palm and fingers of the free hand, as shown in Illustration 3, so that the last loop you collect is the first to leave your hand again, the next-to-last loop is the second to leave, and so on. Don't be discouraged if you have occasional difficulty arranging that this happens just so. After more than twenty years, I still botch it up more often than I really care to admit.

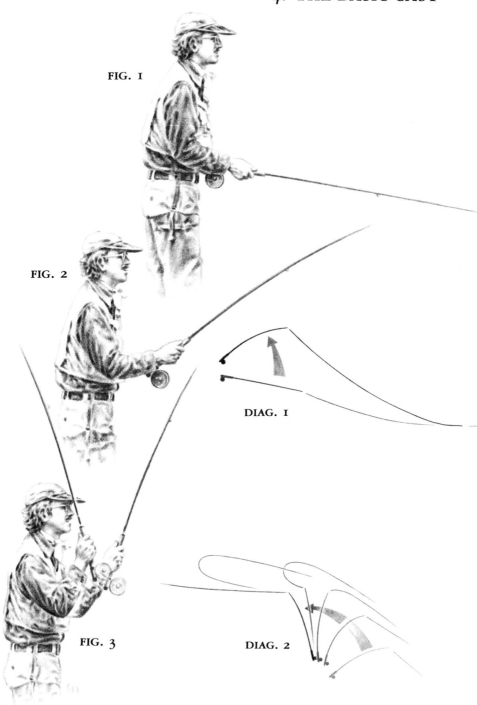

FIG. 1

FIG. 2

DIAG. 1

FIG. 3

DIAG. 2

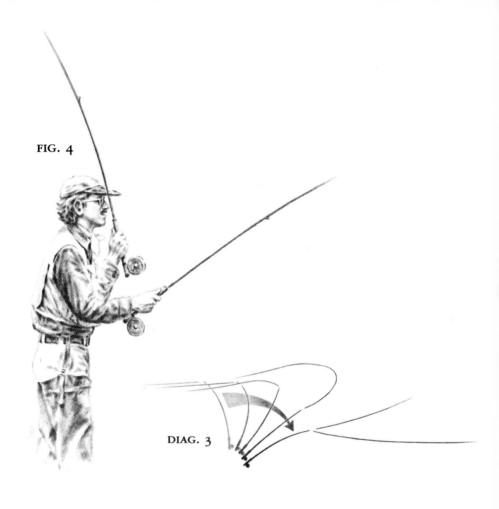

FIG. 4

DIAG. 3

There are about as many fly casting styles as styles for driving golf balls. You could study the styles of a hundred skilled anglers and probably not find two exactly alike. This would be the case even among those anglers who have studied under the same fly casting teachers. The differences in styles, ranging from subtle to dramatic, of course, stem from varied physical and psychological characteristics brought to the exercise by each practitioner.

Illustration 4 depicts the basic casting style I use. I'd like to think it will assist the bulk of my readers, because it is a style evolved largely from the practice of dry fly fishing for trout. Some experienced casters, particularly those who have worked out techniques they seem determined to promote as the only way to go, may view my style as a tad old-fashioned. So be it. It is short on flash, I'll give them that. But it is a style that stresses simplicity, control and accuracy, which, ultimately, should be the primary concerns of every dry fly fisherman.

So, here goes:

1. Walk off about twenty feet of fly line, a 7½-foot tapered leader and a bit of wool tied to your tippet to represent a fly. See that the line from fly to rod tip is straight, and then spot the fly by putting it on a saucer.

2. Now pick up your rod and stand with your feet parallel and slightly apart. Adjust your feet until you feel your weight is equally distributed. Then, assuming you are right-handed, take a half-step forward with your right foot, as if you were going to shake hands with a friend. Next, bend your knees a bit, and you should feel your weight shift to the ball and heel of your right foot and the ball of your left foot. (Some fly casting instructors will argue that you would be better off with your left foot forward. I disagree, since, when standing as I suggest, if you hold your rod as shown in Fig. 1, Fig. 2 or in the final position in Fig. 4, you will find that you can sight along it with your right eye, as if it were a rifle, to the precise spot your fly is resting. Thus, it can be said that you have optimum hand-eye coordination on the side of your body you cast from. However, should you reverse your feet, this hand-eye coordination will be lost. The left eye will become dominant, demanding that you monitor your fly at an oblique angle. Bearing in mind the importance of accuracy in dry fly fishing, such a compromise is totally unacceptable to me.)

3. Grip the rod, as shown in Illustration 1, and clasp the fly line tightly between the pad of your right forefinger and the cork grip of your rod. Be sure the line is secure, or the weight of your working line will likely pull more off the reel and cause you trouble.

4. Now prepare for the pick-up by angling the rod down-ward, as shown in Fig. 1 and Diag. 1. This angle minimizes the slack line you will have to absorb into the pick-up. Be sure that your right wrist is tilted slightly downward but that your fore-arm is virtually parallel to the ground (Fig. 1). Your elbow should be about three inches from your side (Fig. 1). Check your feet to be certain your weight is distributed as before. Okay, you're ready to cast.

5. Using the considerable power generated primarily by your wrist, drive the rod straight upward and back until the tip reaches a point between ten and eleven o'clock above and behind you (Figs. 2 & 3 and Diags. 1 & 2). To get a sense of this pick-up and ensuing backcast, imagine that you have tossed a small stone directly behind you, releasing it at a point just below and behind your right ear. As you rotate the rod upward, try to feel the line loading it (Diags. 1 & 2), imagine a loop forming in the line (Diag. 2) and the line beginning to straighten out high above but directly behind your right shoulder (Fig. 3 and Diag. 2). Meanwhile, you should note that your weight is shifting to the ball and heel of your left foot and the ball of your right foot. During this step, be certain your wrist doesn't rotate laterally (Fig. 3), or the line will flare out at an angle behind you, sub-jecting itself to atmospheric resistance. (You can check this by taking a peek at your reel as you complete the backcast. If you have rotated your wrist, the reel will be cocked either inboard or outboard. Your wrist and reel should look like mine in Fig. 3.) Also try to maintain the position of your elbow as close to your side as practical (Fig. 3), since, as our grandfathers knew well, this represents your best guarantee that you'll be in the correct posture to sight along your cast when you have driven the fly line forward again.

6. Next, wait until your line straightens out behind you (Diag. 2). Your thumb should help you perceive when the line has reached its extremity, but, except among the rarest novice casters, this bit of timing will require plenty of practice.

7. When the line has straightened out, you begin the forward cast by rotating your forearm and wrist ahead, as if you were driving a nail with a hammer (Fig. 4 and Diag. 3). This step

begins at the position between ten and eleven o'clock behind you and ends with the rod at about two o'clock in front of you (Diag. 3). The so-called "power-stroke" or "punch" will propel the line ahead, reloading the rod and increasing your line speed (Diag. 3), as well as causing a new line loop to begin to form (Diag. 3). The power-stroke should be as short as possible, between nine inches and a foot, which will be easy to accomplish, since I do not advocate permitting the rod to drift rearward late in the backcast, as some instructors do today. (This rearward drift, while it occasionally has some advantages, particularly for the sort of distance-casting typically applied on saltwater, wreaks havoc, I believe, with accuracy and line control essential to dry fly fishing.) During the forward cast, you should feel your weight shift again so that most of it will be on the ball and heel of your right foot while the ball of your left foot serves largely to maintain your balance. You will also note that as you drive the line forward, your right elbow will tend to rotate outboard, that is, away from your side (Fig. 4), and while a certain amount of drift is okay, you should endeavor to minimize it, because you will have to adjust for it before the cast is completed in order for the cast to be lined up properly with your right eye (Fig. 4).

8. The basic cast is completed by gently lowering the rod tip to a position on line with but substantially over your target (Fig. 4 and Diag. 3). This step is very important, since it is here that you make the fine adjustments that will insure your fly lands where you want it. For instance, you tuck your elbow in again and check with your right eye that everything is lining up. Now you also make the split second decision whether your cast is going to turn out as you want it, for if not, you will have to compensate quickly by preparing to make another cast before your fly has touched down.

9. When your fly is about to light, you can begin to evaluate your cast by monitoring your rod and body. The ultimate determination, however, is reserved for after the fly is down. If you have made a good cast, your rod, hand and arm should be absolutely still by the time the fly is about to come down (Fig. 4 and Diag. 3). Only your weight should be gradually shifting again so that in the end it will be equally distributed between both

feet. Your fly, meanwhile, should land in direct line but slightly short of the saucer from which you snatched it, the difference amounting to the length of fly line that could be measured between the low point at which your rod tip was located when the cast began (Fig. 1), and the higher point at which it should be found when the cast is completed (Fig. 4). Any wandering of the fly to the right or left means you have some more work to do on your basic casting.

5. SHOOTING LINE

The correct technique for shooting line represents the essence of successful dry fly fishing. It is the shoot, after all, that delivers the fly to the fish. Therefore, the angler must learn how to shoot line in such a way that he is in control of his line at all times. To be able to send fly line whistling through guides is not good enough, for it doesn't guarantee that a presentation won't be too long or too short and thus off the mark, or that the line won't come down with a terrifying splat. Each shoot of the line, then, must be carefully calculated, so that in the end it does the job exactly right. No use pretending otherwise. Shooting line properly is an acquired skill that requires plenty of practice.

Illustration 5 shows the fundamentals of shooting line and, I would hope, a little bit more. Note that the line is held in loops (Fig. 1) collected in the left hand. These loops lie across the palm of the hand, as depicted in Illustration 3. The loops are held at about waist level and in front of the body (Fig. 1) to be certain that nothing obstructs the free passage of line up to the rod guides. Remember that if the line brushes anything, an article of clothing, for instance, resulting friction will alter the line speed you have planned for the cast. Or, worse yet, if your line should catch, say, a button the line will be stopped altogether.

Fig. 1 also illustrates that an angler does not look at his line while he's preparing to shoot it, because he already knows how much line he has collected and where he is holding it while he false-casts. Instead, he concentrates on his target, reassessing the distance, feeling for a sudden change in the breeze, for instance, for which he will have to compensate in less than a second. Similarly, he is thoroughly familiar with the capabilities of his tackle, so that when the time comes to shoot the line, he can predict exactly what the line will do.

Now he makes his power-stroke or punch (Fig. 2), generally when he knows he's built optimum line speed, and simultaneously releases the loops of line from his left hand (Fig. 2). He should feel the loops peel away smoothly (Fig. 2), the line climbing to the first rod guide, called the stripping guide. At the same time, he adjusts his rod to an angle of pitch over the water

5. SHOOTING LINE

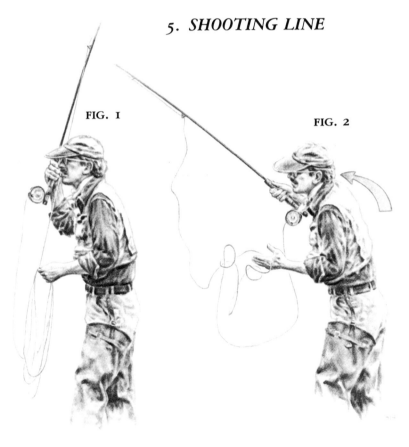

FIG. 1

FIG. 2

that will largely dictate how far and how fast his fly line travels (Fig. 2). Because the line has to climb, working against the law of gravity, the greater the angle of pitch he opts for, the slower his line will travel and, thus, the shorter will be his shoot. But, it should also be remembered that a steep pitch maintains the line high over the water, thereby offering the angler maximum time to control the direction of presentation, as well as how gently or hard his fly, leader and line will come down on the water.

Not all the loops held in the left hand need be released when shooting line, of course. The angler may choose to release only two or three, halting the others by bending the knuckles of his left hand at right angles before further loops can spill off his fingertips. He can also "feather" the line intentionally by causing resistance, either by letting it rub against his hand or, as I prefer, by forming an "O" between his left thumb and forefinger at the last instant before the line is released and seeing to it that each loop of line travels through the "O" as it is unraveling.

Nor does all shooting have to occur on the forward cast. A good false-caster ought to be able to shoot at least a couple of loops of line on the backcast. Not only is this helpful when long casts are needed, but the angler will find it also saves time.

6. BUILDING LINE SPEED AND TIGHTENING CASTING LOOPS

Illustration 6 deals with the line speed, the key to efficient fly casting. It is virtually impossible to build the right kind of line speed if your casting loop, that is, the loop that forms in the line overhead fore and aft, is permitted to remain wide open. (Note the dotted line in Diag. 2 as an example of a poor casting loop, the solid line as an example of a fine one.)

The good caster usually drives his line when false-casting, being sure that the line loads his rod properly (Diag. 1), and that the line straightens out behind him before he begins his forward cast (Diag. 2). Even when a line is driven, however, the casting loop will tend to open if the caster makes a power-stroke that is too long. A long power-stroke causes an uneven line tra-

6. BUILDING LINE SPEED AND TIGHTENING CASTING LOOPS

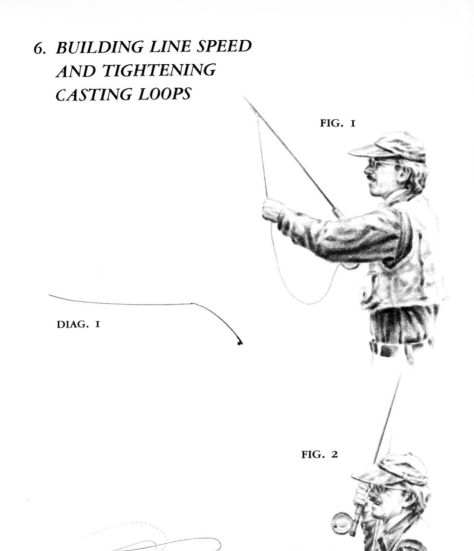

FIG. I

DIAG. I

FIG. 2

DIAG. 2

jectory, which means the best you can hope for is that the line will simply be dragged along. The wide loop that results, then, will become increasingly subject to atmospheric resistance, which, in turn, will inhibit your line speed.

To help increase line speed to an ideal rate, thereby tightening your casting loop, practice the following:

1. Reach up with your left hand and grasp your line below the stripping guide at arm's length, as shown in Fig. 1.

2. Now, as you begin your backcast, pull the line hard down and across your body, until it arrives at an imaginary spot off your left hip (Fig. 2). You should note a marked difference in the width of your casting loop right away (Diag. 2), as well as in the speed at which your line travels as it straightens out behind you (Diag. 2). The name given this pull on the line, by the way, is the *single-haul*.

3. Now make your short power-stroke forward and simultaneously release the line you hauled in at the outset. You will discover that this simple technique, if properly timed, has served to tighten your loop on your forward cast, too, by increasing your overall line speed. This single haul can be repeated with each subsequent false-cast, including, of course, the one at the end of which you will shoot the line.

The single-haul cast can be easily turned into a *double-haul* by permitting your left hand that is holding the line to drift upward toward the stripping guide again as the backcast is completed. Then you exert another haul on the line as you begin the power-stroke of your forward cast. The reader should be cautioned, though, that the double-haul inceases line speed so dramatically that, unless you intend to make a very long cast, it is neither necessary nor desirable when dry fly fishing. The problem is that the line travels so fast that most anglers can't control the most important aspect of any presentation, that is, the attitude of the fly and leader when they hit the water. So, although the double-haul has been widely touted of late, in my opinion it should be used extremely sparingly by the dry fly fisherman. For what it's worth, I would estimate that I show fewer than a dozen trout my double-haul each season.

7. BACKHAND OR CROSS-BODY CAST

FIG. 1

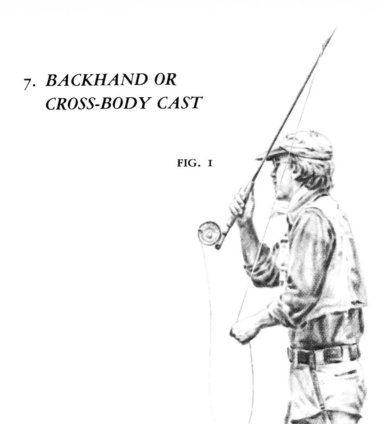

DIAG. 1

Power-Stroke

FIG. 2

Wind can give a fly fisherman fits, particularly a dry fly fisherman who is always playing a "game of inches." A light breeze blowing from directly behind or one that blows gently downstream may actually assist the angler on occasion. But, there's no such thing as a nice wind.

Many inexperienced anglers contend that head winds cause the most trouble. I must beg to differ. A head wind, unless it blows a gale, can be beaten by building exceptional line speed while keeping the line close to the surface; by casting under the wind, so to speak. No, the devil wind has to be the one that blows the line into the angler's body, where, unless he's always ready to duck, his fly is likely to spend considerable time stuck in his skin, hair or clothing. This kind of wind is at its very worst when it strikes the angler obliquely, that is, into him and from the front or rear.

Because a devil wind can actually be dangerous, a few words on safety are in order. The most graphic example of the wind's mischief I can recall occurred while a friend of mine was fishing in Newfoundland. Fighting the wind, he put a number-eight hook right through his lip, but because the fishing was so good, he simply cut off the fly, tied on another, and stayed right at it. By evening when he quit, his lip was swollen so badly around the hook that he had to be shipped sixty miles to receive emergency attention. I have also seen flies lodged in anglers' ear lobes and other parts of the face and head, and although I've been spared seeing one stuck in an eye, I've heard tell of such disasters and am inclined to believe the stories. It is my conviction, therefore, that no fly fisherman, not even the best, should tackle a river under devil wind conditions unless he wears some protective clothing. At the very least, he should wear a hat and a pair of protective eyeglasses.

Illustration 7 shows the best way I know to compensate for a wind that blows your line into you. Here's what you do:

1. Prepare for your pick-up as usual, except that your right elbow should be in line with but slightly forward of its normal position (Fig. 1). (For the normal position, see Illus. 4, Fig. 1.)

2. Now make your pick-up and backcast in the usual manner, except to hold your elbow stationary in its forward position and to couple the pick-up with a strenuous single-haul (Fig. 1).

3. Let the line straighten out behind you (Diag. 1). You will sense the wind pushing the line to your left, until, at the extremity of the backcast, the fly will be located somewhere above and either directly behind or above and behind and to the left of your head.

4. As the line straightens out behind, permit your rod to drift smoothly across your face by rotating your right elbow and forearm to the left, until the elbow is located in about the middle of your chest and the rod grip is just off your left cheek (Fig. 1). (The rod should remain in its one o'clock position —;Fig. 1 and Diag. 1—(and should be brought to the left only to the extent that it lines up directly with the fly line behind you, as indicated by Diag. 1.)

5. Now lean into your cast, that is, bend at the waist (Fig. 2), and make a short power-stroke to the left of your head, as shown in Diag. 1.

6. After releasing the line (Fig. 2), drop your right arm slightly (Fig. 2) to continue the forward cast, as shown in Diag. 1. Then return your right arm across your body again, drifting it smoothly but in plenty of time to make final adjustments in your presentation before your fly hits the water.

8. ROLL-CAST

Although not nearly so popular among American anglers as among those abroad, notably in the United Kingdom, the roll-cast represents a potentially rewarding technique for virtually every dry fly fisherman. Its principal advantage results from eliminating the need for a backcast, and thus the cast is of particular value to the angler who fishes tight places. Small streams or water below steep banks are good examples.

The cast isn't widely used here, I suspect, because it neither complements our typical rod designs well (a tip-heavy rod is best for roll-casting), nor is it applied with particular efficiency to the weight-forward lines that increase in popularity among American anglers every year (double-taper lines work best when roll-casting). Therefore, the angler who finds he will be doing a lot of roll-casting would be well served to invest in a rod with a European-style action, while every dry fly fisherman, as mentioned earlier, should own a double-taper line that balances his favorite American rod model.

That said, here's how to make the roll-cast:

1. Assuming you are right-handed, strip in and coil the length of line you wish to shoot and stand with your right foot about six inches ahead of your left, your knees bent so that most of your weight is on your right foot. You will also want to lean into the cast by bending slightly at the waist (see Fig. 1).

2. Now, holding your rod parallel to the surface, aim the rod directly at the working line you intend to roll off the water and into your next presentation. The line that you want to shoot should be held in loops in your left hand off your left hip. At this point, your rod, right wrist and right forearm should be parallel to the surface. Your right elbow should be in line with, but perhaps six inches ahead of, its normal pick-up position (Fig. 1).

3. Now draw the line back toward you by raising your rod tip slowly but smoothly until it reaches the one o'clock position, shown in Fig. 1 and Diag. 1. At this point, the arc of your line from your rod's tip-top downward should look like the line in Diag. 1, and you and your rod should appear much as I do in Fig. 1.

FIG. 1

DIAG. 1

189

8. ROLL-CAST

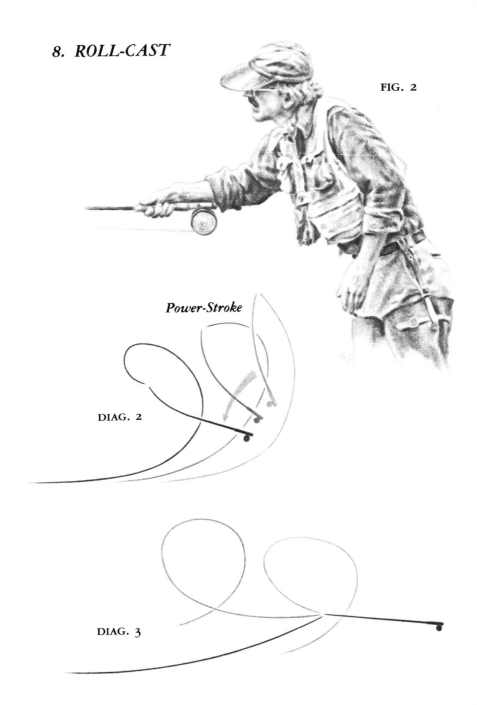

FIG. 2

Power-Stroke

DIAG. 2

DIAG. 3

4. When your rod reaches one o'clock (Fig. 1), begin your short power-stroke (Diag. 2) without hesitation, so that the draw-back and power-stroke become, in effect, extensions of each other, accomplished in a single fluid motion. Wait, however, until the power-stroke is almost completed to release the loops of line held in your left hand. With the power-stroke, you will probably come up onto the toes of both feet, and should note that a wide loop is forming in the working line to your right side, or to your right side and slightly to the rear of your body (Diag. 2).

5. With the power-stroke completed, come back down so that your weight is equally distributed between both feet and then lean even further forward into the cast (Fig. 2), so that your weight will shift gently to the ball and heel of your right foot and the ball of your left. Meanwhile, lower your rod tip gradually (Diag. 2), and you'll see that your line will uncoil and shoot ahead, as shown in the third step of Diag. 2 and all of Diag. 3. At the end of the cast, you should appear much as I do in Fig. 2.

PART 2

DEVELOPING SKILLS
FOR FLY PRESENTATION

A host of dry fly fishing situations call for a dead-drift presentation, that is, one during which your fly floats over the quarry at precisely the same speed as the flow of water along the trout's feeding lane. The perfect dead-drift presentation would be duck soup, if only you didn't have to attach your fly to a leader and line. Since you can't escape that awkward reality, though, the best you can hope to do is to keep the leader and line safely out of harm's way.

The object is to arrange your terminal tackle so that the only current relevant to the presentation is the one that carries the fly over your target trout. Let's call this the objective current and all those currents that pass with the flow between the angler and the trout intervening currents. Intervening currents are the ones that generally cause trouble, because they are the currents that usually cause flies to drag.

Drag occurs because intervening currents have a nasty tendency to grab your line and leader and to pull it along at a speed out of sync with the float of the fly. The most common manifestation of this pull is for a large downstream bow, or belly, to form in the line on the water between the angler and his fly. This belly then tows the fly along faster than it ought to float in order to imitate a natural insect being carried toward the trout by the objective current.

The dry fly fisherman's number-one priority is to show his fly to the trout the way the trout wants or expects to see it during a given period. When the naturals upon which a trout is feeding are drifting idly on the surface, the angler's best hope of taking that fish is to make his imitation do likewise. If he doesn't know how to keep his dry fly from dragging, therefore, he'd be just as well off at home mowing the lawn. It may be possible to have both a dead-drift and drag, but, if so, somebody will have to show me how it's done. As far as I'm concerned, the terms dead-drift and drag-free drift are virtually interchangeable.

This is not to say that drag is always bad. Indeed, several of my favorite techniques, a few of which are described further along in this and in an upcoming chapter, use drag to create the impression of life in my flies by giving the flies some action. However, the critical distinction lies in the difference between intentional and unintentional drag, the latter being an unpardonable *faux pas*. For, if a trout is looking for dead-drifting flies, it is apt to forgive almost anything, except that old demon drag.

The traditional trick for eliminating drag is mending line. Line is mended by presenting your fly across the intervening currents and then, when the line begins to belly, by flicking the bowed length of line upstream with your rod. This is accomplished by rotating the rod with your wrist in the direction counter to the flow, from right to left, for instance, if the direction of flow is from left to right. Thus your fly will float ahead of your line and leader, freeing its drift from the influences of fickle intervening currents that continue to work on the line.

1. UPSTREAM MEND
PRESENTATION
(*Water Flow from Right to Left*)

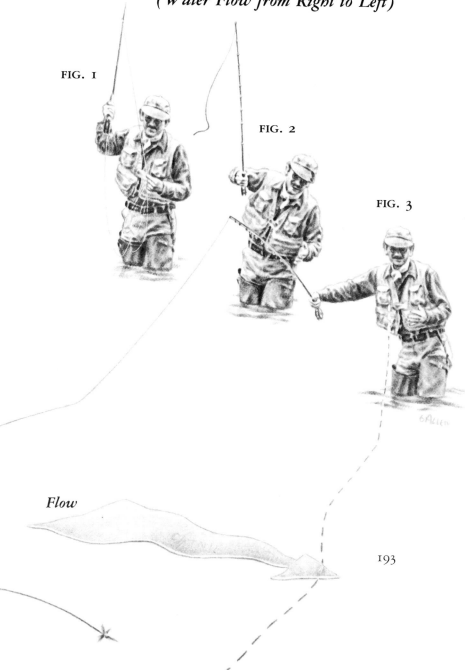

FIG. 1

FIG. 2

FIG. 3

Flow

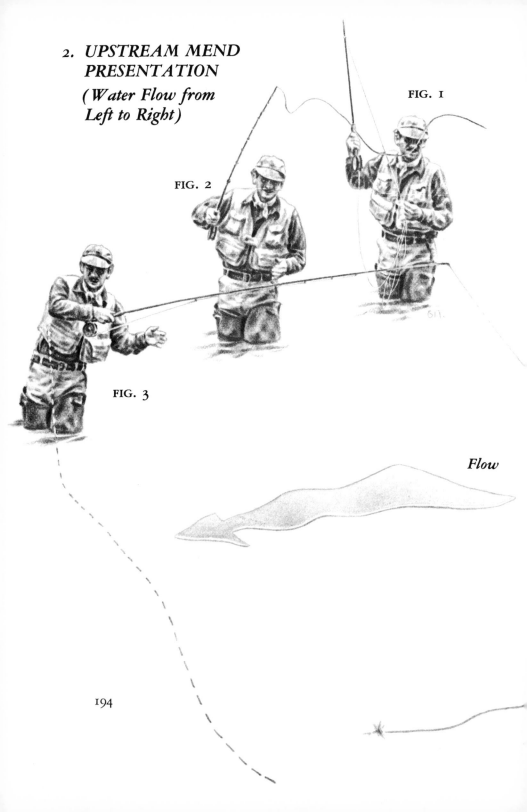

2. UPSTREAM MEND PRESENTATION
(Water Flow from Left to Right)

FIG. I

FIG. 2

FIG. 3

Flow

The trouble with the traditional technique for mending line is that it is a holdover from the heyday of the wet fly, unfortunately not easily reconciled to effective dry fly fishing. It fails, for instance, to accommodate the scant margin for error we have along a dry fly's direction of drift. When you mend line after it is already on the water, the direction of your fly's drift is inevitably altered. Thus the only means by which the dry fly fisherman can adapt the technique to his typical presentation is to cast his fly to a point beyond where he'd really like it to be, so that it will end up in the right place in the wake of his mend. Anglers skilled enough to manage this feat with consistency have no need to be reading books such as this.

Illustrations 1 and 2 show how I have adapted the concept of mending line to presenting dry flies, by incorporating the mend into the cast. The results are much like those observed in the wake of traditional mends, that is, the upstream curve in the line and a fly free to float without drag. But I am able to achieve these ends without the need to alter the direction of drift of my flies. Don't be surprised if, after mastering these simple skills, you find yourself using them in one form or the other most of the time.

First, the *Upstream Mend Presentation* when the flow is from your right to your left (Illustration 1—see page 193):

1. Position yourself so that your target is either directly across or across and slightly downstream from you. Then size up all the intervening currents for which you will have to compensate.

2. Now, with your free hand, strip in and hold adequate line to reach your objective current, plus enough extra to make up the upstream mend you intend to throw into the presentation.

3. Without taking your eye off the target, begin false-casting, as shown in Fig. 1. (Be sure to build sufficient line speed to cover shooting the line you'll need to reach your target and to throw in the mend.)

4. Now make your short power-stroke, as shown in Fig. 2, releasing the line from your left hand just as the power-stroke is completed (Fig. 2).

5. As you complete the power-stroke and release the line, let your rod drift outboard, that is, to the right, until you are holding it at arm's length, directly out from your side, as shown in Fig. 3. This drift should be made quickly but smoothly with your rod continuing to point across the stream. This is done by cocking your right wrist to keep it in line with the rod, until, at the point your arm is fully extended, your wrist will be at an approximate right angle to your forearm (Fig. 3). Properly executed, you will note that most of your weight has shifted to your right foot during the drift of your arm.

6. Now return your rod to its normal fishing position, as indicated by the dotted line in Fig. 3. You should find that you have succeeded in putting a nice upstream mend into your presentation.

Now let's assume that the flow is from your left to your right, as in Illustration 2 on page 194. Here's how to make the Upstream Mend Presentation:

1. Position yourself as in the first example, size up the intervening currents as before, and strip in the line that you'll need.

2. Now, eyeing your target, false-cast, as shown in Fig. 1, until you have built enough line speed to shoot the line to the target (Fig. 2).

3. Make your short power-stroke, as shown in Fig. 2, but this time release the loops of line from your left hand with the onset of the power-stroke (Fig. 2).

4. With the power-stroke completed, let your rod drift to the left across your body, until the rod tip is pointing at an angle approximately three-quarters upstream. The drift of your arm across your body should be made much more slowly than the one you made when the flow was from your right to your left. In this instance, your right wrist need be cocked only to the extent required to angle the rod three-quarters upstream.

5. Now, taking plenty of time, return your rod to its normal fishing position, as shown by the dotted line in Fig. 3, and you should note that you have put a good upstream mend in your line (Fig. 3).

3. A WIGGLE TO CREATE SLACK

Illustration 3 depicts how I make those special presentations to trout that are feeding in places where the flow of water is significantly slower than the general flow along a stretch of river or stream. Side eddies, dead waters and backwashes, shown in my stream nomenclature in chapter three, are typical examples of this kind of water. When you must cast across fast intervening currents to reach a relatively calm spot, the problem becomes to convince your fly to hold in the slow water long enough for a trout to look it over and take it. Trying to keep your fly from dragging hopelessly can drive you crazy. And even when you have mastered the technique described here, often you will get only one shot. So be warned; you had better make it count.

Here's what to do:

1. Position yourself so you are either across or across and slightly upstream of your target. (Across and upstream is decidedly preferable.)

2. Now, with your free hand, strip in and hold in loops enough line to reach the target, plus about one-third more.

3. False-cast up to one-half of the line, holding the rest in your free hand. In this instance, you should only try for moderate line speed, since you don't want to shoot the line beyond your target.

4. Make your usual short power-stroke, as indicated by Diag. 1, but do not release the line from your free hand until you sense the line behind you beginning to dart forward, that is, until an instant after the power-stroke is completed. (A real feel for this step will require some practice.)

5. Now, simultaneously release the loops from your free hand and begin to lower the rod tip smoothly, using your right wrist to wiggle the rod tip horizontally from side-to-side as the line passes through the guides (see Diag. 1). Be sure to begin wiggling the rod soon enough to insure that the action of the rod is transmitted all the way through the line and leader to the tippet.

6. Complete the presentation by bringing the rod tip to its normal fishing position (Fig. 1). Properly executed, you should observe that a number of "S"s have been wiggled into your line, leader and tippet, with which the intervening currents can play while your fly rests idly, like a natural, on the surface of the

3. A WIGGLE TO CREATE SLACK

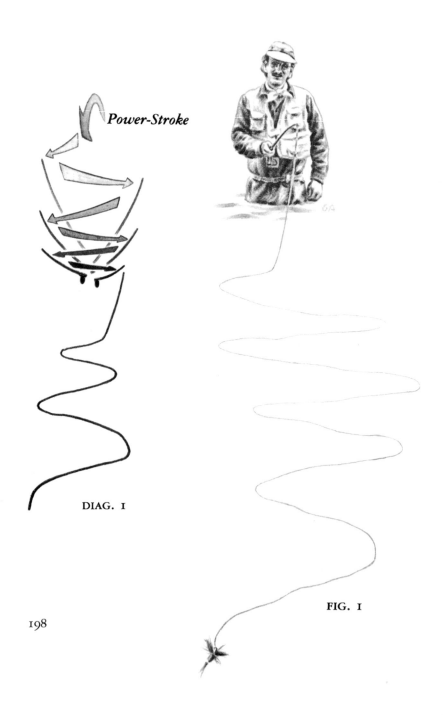

Power-Stroke

DIAG. I

FIG. I

calm water (Fig. 1 and Diag. 1). (Note: It is more difficult to do, of course, but this presentation works even better when combined with the upstream mend presentation described previously in this section.)

4. THE STOP AND DROP

The stop and drop, as I call it, shown in Illustration 4, has emerged in recent years as by far my favorite presentation technique. It is the technique I now use more often than all others combined. I find it ideal for a wide range of dry fly fishing situations, including, among others: presenting either dun or spinner imitations during hatches or falls, whether the water I'm fishing be broken or flat; fine work with midges, particularly when presenting them in a generally downstream direction; the kind of fishing with large terrestrial patterns and attractor flies when you want to minimize false-casting; and prospecting water of almost any kind during periods that no fish are rising. Further, the technique has proven ideal to couple with, for instance, the upstream mend presentations, already described, to develop a host of useful variations on the theme. I hope that many readers will discover interesting ways to apply this technique to tricks they've developed on their own.

The stop and drop should not be confused with the so-called steeple cast that has become popular over the years. I have worked extensively with the steeple cast under the tutelage of some of its principal advocates, and fear the only word I can come up with to describe it is "sloppy." Using the unorthodox casting form recommended and after having allowed my line to tumble to the surface without apparent care or design, I just can't escape a feeling akin to the one you'd experience when trying to pick up Jell-O with your hands.

The beauty of the stop and drop, by contrast, is the sense of absolute control you maintain throughout each presentation. Although that may be its chief advantage over the steeple cast, the stop and drop also permits you to drift a fly over a piece of water in such a way that any trout lurking there will see the fly before it sees the leader tippet. Meanwhile, the angler can feel secure

4. THE STOP AND DROP

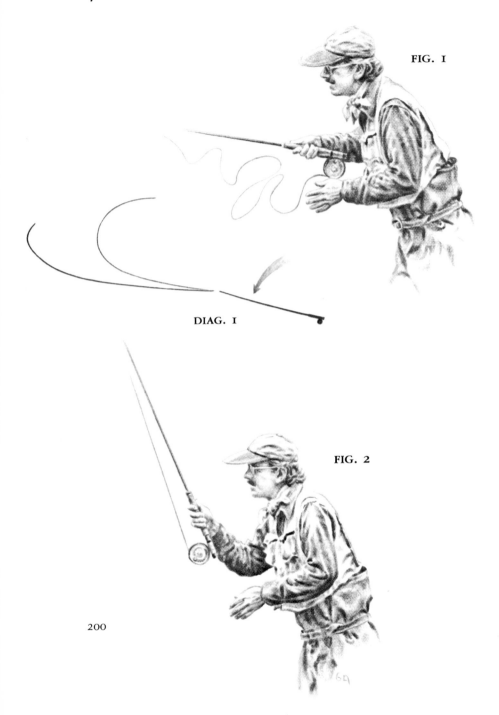

FIG. 1

DIAG. 1

FIG. 2

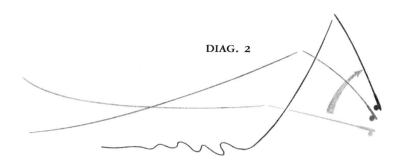

DIAG. 2

that his fly is floating without drag and that should the eventuality arise, he will be able to set the hook without the need to resort to such extraordinary devices as an abbreviated roll-cast hook setting technique, which, believe me, is a whole lot easier written about than accomplished.

The stop and drop is executed as follows:

1. Try to position yourself across and somewhat upstream of your target.

2. False-cast your line, when practical, using the single-haul to build up plenty of line speed. (Check to be sure your casting loop is tight.)

3. Now make an extremely short power-stroke to drive your line forward, as shown in Diag. 1, and you should feel the line slithering up through the guides, as shown in Fig. 1.

4. Lean into the cast and lower your rod tip (Fig. 1 and Diag. 2). Then, when most of the line has passed through the guides, raise your rod tip abruptly again, as shown in Fig. 2 and Diag. 2. If you have driven the line properly, you will feel a decided thump through the rod as the pitching rod stops the line. With the shock of the stop, the line will spring back somewhat toward you and then will drop to the surface in a series of clean "S"s (Diag. 2). (Note that if the line springs back too violently, your fly will either land in a bird's nest of tippet material or will light so that it actually floats behind some of the leader.)

5. Now that the fly is on the water, it should begin to drift downstream with all the "S"s straightening out uniformly behind it. As this occurs, lower your rod tip gradually, until, at the extremity of the drift, it is in its normal fishing position.

5. POPPING ONTO POCKETS

Pocket water fish are sometimes the most forgiving of trout. This is likely true, in part, because the nature of pocket water tends to break up the images of fly and tippet floating overhead. Even more important, though, is that pocket water trout seldom have much time to look their food over. A fly bursts into view, perhaps tumbling through some white water at the head of a pocket, and in a flash it's gone. The choosy pocket water trout is apt to be awfully skinny.

This is not to say that the angler who fishes pocket water ought to throw caution to the wind. For, even on the most turbulent pocket water, an angler who observes the rules of precise presentation should outfish a klutz almost every time. It is rather that pocket water presents a special set of problems to which the skillful angler must attend, chief among which is covering as much of the water as possible with minimum effort.

Over the years I have experimented with a number of alternative techniques in an attempt to discover the best to accomplish that end. In the extreme, I tried positioning myself so that there were pockets all around me, and then fished them by rotating 360 degrees, until I had worked out all the line I could handle. In some cases this method worked fine, particularly on a few streams where wading was so treacherous you dreaded every step. However, I also found that by fishing long to pockets, I was substantially compromising my control over my terminal tackle, including my fly, while to hook a heavy fish raised far out could be an unrewarding adventure. Further, in my typically unscientific manner, I noticed an irrefutable decline in the number of trout raised, hooked and landed, as the pockets I fished became further away.

Luckily, I also discovered that I could approach pocket water trout much more closely than I had ever supposed by simply exercising a modicum of caution. Along many waters I found that by approaching pockets from downstream, keeping a low profile, watching my shadow and being sure not to disturb the bottom too much, I could actually take fish just off my rod tip. Con-

FIG. I

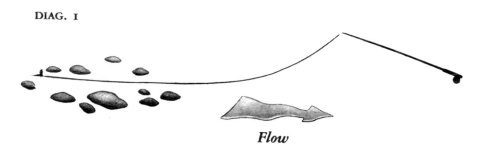

DIAG. I

Flow

5. POPPING ONTO POCKETS

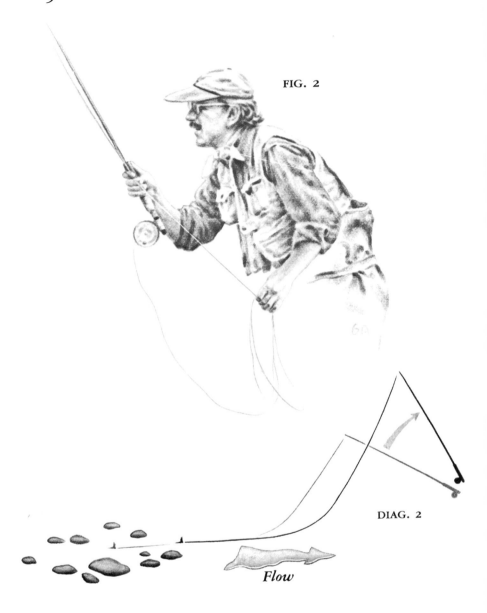

FIG. 2

DIAG. 2

Flow

sequently, fishing a short line to pop dry flies onto pockets remains my favorite technique for that kind of water to this day.

Illustration 5 shows how I go about it:

1. Choose a series of promising pockets and approach one
from directly downstream. Try to stay low, as shown in Fig. 1,
and as you move along, plant your feet firmly with each step, in
order not to disturb the stones on the bottom. (The sound of
stones either grating or banging against each other carries to fish,
even to those lying upstream.)

2. Try to approach the tail of your target pocket as closely as
prudent, making sure there are no difficult intervening currents
between you and the surface of the pocket you intend to fish.

3. Now grip your rod for doing short work (see Fig. 1), and
hold some extra line in loops in your left hand. (A short leader
works best, since it gives you more working fly line with which
to control the presentation. The extra line in your left hand is to
handle the initial run of a hooked trout.)

4. Now false-cast briskly and pop your dry onto the water
near the head of the pocket, as shown in Diag. 1. Keep your
power-stroke extremely short, so that when you shoot the line,
its speed will automatically throw a bit of slack into the tippet
behind your fly. After the fly has landed, you should look somewhat as I do in Fig. 1.

5. As the fly drifts downstream, raise your rod gradually, as
shown in Diag. 2, until it has reached the pitch shown in Fig. 2.
The rate of inclining the rod should correspond exactly to the
speed of the downstream float of the fly. (If you can't keep up
with the fly, take out extra slack line by drawing it into loops
with your free hand.)

6. When the fly reaches the tail of the pocket, the pitch of
your rod should not be steeper than mine in Fig. 2 and Diag. 2,
since you must retain sufficient leverage to set the hook if a trout
takes your fly. You will also note that as the presentation is completed, you will be in an ideal position to initiate another presentation by simply making a quick roll-cast to get your line into the
air before false-casting and shooting as usual.

6. THE MEND-AND-TWITCH

While the dead-drift, drag-free float is unquestionably the most frequently applied technique in dry fly fishing, there are numerous situations in which the dead-drifting fly must appear just as suspicious to a feeding fish as a dragging one does when all the naturals are drifting idly by on the surface. Remember that even some mayflies struggle frantically before leaving the surface after they hatch. Caddis and stoneflies are particularly prone to fluttering all over the place during periods that they are on or near the water. Likewise, an angler will seldom observe large terrestrial insects, such as grasshoppers, crickets, beetles or moths, simply going along for rides with the current. The surface of a trout stream, after all, is an unnatural and hostile place for terrestrials to find themselves.

Dry flies that are presented to imitate any of the insects described above, among others too numerous to itemize, must be imbued by the angler with action that creates in trout the impression of fluttering or struggling naturals. The angler should also find that, by imparting such action to his flies, he can sometimes wake up fish that are seemingly uninterested in imitations drifting by casually. To just allow your dry fly to drag, though, isn't good enough. Imparting action to your fly must be a calculated maneuver to which you bring the same degree of expertise you do to obtaining the drag-free float.

An angler could probably dream up a thousand ways to make flies bob, weave, streak, dodge or skitter, all based on a single fundamental principle: Where the rod goes, the line, leader and fly must follow. To verify this principle, take a rod with about eight feet of line and a leader outside its tip-top and spin the rod over your head as if it were a lasso. You'll note that as you revolve the rod, the line and leader will describe a perfect circle in the air. And so it will be on the water: the line, leader and fly will react to every movement you make with your rod.

Bearing the principle in mind, here, as shown in Illustration 6, is the mend-and-twitch, one of my favorite tricks for giving action to dry flies:

1. Present your fly either across or across and slightly downstream, as shown in Fig. 1. (A long cast works best.) Try to

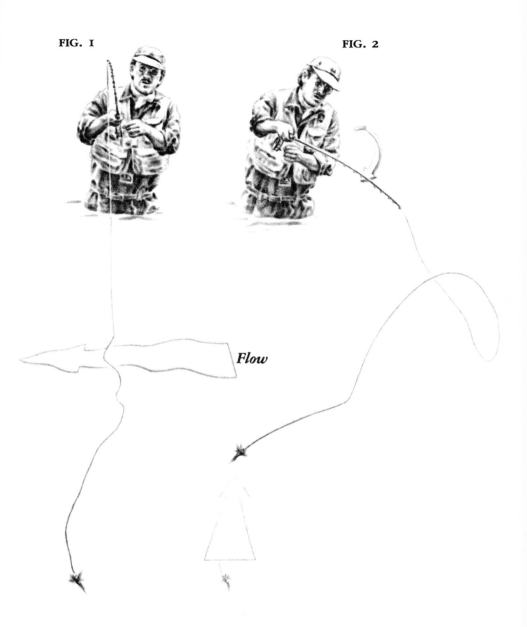

FIG. 1   FIG. 2

Flow

6. THE MEND-AND-TWITCH

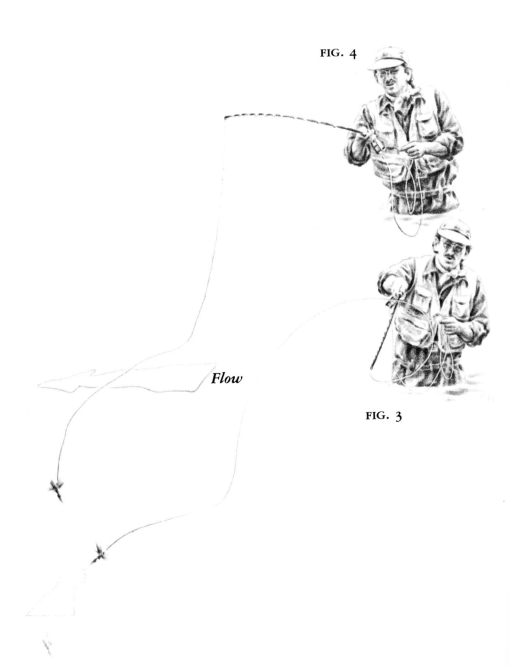

FIG. 4

FIG. 3

Flow

minimize the number of "S"s in your working line, in order to get on with the business of the presentation as soon as possible.

2. Now permit the intervening currents to take hold of your line, either straightening it out, as shown in Fig. 1, or causing a belly in it.

3. When your line is taut, make a mend by rotating your rod in an upstream direction, as shown in Fig. 2. The mend should be just big enough to twitch your fly and drag it toward you in an arc of several inches. (The mend shown in Fig. 2 was exaggerated by the artist to illustrate the principle.)

4. Next, strip in the slack line created by the mend (Fig. 3), and when the line becomes taut on the water again, make another upstream mend just like the first (Fig. 3). After this and each successive mend, all excess line should be stripped in while you return your rod to its normal fishing position (Fig. 4).

5. The series of mends which result in the twitches and short drifts of the fly should be repeated until either all the productive water is covered or your fly is dangling in the current directly downstream, whichever comes first.

7. *SKITTERING A SKATER*

Illustration 7 depicts another more dramatic approach to imparting action to a dry fly. It is particularly applicable to fishing skaters and other bushy patterns, but with minor modifications can be utilized with virtually any dry you want to cover a piece of water in an erratic fashion. The technique was developed primarily to trigger strikes by appealing to that impulsive side of a trout's nature that makes it react violently sometimes to flies, perhaps out of excitement, playfulness or anger. No matter, really. The important thing is that the technique works.

Here's how it's done:

1. Assuming you are right-handed, present your fly across or across and slightly downstream, being sure to build sufficient line speed to be able to shoot all the loops held in your left hand.

2. As intervening currents straighten your line, bring your rod smoothly across your body to the position shown in Fig. 1.

7. SKITTERING A SKATER

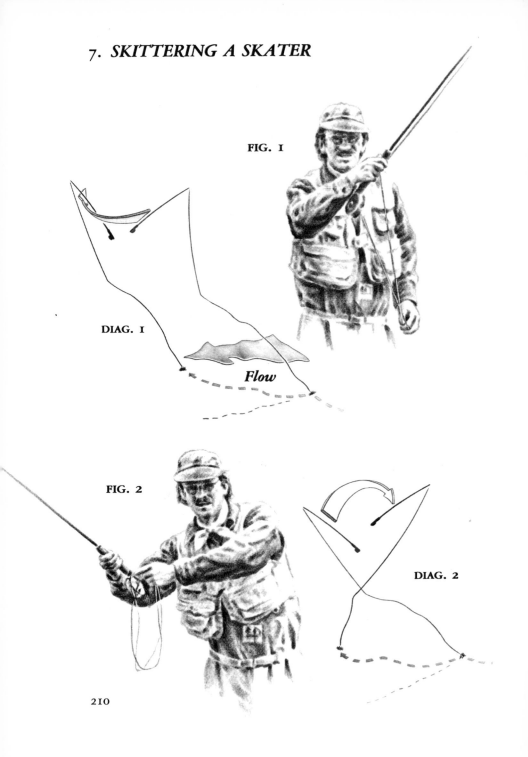

FIG. 1

DIAG. 1

Flow

FIG. 2

DIAG. 2

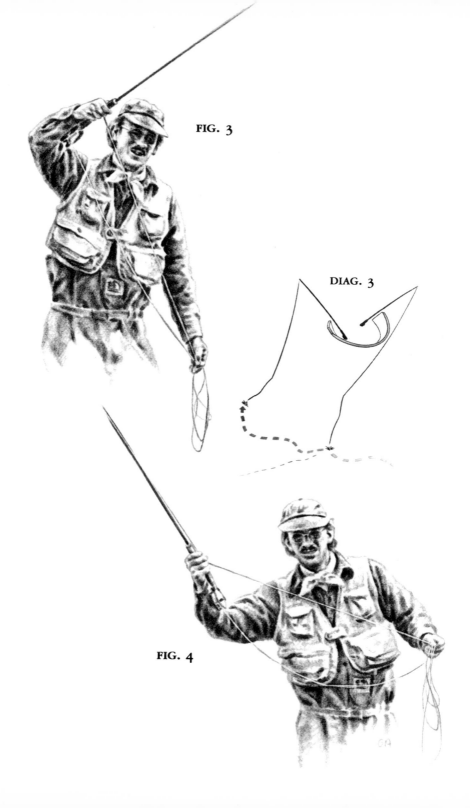

FIG. 3

DIAG. 3

FIG. 4

3. As you are rotating the rod, reach up and clasp your line near the rod grip with your left forefinger and thumb, and pull an arm's-length of line downward to an imaginary point off your left hip (Fig. 1). The fly, you'll note, will cock up and begin to skitter toward you, as indicated by the beginning of the heavy dotted line in Diag. 1.

4. Before the fly has had a chance to skitter far, sweep your rod to your right, following the path depicted by the arrow in Diag. 1, and when the rod has arrived at the position shown in Fig. 2, reach up and clasp your line with your left hand again (Fig. 2). The fly should be skittering downstream and somewhat toward you, as indicated by the heavy dotted line in Diag. 1. (The fine dotted line, shown in this and all the diagrams, indicates the path your fly would have taken were it not for your manipulations of the rod and line.)

5. Now rotate your rod up and to your left, until it reaches the position shown in Fig. 3. The rod should be swung smoothly in a broad arc over your head, as indicated by the arrow in Diag. 2. Simultaneously, draw another arm's-length of line downward to the spot off your hip (Fig. 3). If properly executed, the path of the fly will be similar to that of the heavy dotted line in Diag. 2.

6. Next, holding the loops of line stationary off your hip, rotate your rod downward and to the right of your body, until the rod is positioned as shown in Fig. 4. The rod's path is depicted by the arrow in Diag. 3. If you have made this movement correctly, your fly will skitter along a path similar to the one shown by the heavy dotted line in Diag. 3.

7. From the position shown in Fig. 4, note that the angler can begin another presentation by simply tucking his elbow into his side, thus assuming his normal casting position, reaching up with his left hand again to clasp his line near the rod grip, and driving his line into the air by initiating a single-haul.

CHAPTER THIRTEEN

The Correct Approach

THE UPPER MAIN STEM of the Delaware River alternately slides and tumbles through a valley carved in antiquity between twin ridges. The upper river is the boundary between two states, New York and Pennsylvania, as well as, curiously enough, between two mountain ranges, since geographers somehow concluded that the ridge in New York is part of the Catskills while the one in Pennsylvania belongs to the Appalachians. Although the Catskills in New York are generally assumed to lie entirely east of the Appalachians in Pennsylvania, flowing water has a funny way of turning things around, and so when fishing some of the Delaware's most productive stretches, an angler may find himself in a spot where the sun goes down behind the Catskills.

From mid-May to mid-June the Delaware unquestionably becomes among the world's finest fisheries for free-rising brown and rainbow trout. Its environment is ideal for generating luxurious hatches of mayflies, caddis and stoneflies, including one species, the brown drake, virtually unknown anymore elsewhere in the East. Fortified by the insects, plus a bountiful supply of baitfish, including baby shad, the river's fish grow large and powerful. In fact, inch for inch, the Delaware River rainbow is the hardest fighting trout I've encountered anywhere on earth.

One late afternoon, or early evening, depending on how the clock is interpreted during that time of year with the most daylight hours, the river burst to life, first with millions of emerging mayflies and soon thereafter with rising trout. Behind my back over the Catskills the sun seemed to be hanging just above the rim of the ridge. Before me in a riff, dozens of trout rolled and sucked and splashed, taking their dinner. Alone on the New York side, I had paused to replace a soggy Adams when an angler appeared slogging upstream from a bend in the river near the Pennsylvania shore. It didn't take him long to arrive opposite me. "Getting any?" he shouted across the broad flow.

"A couple," I called back without looking up from my knot.

"Don't see anything moving," I heard him say, almost as if he doubted my word. It was unnecessary to look up, however, so certain was I that trout were working all around. "Wait a second," he said excitedly. "I just heard one somewhere between us, I think. Sounded good, but I didn't see it."

Glancing up, I noticed he was hunched over, and the look of that, coupled with the way he had to squint into the glare, reminded me of a kid who'd stuffed himself with green apples. "God, I keep hearing them," the angler wailed, "but I can't make out a one. Can you see them?"

"Yeah, they're working all over the place," I replied with a sympathetic shrug.

Like a drowning man, the angler began flailing casts haphazardly here and there in hopes, I suppose, of lucking into a cruiser. On the big Delaware such a hope is almost futile.

Meanwhile I'd completed my chore and my first pitch had hooked a rainbow that was running downstream, taking me into my backing in characteristic style. I was trying to organize my feet in the heavy current to begin the inevitable chase when the angler

The author plays a rainbow on the New York side of the upper Delaware River, while his companion, Ed Van Put, presents his Adams to another fish rising on the Pennsylvania side. Note, however, that Van Put has skillfully positioned himself so that the glare of the sun is to his back.

sang out again. "What did you hook him on?"

"Adams," I answered, "number 12."

"Same thing I'm using," he lamented, "but I can't buy a hit."

Can't catch what you can't see, I thought before saying loudly, "Too much glare on your side." I pointed over my shoulder at the descending sun.

"Can I cross?" he wailed.

"God, no." I almost fell in. "They'd be dragging you out in Trenton. Hold on. It'll be better once the sun gets down below the ridge."

"Yeah," he muttered in at tone more reminiscent of sour grapes than sour apples.

Having observed an awful lot of anglers applying their tactics to all sorts of waters, I'm frankly bewildered by how little attention many seem to pay to determining the best approaches to every stretch of river and stream, or, indeed, to every trout that inhabits it. For each presentation, of course, there's a correct approach, a precise position from which a dry fly can best be delivered. Sometimes that position is readily apparent through the angler's capacity for reading water, although more often than not other factors, such as sun location and wind velocity, are also brought to bear. Analyzed collectively, these determining factors frequently dictate a measure of compromise by the angler—as was the case, incidentally, when I opted to position myself toward the New York side of the Delaware River riff mentioned previously. Given another time of day, or, for that matter, enough cloud cover to obscure the sun, and I would have been fishing it from the Pennsylvania side, where the nature of flow promises a uniformly better fly drift.

Detecting the choicest spot from which to work over a fish or piece of water is a skill acquired and refined with experience. In time along familiar streams it should become an almost reflex action, a matter of second nature; but while the veteran angler ought to be able to project what he's gleaned from one fishery to another, it still behooves him to reflect on his battle plans before rushing to have at the trout, especially when confronted with unfamiliar surroundings.

Whether presenting flies to rising trout or simply covering a piece of water, the primary concern has to be how well you can direct the behavior of your offerings. Foremost in your mind must be that you are the puppeteer while the fly is the puppet. The angler must ascertain in advance, therefore, precisely the nature and length of drift required to properly cover a trout's feeding station, for instance, and from where in 360 degrees around the station he'll best be located to achieve that end. Although it's probably true that the exact spot will differ somewhat from angler to angler, there are certain principles that can be represented as virtually axiomatic: (1) The closer you can approach without detection, the easier your ultimate task will be; (2) You must choose a spot to which you can wade in safety; (3) The fewer confusing currents your line and leader must lie across, the better

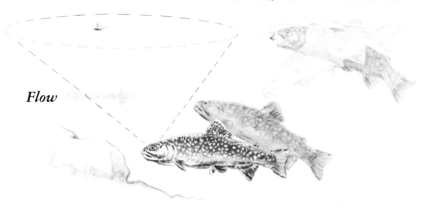

Flow

Learning to be able to estimate a trout's field of vision of the surface of a river or stream is absolutely essential to presenting dry flies effectively. This sequence shows, not only the trout's window, but also how the fish may be expected to rise to take the fly.

off you'll be; (4) A slight downstream breeze is usually preferable to one blowing upstream; (5) There should be no snags along the line of drift; (6) The sun should be positioned so you can clearly monitor the float of your fly; (7) There should be adequate room to make backcast; (8) The position you choose mustn't compromise your chances of working to other nearby fish; (9) If a trout takes, you'll be in good position to fight it.

The object of all good dry fly presentations is to show a trout only the fly, regardless of the technique employed by the angler. There is no technique with which I'm familiar that calls for permitting a fish to see leader, line, rod or angler. How the trout should come to see the fly, though, may vary substantially from technique to technique. Conditions may dictate, for instance, that the fly drift into a trout's range of vision, called its *window,* or that the fly light on the surface somewhere within that range, even directly over the fish's nose. Whereas in the former instance the angler must be positioned so he can effectively "lead" his quarry, in the latter no such requirement to reach out is called for. Lead or no lead, however, the angler's first concern ought always to be that he's positioned so that when he makes a presentation, during the span of time his fly is observed by a trout it will manifest no unnatural behavior—including, of course, drag, the ultimate curse.

A trout's window is cone-shaped, as shown in the accompanying illustration. The circumference of its outward extremity increases in direct proportion to the depth at which the fish is lying. The area of a trout's vision of the surface of a river or stream, in other words, is greater if the fish is holding in deep water than if it holds in the shallows. Learning the approximate depths of all the waters you fish, therefore, becomes a very helpful insight each time you're considering where to position yourself to present a fly.

The conventional practice for approaching dry fly presentation calls for positioning yourself somewhat downstream and across from the prospective target (see Fig. 1 in the accompanying illustration). Tradition, then, directs that the fly be three-quartered upstream and allowed to drift over the trout or the typical holding water the angler hopes to cover. Like most fishermen, I accepted this concept for years without really understanding its essential purpose, although through it all I knew I disliked the oblique attitude that makes it virtually impossible to compensate for currents playing with the line. The only redeeming quality I eventually perceived in the technique was the secure feeling you get that you won't be detected by the trout and, for that reason, I continue to use it when I fish a short line to rough pocket water and on the rare occasions I fish tiny brooks.

In most situations I like to present dry flies from a position directly across from, or across and slightly upstream of, my target, as shown in Fig. 2 in the drawing. From such a vantage I'm able to (1) accurately judge the distance each presentation must cover; (2) identify the number and potential influence of intervening currents, as well as effectively compensate for them with one or more of the presentation techniques illustrated in chapter twelve; (3) meticulously monitor the progress of my fly along its line of float; (4) engineer the optimum drift both ahead of and behind

DRY FLY PRESENTATION POSITIONS

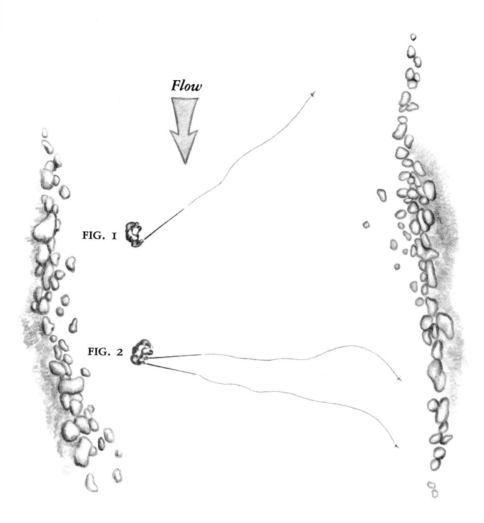

Flow

FIG. 1

FIG. 2

Fig. 1 shows the conventional position used by generations of anglers for presenting dry flies three-quarters upstream. Fig. 2, by contrast, shows the position preferred by the author to present his flies either directly across or across and slightly downstream.

my target; (5) get the best perspective on a trout rising to and taking my fly; and (6) set the hook gently, usually with a minimum amount of slack line to take up in the process.

Accurately assessing the distance between your position and your target, of course, tells you how much line will be needed to make the desired presentation, if you correctly factor in the amount of extra line necessary to compensate for currents. Bearing in mind that you want to show a trout only your fly, the estimate must be refined to inches. With practice the skilled fisherman learns to gauge how much line, including leader, is outside his reel—the sum of line beyond his rod's tip-top, along the length of his rod and within the spirals held in his hand. A beginner should find it helpful to strip line off his reel in his accustomed manner and to measure the length gained each time. Then he should endeavor to strip line uniformly thereafter, so that by starting out with only his leader outside the rod and adding to it the length of the rod plus the number of line strips he holds in his hand, he becomes consistently aware of the amount of working line he has available to make a presentation. For anglers who find this process either too confusing or too much trouble, lines can always be color-coded with indelible ink in five- or ten-foot intervals—black for five feet, red to ten feet, etc.

In most instances, as I approach dry fly presentation, my chief concern is *drift*. Do I want a long drift or will a short one suffice? Must I lead a fish, or do I want my fly to come down right over its nose? Is a dead drift or, perhaps, some twitching or skittering in order? While to work on a stretch of water blind—to pound up trout that aren't rising on their own—the ultimate choice of technique from among many available options may depend upon the individual angler's whim as well as prevailing conditions, to present your dries to rising trout is quite another matter, one that necessitates a substantial degree of precise and objective calculation by the angler.

Let's assume, for instance, that you've marked a trout leisurely rising to emerging mayflies on the far side of a slick that flows from left to right in front of you. The stream's velocity permits you to cross one-third of the way to your target. Standing directly opposite the trout's last rise form, you figure the remaining distance between you to be thirty-five feet. Next, you determine that the trout is rising about four feet from the bottom to the surface, meaning that from its lie it should spot your dry on top when the fly has floated to within about three feet in horizontal distance. Because all the flies you've seen the trout take have drifted into its window, you conclude yours should do likewise. However, then you happen to observe that your quarry isn't grabbing each natural the instant the fly passes over its head, but rather that the fish occasionally drifts along under one, taking it about five feet downstream. Simple arithmetic, then, stipulates that you may need as much as nine feet of drag-free drift—about a foot ahead of the trout's window, three feet within the window, and five feet downstream in case the fish decides to follow.

Now, an optimum drift while locked to your present position would oblige an upstream mend, which requires shooting extra line, and at least five additional feet beyond that in the mend, in order to reach the upper limit of your presentation. All this you perceive at first as feasible. And yet, further analysis indicates a potential for trouble as the slick carries your line downstream. In particular, you note a chance for disastrous drag once the fly has passed beyond the trout's holding station. Is the situation untenable? Must you accept drag below the trout to assure dead drift above? The answer is no, certainly not, if you adjust your approach by wading not more than six feet upstream, that is, to your left. Thus positioned a tad above your target, by combining the principles of the upstream mend and the stop and drop cast, both of which are illustrated in chapter twelve, you'll find you can plan for a full course dragless drift without needing one extra inch of line.

It's often said of master pool players that they are endowed with an extraordinary capacity to look ahead. A shot one of them is about to make had to be planned several shots back and will be considered really successful only to the extent it positively impacts on the remaining shots required to clear the table. Perhaps no concept in any sport applies so neatly to fishing dry flies to trout on moving waters. In countless angling situations, choosing the correct approach to presenting a fly to a fish translates into developing a knack for *evaluation* and *anticipation.* Both are, in essence, products of exercising common sense. For example, when finding two large trout feeding one behind the other, your most practical approach to a shot at both of them is certainly to position yourself to cover the rear fish first with a preconceived plan as to how to lead it away from the upstream trout without disturbing that one's feeding rhythm. Similarly, when confronting two trout rising parallel to each other, the best tactic must be to try the closer one first, for to reach out to the farther fish initially would compel showing leader, line, or both, to the one nearby, a mistake almost certain to put it down.

The same concept can be applied to approaching entire pieces of water, whether the angler aims to position himself to present dry flies to rising trout or to develop a strategy for prospecting a spot where he doesn't see a single rise. The following two illustrations represent a comprehensive approach to engaging a hypothetical but typical trout pool. In illustration A, however, the pool's fish are rising freely to a hatch, while in illustration B all the trout are "down and dirty." Note how each situation dictates a vastly different approach to presenting a fly, and yet how throughout the course of covering all the potentially productive water the angler always commands a position from which he can get the most from his fly while he's least likely to compromise all his presentations still to come.

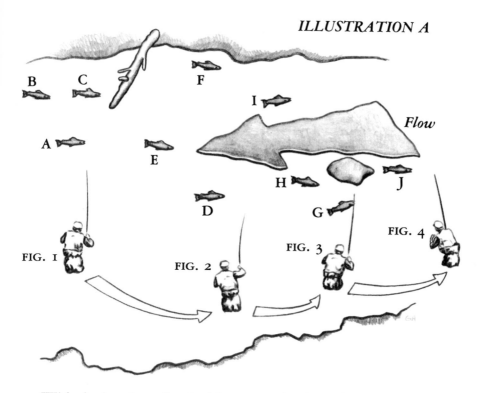

B   C   F

I

Flow

A

E

H   J

D   G

FIG. 4

FIG. 1

FIG. 2

FIG. 3

With the location of each rising trout clearly visible to him, the angler begins fishing the stretch by positioning himself either across or across and slightly upstream of each target trout. He then rotates his position in a generally upstream direction, from the position shown in Fig. 1 to that in Fig. 2, Fig. 3 and, finally, to Fig. 4. From Fig. 1, he presents his fly, in turn, to fish A, B, and C; from Fig. 2, to fish D, E, and F; from Fig. 3, to fish G, H and I; and from Fig. 4, to fish J. Note that in each instance he presents to the closest trout first, moving on then to those feeding in locations downstream from the other fish. In this way he is certain neither to drape his line or leader over a trout he still intends to fish to, nor to permit any of the trout he hooks to spook the others he will present to later. Each angler should determine such strategy before attacking a piece of water.

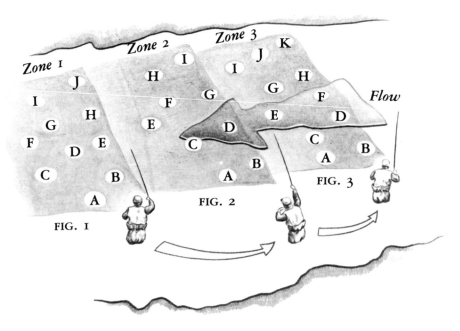

FIG. 1

FIG. 2

FIG. 3

Now, when prospecting a stretch of water where no trout are
rising, the angler divides the stretch into zones and rotates his
position for presenting his fly in a generally upstream direction,
as from Fig. 1 to Fig. 2. to Fig. 3. Within each zone of coverage
he also determines the most likely spots to bring up trout, shown
here by the circled letters. In each instance, he positions himself
at the head of the zone, so that he can present his fly either
directly across or across and slightly downstream to the spots he
figures most likely to hold trout. Then he covers those spots
nearest to him first, always following a sequence that begins with
the spot furthest downstream. Thusly, he covers each likely spot
without either "lining" any other potentially productive water or
chancing that he spook one fish by hooking another. Following
this procedure, an angler should substantially increase his yield
from stretches where the fish must be pounded up.

CHAPTER FOURTEEN

~~~~~~

Tactical Tips and Innovations

NEW SLANT ON THE ANT

March 18, 1978, according to my stream notes, was one of those "in between" days—not still winter, not quite spring. Ice-out on the Willowemoc had gone easier, Catskill natives allowed, than for decades, and in its wake, thanks to warming days but frosty nights, snow runoff proceeded at an imperceptible rate in the stream. The slithering water appeared hungry for warmth from the sun, but, although the air had reached the mid-40's, the sky remained the color of cold stove ashes. No sun would shine that day.

I'd decided to use a sinking-tip line, heavy leader and Black Ghost streamer. I don't recall whether catching trout seemed important after typewriter marathons all winter. What mattered, I think, was to feel a vest heavy on my back again, a wader belt

Ed Sutryn named his patented creation, the McMurray Ant, after his hometown in western Pennsylvania. Here he prepares to have at the trout of Willowemoc Creek in the Catskills of New York.

cinched tightly at my waist. Trout are lucky, I reasoned, almost as lucky as bears or woodchucks. Metabolism protects them from restlessness and cabin fever.

Fishing the streamer means nothing to this chapter, except that had I not worked downstream shooting it for the far bank, I might not have spotted a small trout sipping at the surface. Tight to the bank it poked its nose up each few seconds to suck something I couldn't see. No flies were apparent on the water, not even the midge we call the *snow fly* for its appearance in dead of winter. Yet, like most fly fishermen, I wanted winter to push by and give us spring, and a rising trout somehow seemed to shepherd that moment closer. So I reeled in and slogged ashore to rig my rod for a floating line.

What fly to choose—that became my concern. Cold hands call for one you can stick with, and the stream offered no clue. Rifling through boxes, I'd almost settled for a size 18 Adams when the gist of a friend's letter suddenly drifted back to me. Jim Hepner wrote that he had met a fascinating little guy, Ed Sutryn, of McMurray, Pennsylvania, who manufactured ants out of balsa wood, monofilament and rooster hackle. "Absolute dynamite," Jim assured me.

Now, I've been in this business long enough to develop a "dynamite" case of cynicism, but it hadn't deterred me from billeting the samples Jim enclosed in a box I always carry.

What the hell, I mused, fingering through it until I found a size 22. Magazine articles are born of innovation. If I try it, no one can claim I wasn't working. Doing research.

I was false-casting when I reached center stream. The trout still sipped, so I punched the ant to a point about two feet above it, allowing enough slack to insure a dead drift. The fish rose without hesitation to inhale the fly. I recall responding much like the fellow who wants trouble and, finding none, feels cheated. I set the hook by reflex, and in less than a minute a little brown writhed in the belly of my net.

"Is that all she wrote?" I grumbled, scanning the water below both banks for more rises. Seeing none, however, I began trudging ashore, trying to reckon myself lucky to have even one trout on a dry so early in the year. Before I made it, though, a tiny bulge near the root of a dead elm tree caught the corner of my eye, and, sensing dissatisfaction beginning to melt away, I ambled with the light current abreast of another feeding fish.

Sparing the reader further play-by-plays, suffice it to report that I hunted up nineteen rising trout that afternoon and hooked eighteen of them, all on the McMurray Ant. Fourteen took the first presentation. The next day, bitter cold, the ant fooled eight of nine. Thanks to Jim Hepner I had myelf one helluva fly.

The word *fly* requires emphasis because, unfortunately, there are always those who derive more pleasure from picking nits than sticking trout. Obsessed with "purity," they insist a bug tied with wood must be called a *lure*, not a *fly*. If it weren't for the argument's potential impact on management of some Fly-Fishing-Only waters, I'd consider it no more worthy of comment than one that maintains that the American League hasn't played baseball since the first designated hitter stepped to the plate. The sport, I believe, would be no worse off for universally accepting balsa wood fished fairly, because that is certainly no less "pure" than to squeeze split-shot onto leaders to dredge the bottom for sluggish trout.

I'm frankly at a loss to find a time or place when or where the McMurray Ant won't catch trout. Although difficult to sink, if it does it seems to make no difference. Trout hit it anyway. They hit it dead drift or when it's dragging. I've now taken browns, brookies and rainbows on both the black and cinnamon patterns from March through October along rivers and streams in the eastern U.S., Great Britain and France. A 5½-pound brown slammed a size 18 on a northern Icelandic river as if the trout hadn't eaten for weeks. While I've had no chance to test the fly on new Zealand or South American waters yet, I'd be willing to bet my last buck they'll work there, too. My only caution is that the smaller sizes (18–22) work best.

Most impressive to me, however, is how beautifully these ants handle finicky trout. Time after time, even during hatches, if standard patterns are rejected, I cinch on a McMurray Ant, and *bingo.*

During public appearances I'm often asked what dry fly I'd choose if I only had one to fish with. I've always answered less than enthusiastically, the Adams. Now, however, I've changed that tune, and my answer is born of confidence. If I had only one fly—wet or dry—to fish from ice-out to the first freeze of the following winter, make it the McMurray Ant, the deadliest pattern, I believe, ever to shake hands with a leader.

McMurray Ants are available in black and cinnamon (sizes 12–22) from The Hatch, DeBruce Road, Livingston Manor, N.Y. 12758.

PICKING THE POCKETS

Trout require much less space to flourish than anglers sometimes appreciate. Given adequate flow, hospitable temperatures and a lane along which abundant food passes, a spot of no more than 324 square inches (about 1½′ × 1½′), eight to twelve inches deep, can hold a nice fish the year through. Known as pocket water, reaches of this sort commonly sustain more fish per surface acre than any other kind of trout habitat, including a fishery's most spacious pools. A stretch of pockets, typical of a surface water river or stream, can accurately be described as a trout apartment complex where, separated by the rocks that divide the units, fish coexist in greater density than would be possible under wide open conditions.

Pocket water tends to be swift—at least relative to pools, eddies, runs and slicks—and this velocity, when coupled with the limited space the fish have to maneuver, generally prescribes that pocket water trout be decisive feeders; that is, that they take little time to look food over, accepting or rejecting it without much ado. Some-

Francis Betters of Wilmington, N.Y., originator of the Ausable Wulff, plies a typical stretch of rugged pocket water on his beloved West Branch of the Ausable River. Having devoted a lifetime to this kind of angling, Francis is the only dry fly fisherman the author knows who consistently handles both long lines and rough pockets well.

what reckless feeding habits demanded by habitat, plus a propensity for complicated surface currents that break up images and inhibit the capacity of trout to differentiate between artificial flies and the real McCoy, makes pocket water unquestionably among the most forgiving of an angler's mistakes and, therefore, among the most adventageous for him to fish. Further, the proximity of pockets to each other enables an angler to cover maximum fish in minimum time, thereby enhancing the knowledgeable fly fisherman's odds for success.

Tricky currents can make pocket water mighty tough to fish, however, particularly with a dry fly on a long line. (Of all the anglers I know and fish with, only Francis Betters, dean of present-day fly fishermen on the Ausable River in New York's Adirondack Mountains, handles very long lines and complicated pockets really well. He's devoted a lifetime to little else.) These currents are caused by water being buffeted by boulders, rocks and stones, as well as swirling over, under and around them. The breadth of a stretch of pockets may contain scores of such currents, each of which can foul up the float of your line, leader and fly during a presentation. No set of circumstances, with the possible exception of attempting to present flies from fast water into slow, is more apt to result in fly drag beyond the tolerance of even the most unwary trout. What is a long line for pocket water? Most fishermen I've met have plenty of trouble handling more than fifteen feet.

To fish pocket water effectively, therefore, requires the shortest line feasible for prevailing conditions. (When circumstances oblige a long line, try the stop and drop presentation from a position either directly upstream from the target or as far as possible upstream and across.) Getting the most from a short line calls for a short leader (6'–7½') too, since you want all the working line you can get outside the rod's tip-top. A rod with a sensitive but quick tip to flick your fly out onto the pockets is helpful, as is a double-tapered fly line from which the first couple of feet have been lopped off to give it more "body."

Because trout normally lie facing into a flow, they are vulnerable to close approach from behind. Unless the sun causes the angler to project a shadow over a fish, by treading softly it's easy to take up a position no more than ten feet below a feeding trout or a pocket in which the angler is reasonably sure one is stationed. In fact, if currents don't decree otherwise, the angler may be able to cover at least a dozen small pockets within fifteen or twenty feet upstream without altering his location by a single step. He must, however, attend to the nearest pockets first or risk paying for his eagerness by draping his leader or line over fish that happen to be fanning there.

Almost without exception, pockets don't require long fly drifts, but the more time an angler's dry spends on the water, the better his chances of raising fish. False-casting, therefore, should be limited to the minimum essential to keep the fly afloat.

As is true of all dry fly fishing techniques, the angler plying pocket water should choose a pattern that represents at least a reasonable facsimile of an insect he knows will interest his quarry most. Because trout in rough pocket water are likely to be "forgiving," though, the choice of fly should key most of all on its buoyancy, that is, how well the pattern floats. The accelerated rate at which everything happens on pocket water also dictates using flies that are readily visible, both to angler and to fish. A good rule, I've discovered, is to opt always for the largest, highest floating fly I'm confident the trout will take, even if it doesn't look very much like the naturals I spy floating on the very pockets I'm about to fish.

ASSAYING THE ''ALL THAT GLITTERS'' RULE

In May a few years ago, friend Mike Kimball, of Ithaca, N.Y., was hurrying up the road that parallels the Beaverkill just two miles from my home. Parked along one stretch were about thirty cars, according to Mike's estimate, each of which must have toted more than one angler to a weekend's sport by the look of the convocation in the river. Approaching an eddy, Mike's disciplined eyes instantly picked up that it was frothing with feeding fish as well as fishermen; in that instant his eyes also spotted countless insects over and on the surface of the river.

"What struck me as weird, though," Mike recalled later, "was that nobody, I mean *nobody,* had a trout on. Wouldn't that be enough to make you stop to check things out?"

Mike grabbed a parking space between two vans, got out of his car and leaned against the left front fender. "Henricksons and Red

Quills were coming off, millions of them," he observed, "but my eyes hadn't been putting me on. Nobody was catching any fish. . . . Not even raising any, as far as I could see. I think a lot of guys were ready to break their rods. I don't remember seeing anything quite like it before."

Among the most skillful anglers I know, Mike is obsessed with problem solving. "I didn't really feature getting into the fray," he said, "but I just had to have a whack at it—to find out if trout could be that stinky."

Keeping one eye glued to the eddy, Mike geared up. In the time before he edged into the water, he still hadn't seen a trout caught, although the fish continued to feed like crazy. "Like everyone else, I guess, I did the logical thing," Mike recounted. "I put on a Hendrickson, picked the first fish I could get at and made a cast. The fly drifted right on the money, but the trout never moved. I cast again. No soap. Again—and the fish came up and grabbed something right next to my fly. The strange thing was, though, I didn't see the natural the trout took.

"So, I figured, 'they're taking emergers,' and that's what finally got my nose down to the surface for a closer look. Would you believe the top was carpeted with little spinners? Then I checked the air and, sure enough, there were millions of them over the water too, so small that, with all the big duns around, nobody, including me, had been paying any attention to them."

Except, apparently, the trout, that is. Mike snipped off his Hendrickson, extended his leader by splicing a short section of 5X material and a 6X tippet, and tied on a size 20 Rusty Spinner. Then he tried the trout again. "It rose pretty as you please," he said, as did sixteen others Mike caught while picking his way among the crowd of anglers. "You know the craziest thing of all, though, wasn't the fact the trout were skipping the duns and taking the spinners, or even that I didn't pick it up at first," Mike commented over dinner at the Antrim Lodge that evening. "The really crazy thing was that nobody who watched me taking all those fish bothered to ask what I was doing."

Any experienced angler who says he's never been distracted by a hatch would be in big trouble if he repeated the statement under oath. Many fishermen devote years to streams without perceiving their multiple hatches or, for that matter, the hatches that dovetail with spinner falls. The Beaverkill's annual Hendrickson emergences coinciding with falls of rusty spinners isn't by any means unique, but is only one example from among hundreds that might be cited as existing on U.S. waters alone. Unfortunately, though, hatching flies seem to get most of the play among anglers, the result, I suppose, of a sort of complacency born of tradition. The more I've fished, however, the more I've come to understand just how much this indulgence has cost us through the years.

Experimentation has proven that, given alternatives of plentiful hatching duns and lots of falling spinners, trout frequently opt to feed on the latter, regardless of which of the two happens to be the larger insect species. The motivation represents a sterling illustration of a trout's natural inclination to be opportunistic. Whereas hatching duns, large or small, have a nasty way of eluding the jaws of feeding fish, spinners floating on the water, incapable of flight, constitute a *sure thing*. Taking spinners, therefore, becomes for a trout a simple matter of assuming a position under the surface and establishing a leisurely feeding rhythm. The position and rhythm enable the fish to eat its fill of tiny spinners at the expense of much less energy than would be required to consume an equal volume of larger duns.

The essential lesson is, therefore, not to take a fishery for granted, even one you've known for years. The river or stream doesn't exist that hasn't its share of surprises to deal out. Look each situation over carefully before jumping to conclusions, for the success of many an outing hinges on the angler's capacity to discriminate between the insects trout *seem* to be feeding on and the ones they are *really* taking.

Flights of caddis like this one in May on New York's Beaverkill are typical of many rivers and streams, both in North America and abroad.

CADDIS FARE

There's nothing revolutionary about the importance of caddis flies to the diet of North American trout. It is only relatively recently, however, that some anglers here have begun to recognize the role caddis play as a food source, or how to take advantage of the caddis–trout relationship to enhance their fly fishing strategy. By now it's hoped that all savvy American dry fly fishermen would be carrying at least one caddis pattern among their flies— something our European counterparts have been doing for generations—and that as we fish it, we recognize that to use the caddis as we might most traditional mayfly imitations will garner us precious little success.

235

To imitate the behavior of any insect species accurately requires considerable streamside observation on the part of the angler. Whether he be imitating a species of mayfly or caddis, his chances of attracting trout improve with his knowledge of the typical behavior of that species and his ability to mimic the peculiarities he perceives within seeing distance of his quarry. To believe, for instance, that uniformly presenting all patterns dead drift is sufficient technique to carry you on very many waters is to misunderstand the fundamental principle of *fishing* dry flies for trout on rivers and streams. To wit: *There is a critical distinction between fishing dry flies and dry fly fishing.* And it's only by learning the lessons of the former that the angler can become true master of his fate.

Caddis behavior illustrates the point particularly well. Caddis can be observed at times, for example, floating idly on the surface, skittering madly on top, fluttering over the water, touching down, or any of these in combination. All behavioral patterns, of course, can be telegraphed by the angler to his artificials by a host of means, including precise placement of each presentation, varying the duration he permits his fly to ride on the water, and twitching or raising his rod tip during the drift, among others. The significant factor is, though, that he practices each variation thoroughly when it doesn't count, so that, given occasions when it does, his ministrations will have the sensitivity essential to fool the wariest trout.

It's not uncommon for even schooled observers to confuse a swarm of ovipositing caddis with those of a hatch. As noted earlier, some caddis oviposit by plunging through the surface of a river or stream, swimming to the bottom, depositing their eggs and swimming to the top again. Although trout chase the insects underwater on occasion, evolution has taught the fish that the caddis is singularly vulnerable during the several seconds to half a minute it rests in the surface film before taking off. There, it rides the flow virtually motionless and makes an easy bite for a hungry trout.

Although standard caddis patterns sometimes prove effective

Few flies could be simpler than this one designed by the author to represent an ovipositing caddis, called the Shad Fly, that appears on his home river, the Beaverkill, each spring. The wing material is intentionally clipped bluntly at the head to allow an air bubble to form while the fly is drifting in the surface film.

for trout feeding on these weary flies, more often than not, it seems, the fish pass them up. My inclination is that rejection occurs because the high silhouette of the standard floating fly appears to represent an insect about to leave the water or one the trout is likely to miss. Fortunately, a fine alternative dressing is among the easiest to turn out, tied by simply winding a dry fly hook shank with buoyant dubbing material, such a muskrat or fox, and adding a single wing of coarse polypropalene yarn (the finished product should appear as in the accompanying photograph). Or, in a pinch, a well-greased wet fly with its hackle and tail snipped off, fished dead drift, makes a reasonably operative substitute.

''PEACHES AND CREAM''

When was your fishing last "strangled" by a hatch? To answer "never" probably means you have access only to waters with marginal fly life, since because the more copious hatches are on a river or stream, the more likely the sport is to be suffocated by them once in a while. The customary sign of this paradoxical and frustrating phenomenon is for hosts of ravenous, free-rising trout to snub the best imitations of an insect species you have to offer at the height of a hatch, leaving you talking to yourself like a character in a Beckett play.

Although many American trout fisheries, thank heavens, remain blessed with abundant hatches, an angler finding himself confronted with a blanket of floating flies shouldn't necessarily prepare to celebrate—except, perhaps, to extol the bounty of nature—until he's scapped a few trout with his net. From a purely practical perspective, a hatch on such a grand scale can produce one of the sport's most humbling ordeals, that is trying to hook any fish when your fly becomes just one more face in the crowd.

No matter how long or how widely an angler has fished, only a victim of cystic emotions could fail to be dazzled by the sight of a really big hatch, the wondrous spectacle that betokens the soul of our sport. The wits melt even as the reflexes turn to jelly, and soon novice and war horse alike are lost to a spell that has them fishing like so many sleep-walkers. Thus possessed, what pattern of fly to use is seldom considered, at least not in depth. Indeed, for many anglers the thought of turning to a pattern other than one suggestive of the hatch in progress would be foolish, if not downright sacrilegious.

The essential enigma is, then, whether or not catching fish is important. For those who contend that it is not, any pattern at all, I suppose, is fine. When and if the trout turn down well-presented hatch imitations, though, and the angler admits he'd like to catch

238

Lee Wulff, dean of American fly fishermen, presents one of the many patterns that bear his name to a rising trout on the upper Beaverkill where he and his wife, Joan, settled several years ago and now operate a fly fishing school. Also the originator of the fly fishing vest, Lee continues to wow all who know him with his undiminished passion for the outdoor world and innovative fly fishing.

one or two, he's left with but a couple of options; (1) to find a stretch with fewer emerging flies, or (2) to come up with a pattern that will create some interest.

Lee Wulff, unquestionably one of America's finest and most innovative anglers, has a strategy for such situations that he calls "Offering a trout *peaches and cream.*" The technique involves showing hatch-feeding fish the biggest, bushiest flies in your boxes, and preferably those that look nothing at all like the naturals upon which trout are working. The key to successfully implementing Lee's concept, I've found, is to throw inhibition and caution entirely to the wind. Not only should the fly pattern not resemble the prevailing natural insects, but the behavior engendered to it by the angler should be as eccentric as possible. Try twitching or skittering, for example, or repetitive placement of the fly right over the trout's nose. In this manner, if the bug you are using doesn't happen to appeal to a trout's palate, it may well excite its anger, which is okay, too.

"'STONING THE POOL''

Trout fishing in England has left me with a decided impression of the typical British angler as being rather staid. In light of this seemingly universal characteristic, therefore, I have a difficult time imagining a member of the venerable old Houghton Club, for instance, "stoning a pool" on the equally venerable River Test. The technique—that is, chucking big rocks into the water to "wake up" listless trout—is recommended by old and venerable English angling books, but, having experienced the rule-impacted brand of fishing traditional to the Isles, I'd frankly have to catch somebody right in the act of pegging to believe they really do it.

Most of all, I'm doubtful whether British anglers could stone chalk stream pools even if they ever got so giddy. My skepticism is grounded on the fact that along most streams, like American limestone streams, rocks suitable for stoning are very hard to find. On the banks of the Test, among other English chalk streams I've fished, I don't recall tripping over a single rock worth bending down for. My guess is any that were found lying around have long since been tidied up to make the walls the British gentry seems so obsessed with building to separate one's holding from another's.

It's conceivable, of course, that all the best stoning stones were simply used up by stoners in the heyday of Halford, and thus that by attrition the British pool-stoning corps went the way of all cavalry colonels who've ever ridden a horse. Upon reflection you

When conditions are right, the trout that inhabit English chalkstreams require no "stoning" to convince them to take your dry flies. Here, the author plays a brown hooked on a tributary of Britain's most famous such stream, the Test, located near Stockbridge in Hampshire.

should agree this theory has real possibilities, given the propensity of the British Foreign Office in the glorious era of Empire to maintain unapologetically that the world's natural resources were virtually inexhaustible, unless somehow they got into the hands of the Irish.

Or, an American fisherman of Gaelic descent, given a cynical streak, might just ask you to try on a theory that the most vocal proponents of stoning the pool were themselves endowed with the gift of the blarney. After all, if you could convince the bloke who was fishing the beat in the morning that you had drawn for the afternoon to give the water a thorough stoning, it's reasonable

241

to assume that most of the stretch's trout would be sufficiently
over their hours of terror to gobble your flies before afternoon tea.

BETTER THAN STONING

I doubt a trout stream exists in which most of the fish don't get
listless and uncooperative occasionally, despite conditions that
would appear ideal. While listless trout are to be expected, of
course, when waters are too warm or too cold to stimulate feeding
(circumstances that are seldom reversible until Mother Nature
has played out the hands), there's no predicament more frustrating than seeking to contend with trout that refuse to recognize
that now is the perfect time to eat. In a stream of subterranean
origin, a spring creek or limestoner for instance, where both temperatures and food supplies remain relatively constant, trout will
suddenly and inexplicably take a dive and remain hidden for protracted periods under banks, in deep channels, or among the generous growths of weed prevalent in such waters. Given no clues as
to motivation, it's understandable that many dry fly fishermen determine they have little choice but to work to the trout down
deep or to write off their outings altogether.

Experimentation has disclosed, however, that there's virtually
no instant when a trout is entirely unaware of what's going on
overhead, regardless of how well concealed from the angler's sight
it may be. It follows, then, that if the fish continually monitor the
surface, the problem is reduced to turning up something to put
there sufficiently provocative to prod them out of their reverie.
Often, you'll discover, the answer is a *Skater.*

The trick for effectively fishing a Skater is to cover the water
systematically without letting the fly appear to rest, the object
being to prompt a trout to respond much as a kitten does to a
wad of cellophane dragged by a string across a linoleum floor.
Casting loops should be tight to insure high-riding floats with
minimum false-casting. The culmination of each presentation
ought to find the rod in a position as nearly as possible on a hori-

zontal plane over the water. When the fly touches down, the rod tip is raised immediately, in an uninterrupted arc when the intent is to skitter the Skater evenly across the surface, and in a jerky one if you want to impart an unmistakable air of recklessness to the fly. Repeat the process several times on each area of water you cover, inclining toward a more agitated retrieve with every successive presentation.

Fishing Skaters has a way of producing truly astounding results. Apparently fishless stretches literally come alive with ruffled trout competing to catch up with the flies. Sometimes trout push big wakes several times chasing Skaters before finally grabbing on, but even when a fish ultimately refuses to return to the maddening offering, the spirit of the chase is frequently found to have been sufficient to rekindle its desire for a more conventional pattern.

"Won't fine leader tippets needed on many streams twist hopelessly as you try to cast big Skaters?" an experienced angler might legitimately ask. If it weren't for the knot shown in the accompanying illustration, the answer would have to be affirmative. By adapting the handy surgeon's knot, however, a large fly remains free to spin independent of the tippet, thus making it impossible for the tippet to twist no matter how minute its diameter.

Here's how to tie this useful knot:
1. Pass the fine tippet through the hook eye from left to right, so the head of the fly faces the leader butt (Fig. 1). Release the fly and permit it to hang on the tippet (Fig. 1).
2. Now cut a section of tippet material three or four inches long and several sizes heavier than the tippet attached to the leader you're using (Fig. 1). (For a size 10 fly and a 7X tippet, for instance, you'll want a short section of 2X or 3X material.)
3. Connect the short section of heavy material to the end of the fine tippet by means of a surgeon's knot (Fig. 2).
4. Clip excess material close to the body of the surgeon's knot, leaving only your tippet intact (Fig. 3). This requires clipping the three tabs, as shown in Fig. 3. (Note: It is important that the excess material be clipped extremely close to the body of the knot in order to prevent jagged ends from catching the hook eye or forward portions of the fly while casting.)

THE SURGEON'S SWIVEL

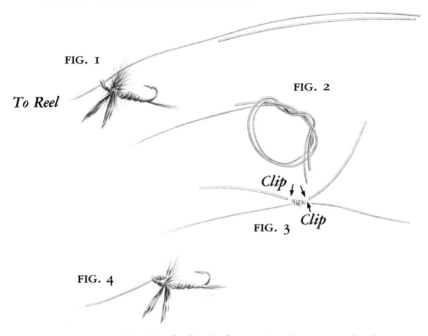

FIG. 1

To Reel

FIG. 2

Clip

FIG. 3 *Clip*

FIG. 4

5. Now slide the fly back down the tippet, so the knot rests gently against the rear of the hook eye (Fig. 4). Check that the body of the knot is larger than the diameter of the hook eye, so it can't sneak through when fishing.

6. Grasp the fly in one hand, the leader in the other, and try revolving the fly. If the knot is properly tied and situated, the fly should revolve freely while the tippet remains stationary.

THE RUDE AWAKENING

To get the most out of waters where trout aren't rising, burly attractor patterns make imposing "spotter" flies. In angling jargon, spotters are flies capable of bringing up otherwise disinterested trout, although more often than not the fish refuse to take them. The rise to a spotter is characteristically savage, culminating in the trout buffeting the fly with its body, drowning the fly amid a rush of water, or slapping the fly viciously with its tail—all of which would seem to serve the angler no useful purpose were it not for a curious but certain connection between a trout's attack on a spotter fly and the fish's almost immediate responsiveness to more conventional patterns.

The rule for spotter flies, I've found, is *the bigger the better*. Patterns such as the White Wulff, Dutchman, Ausable Wulff and Hornburg, in sizes as large as 6 or 8, work exceptionally well. It also helps, I think, to opt for artificials as dissimilar as possible to any naturals you observe on the water.

The real trick, though, is to keep a standard pattern handy all the time you work a spotter. (The conventional fly, by the way, should approximate the naturals around in both size and shade.) The surface over likely lies must be plied thoroughly with the spotter, since repeated presentations are often required to bug a trout enough to bring it up. The more time the spotter spends on the water, of course, the better the odds of raising a trout, but most crucial of all is that each presentation be watched carefully if the angler hopes to coordinate a rise to his spotter and the subsequent presentation of his standard fly.

When a trout shows, *don't* offer it the spotter again. Instead, clip the big fly off as quickly as you can and replace it with the standard. Then have another go at the fish. If it doesn't rise to your first presentation, don't give up on the conventional fly. Frequently it takes patience to be rewarded, and while you wait you can at least find comfort in the assurance you are working over an active fish.

IN SPITE OF A SPATE

Two full days and nights of rain had left the river awesome and ugly. Full to the banks, it hauled along the color of cocoa, swamping even boulders that rise two or three feet above the surface under normal conditions. It was the sort of day the Antrim bar would be stacked three deep, while at the fishing clubs far upriver members would be exchanging nickels, dimes and quarters in deadly earnest over poker tables.

My car had to creep along with little guidance from me, because most of my attention was being accorded the river, looking for a spot—any spot at all—where the water was sufficiently deflected to allow me to get in. As spates go, this was a pretty fair one for drowning, I understood, but it had been a fishless week and, besides, there were all those March Browns bursting from the surface. There's gotta be a spot, my heart insisted, while my mind told me it wasn't to be.

I parked in a pulloff alongside a favorite stretch of pockets. The sound of the angry flood hissing by carried through the alders creating in me an exquisite fascination, akin to the kind you experience approaching the edge of a cliff. At the bank I could see the bed was carrying every drop it could hold, and that here and there surplus flow had pushed over to make wee eddies that turned gently in the shadows of streamside foliage. In one of these small backwaters I spotted a pair of newly emerged March Browns winding in the oval current, but I must have glanced away, for suddenly, one of the flies was missing and I couldn't swear where it had gone, whether or not it had flown away. Then as I watched, puzzled, a nice brown trout materialized in the little hole below my feet, rising to inhale the second fly I'd been watching intently. A few steps downstream I noticed another similar pocket, and sure enough, a trout was working there too, feasting on insects confined to the revolving water not two feet off the bank. Just forty-eight hours earlier, I mused, each of these pockets, and many more, had been as dry as bone.

Although most trout are by nature territorial, during periods of extreme water fluctuation, high or low, they frequently abandon accustomed quarters to seek more comfortable haunts. During spates, periods of high water running off, the fish generally tend to wander toward shore, where once situated free from troublesome currents, they're apt to feed heartily both on and below the surface. Wearing only hip boots because there's no need to walk in the water, the angler can pick his way along the bank, taking

Small side-eddies, like the one pictured here onto which the author is popping his dry fly, are apt to be where most trout are surface feeding during periods of heavy runoff, called spates.

fish after fish without a need to present his flies more than fifteen feet. On most rivers and streams I fish this way, trout seem to be relatively unconcerned with my presence. A spate is, in fact, the only water condition I can think of during which normally wary trout appear almost ready to eat out of your hand, an especially delightful turn of events since there are usually so few other anglers around to help feed them.

CHEATING SUNDOWN

Without the gift of exceptional eyesight, gathering darkness is certain to blunt an angler's edge, particularly when he's fishing dry. As sunlight expires, precise presentations help brighten up declining conditions, of course, by enabling you to judge with respectable accuracy where your fly is at all times, including those when you cannot see it. Even this evidence of expertise, however, introduces a measure of guesswork and luck, neither of which does (nor should) inspire the pitch of self-confidence needed to keep you really loose. Confronting semi-darkness, then, it's no wonder so many dry fly fishermen either switch to wets, nymphs or streamers, or, unhappy but resigned, pack it in for another day. It's an awful thing to lose the use of your eyes.

Feeling obliged to quit is particularly unfortuanate since evening often offers the best dry fly fishing of the day—in fact, the *only* dry fishing on some waters during the warmest months of the year. Notably, it's very common that sunset and later represent the time reserved for the mayfly spinner fall, when having seen through the perils of being small and fragile in a world dominated by strength, the insects celebrate the immortality of their kind in a glorious but terminal orgy under the gaze of the eternal sky.

Despite having dabbled with all sorts of devices, I've never been able to improve my so-called "night vision" a bit. So I've had to learn to cheat. Several years back, for example, I discovered quite by accident that from dusk to darkness, and sometimes thereafter, trout will hit artificial spent spinners dragging across the surface on tight lines, these being the same fish that would refuse wets fished in the traditional downstream manner and would spook at the mere suggestion of drag from a conventional dry.

Although I have no evidence from authoritative sources to support my thesis, a clue to explaining such extraordinary behavior is to be arrived at, I believe, by simply observing spinners as they land upon the water after mating. You'll notice that most aren't dead when they light, but rather that they remain alive for from several seconds to several minutes. During that time they are prone to buzz across the surface, describing a series of little arcs in a vain attempt, I guess, to gather enough momentum to take off again. Virtually always lateral, that is, from side to side, the movement of spinners covers distances of from just a couple of inches to a few feet, depending upon the pluck left in the dying insect. There is no question, however, but that their movement is strikingly reminiscent of a dragging spinner imitation. The secret, then, becomes to locate a rising trout, and, positioned upstream and across from it, to three-quarter your spinner downstream, making sure the line of drag puts the fly right over the trout's nose. Usually, you'll find, the fish take the fly as it passes by, although occasionally, I was surprised to discover, something about the action of the spinner in the surface film prompts a trout to chase a fly halfway across a pool. In either event, given the tightness of the trailing line, setting the hook is seldom if ever necessary to lock a fly securely into your quarry's jaw.

~~~~~~~~~~~~~~~~~~~~~~~~~~~~~~~~~~~~

CHAPTER FIFTEEN

Hooking, Playing and Landing Trout

WHAT PERCENTAGE OF TROUT that you raise do you hook, and what percentage of trout that you hook do you land? No angler, not even the most adroit, of course, will score a hundred percent. There are just too many ways to miss or lose fish, some of them clearly unpreventable. Yet, perfection is the goal to shoot for with every trout every time out, since to strive for the unattainable constitutes the best hedge against those little slips that cost us dearly when it really counts.

There is a correct procedure to hook and to play each trout that takes a dry fly, if only the angler could dope it out. The elements of that procedure, however, may vary considerably from fishery to fishery and, indeed, from trout to trout. It's predictable, then, that seasoned anglers will boast somewhat higher success percentages on waters they know intimately than on those to which they are relative strangers. That isn't to say, though, that there aren't fundamental rules governing hooking, playing and landing trout that, once understood, mastered and put to work, will serve the angler admirably anywhere he travels. There are, in fact, such rules aplenty, and it is to analyze them that this chapter is devoted.

The dimension that sets fishing dry flies apart from alternative techniques is that the entire show evolves under the scrutiny of the angler. It is inconceivable that any angling experience could be more gripping than to follow the course of a floating fly, always expectant yet inevitably startled, if not entirely unstrung, when a trout suddenly materializes to dispatch the offering before your eyes. A more delicious irony for enhancing a sport would be impossible to orchestrate than to unite its most stimulating and yet prejudicial element, the miracle of the rise, in such a way that each repetition turns out to be a confrontation' between instinctive emotional stimulation and the need for intellectual self-discipline. Because, unless an angler recognizes and learns to control his tension and excitement as each trout prepares to take his fly, he's bound to set the hook incorrectly on an awful lot of fish.

Dry fly fishermen have to recognize that setting the hook is one instance when the behavior of the trout must be accommodated. While it is wise to factor in the business of hooking up when positioning yourself to present a fly, there's no way to escape the plain truth that to connect with a trout demands that the set be timed to correspond precisely with the period a fish retains the fly in its mouth, a period that may vary in the extremes from a blink to a nod. Fortunately for trout, their dispositions respond to no internal or external metronomes, and thus no trustworthy tempo to measure the interval between when they take hold of and spit out artificial flies is demonstrable for national, regional or even local application, at least not by me. Frankly, I'd hate to have my last buck down on predicting the comparative fly-taking behavior of two fish lying side by side in the same pool on the same day during the same hatch.

That stated by way of employing a literary style reminiscent of malpractice insurance, I feel free to proceed to contradict myself

From the instant his fly touches down, the angler must be prepared to time the setting of the hook to correspond with the period a rising trout will mouth the fly. It can be particularly difficult along stretches of water such as this, where numerous intervening currents are troublesome and the rise of a fish to a small fly may be hard to detect.

by pitching a baker's dozen of propositions, gleaned from observation and experimentation on the water. These contentions I believe worthy of attention by anglers sufficiently flexible to adapt to their experiences somewhat imperfect but, nevertheless, functional generalities about an elusive subject without feeling the information should apply neatly to every fishing situation: 1. Trout inhabiting swift, broken water seem less prone to tarry with flies than those found in slower stretches; 2. Trout feeding on hatches often mouth artificial flies longer than fish pounded up by anglers; 3. A trout rising into the flow—that is, in an upstream direction—may spit your fly less hastily than one that takes it while swimming with the flow downstream; 4. Small trout, notably stockers, appear more apt to take flies deeper and hold them longer than large wild fish; 5. Fish observed making splashy rises are frequently quicker to eject artificials than those seen feeding in leisurely rolls, given of course, that the character of their rises doesn't change when they turn to your artificials; 6. The more angling pressure a stretch of water endures, the greater the chances its fish population has learned to differentiate in a flash between natural and artificial flies; 7. Trout you tease to the surface tend to gulp flies deeper than fish working rhythmically to a hatch; 8. Trout seem prone to inhale midges further into their mouths than larger flies, thus increasing the duration tiny patterns remain well placed for hook-ups; 9. Most fish won't abide caddis imitations as long as flies that represent mayfly duns, but neither will they stay with dun patterns as long as artificial spinners; 10. Patterns dressed with soft materials consistently trick trout into mouthing them longer than flies of more rigid construction; 11. Prickly patterns are usually rejected lickety-split; 12. The hour of day or night seldom significantly bears on the amount of time trout retain flies; 13. Fish you can coax to hit skittering or dragging flies are frequently hooked by the sheer momentum of their rises.

Perennial causes of missed sets include:

1. *Striking too early,* thereby snatching flies away from trout before the fish have a chance to engulf them;

2. *Striking too late,* or after a fish has expelled the barb beyond a point where there's enough meat or bone to bite into;

3. *Striking too hard;* that is exerting force from arm to rod to terminal tackle, either in excess of the capacity of trout tissue to stop the hook from cutting all the way through, or out of proportion to the breaking strength of tippet materials or knots.

Even among skilled fishermen, striking too soon and too late are likely to remain lifelong problems, since they're attributable to timing errors, as often as not promulgated by erratic fish behavior. The practiced angler, though, has no one to blame but himself for heavy-handedness, and therefore should find a tendency to strike too hard as easy to remedy as exercising a modicum of self-restraint.

There's next to nothing an angler can learn between the covers of a book about adjusting his timing for setting hooks on rising fish, so brief are the intervals trout hold onto artificial flies. The fact that I've been unable to think of a reliable means to measure these durations is itself evidence of sorts to illustrate how reflexive the fisherman's responses to rises must become if he hopes to minimize his penchant for error and disappointment. Asked to guess, however, I'd speculate some trout are altogether capable of differentiating between natural and bogus insects in, perhaps, a tenth of a second, while fish that might take a full second to do the job would become pretty good candidates for the frying pan sooner or later, and probably sooner. The key, then, has to be anticipation, as in always holding your rod at an angle to expedite setting your hook (see Fig. 1 in the accompanying illustration), and determining in advance precisely how much slack line and leader must be taken up in the process of setting to make optimum use of your reaction time.

I've had occasion to witness countless hook settings through the years, and were I to try to underscore a single flaw as epidemic, it would have to be the tendency for exaggerated, jerky motion as the rod is raised to drive the barb home. So prevalent is this misapplication of tackle and technique among novice and experi-

SETTING THE HOOK

FIG. 2

FIG. I

Setting the hook should be perceived as a logical extension, rather than a disruption, of fishing a dry fly through its drift. Therefore, all the time your fly is on the water, the attitude of your rod must be maintained so that no major adjustments of, for instance, its angle of pitch over the water are required prior to initiating the procedure for setting the hook (Fig. 1). Your head should be positioned so that you can monitor your fly by sighting along the rod. Then, when ready to set, you rotate your rod directly upward by rotating your forearm in a gentle, uninterrupted arc from its normal fishing position (Fig. 1) to the position that culminates the set, indicated by Fig. 2. Note that your wrist plays no active role in setting the hook. Flicking or snapping the wrist, a common error, causes abrupt line and leader acceleration, which, in turn, is likely to cause your tippet to part as a consequence of the resistance introduced by the weight of the fish.

255

enced anglers alike that I can only assume it to be the consequence of a failure by many fishermen to perceive how little force
has to be exerted to promote sufficient line and leader velocity to
propel a hook securely into trout tissue, whether such tissue be
skin, bone or both. Without bogging down in principles of phys-
ics, it should be pointed out that a fly fishing rig—rod, reel, line
and leader—is integrated by design and balance to maximize line
acceleration and speed with minimum effort. This is standard, particularly among outfits coordinated for dry fly fishing. Thus, when
a rod is arched a given distance, say a foot, in the act of striking,
the relative response of the line and terminal tackle outside its
tip-top will vary significantly with the amount of power generated
by the angler in moving the rod that distance.

Experiment on your lawn. Walk off about fifty feet of line and
leader, being sure to affix a bit of bright yarn to the end of your
tippet to represent a fly. Next, holding your rod at about ten
o'clock, strike abruptly and vigorously to the vertical position.
Note how the line, leader and "fly" leap back at you, and try to
visualize the impact of the shock were a hook in the "fly" to be
stopped suddenly by the jaw of a heavy trout. The result, you'll
realize, would be disastrous. Now repeat the exercise several times,
attempting slower, more fluid upward strokes with each successive strike. You should observe that while your line, leader and
"fly" cover ever decreasing distances as the energy you impart to
them through the rod diminishes, sufficient force remains, even
after you seem to be setting listlessly, to lock the hook into any
trout. Herein lies the secret, then, for setting hooks efficiently.
Whether circumstances call for a quick set or a delayed one,
whether the trout is close to you or far away, when you strike
make it the steadiest, smoothest, most restrained flex of the rod
feasible to carry sufficient authority to hook a fish. Most instances,
you'll discover, will be sterling examples of *less is better*.

Playing a trout should be thought of as an extension of setting
the hook. The degree of dexterity exercised when striking a fish,
in fact, commonly establishes the tone of the entire battle to fol-

low. While the response of a trout to a violent strike is liable to be immediate and absolute panic, a more composed set may leave the fish relatively unruffled, at least long enough to let the angler organize himself to be in command of the fight from its outset. The object, therefore, is always to set a hook so that it is felt by a fish as a minor sting, rather than as a major jolt. That accomplished, the ratio of trout landed to those lost should increasingly favor the fisherman.

When I was just a kid, the late Chett Osborn, naturalist, artist and inimitable professor of homespun lessons, taught me a trick about setting the hook that continues to impress me from time to time to this day. Chett insisted after each presentation that I draw my thumb backwards along the rod grip until my knuckle jutted upward ominously. Then, if a trout took my dry, he'd direct the strike be made by raising the rod directly toward my face, reminiscent of a soldier saluting with a sword. If my set was suitably gentle, he pointed out, everything would turn out fine. If on the other hand I jerked the rod with typical twelve-year-old exuberance, the bulb of my nose would take a solid jab from my knuckle. The price exacted for overeagerness, I soon found out, could be very painful, although then as now, the pain of a self-inflicted punch in the nose wasn't nearly so severe in the physical sense as it was a blast to my pride.

No two trout can be expected to put up exactly the same kind of tussle. Were hooked fish entirely predictable, playing them would be no fun at all. The ultimate challenge to be derived from fighting fish springs from the angler's capacity to compensate for each move his quarry opts to try by introducing strategy of his own (1) to prevent the move from occurring if he perceives in it dangerous potential, or (2) to make the trout pay dearly for the move when, indeed, circumstances dictate the fish temporarily be given its head. Above all else, however, one concept is crucial to handling trout successfully. The angler must never permit his degree of control to deteriorate to a point at which a reversal of fundamental roles is manifested between himself and the opposition. *For the surest way to lose a fish is to let it manipulate the action.* Only the most inept fisherman, I believe, could even conceive of allowing a trout to play him. *A skilled angler plays a trout by remaining always on the offensive.*

Why some waters support harder fighting fish than others I couldn't begin to explain. Nearby streams, inhabited by the same trout species in comparable sizes as distant rivers, are just as likely as not to host fish with spunk, strength and stamina that varies to the extremes. And yet, despite these prevalent and puzzling inconsistencies, I remain convinced it's the make-up of a trout's immediate environment—that is, the habitat in which it goes about the business of surviving from day to day—that largely determines the kind of battle it will put up when its moment of truth arrives.

Consider the following:

1. A trout with lots of room to run is apt to take advantage of it.
2. A fish that spends considerable time hiding beneath an undercut bank tends to make for its hiding place at the first sign of danger.
3. A pocket water trout is prone to try hanging you up around rocks.
4. If snags exist in a piece of water, a fish hooked close by can be expected to attempt to use them.
5. Calm pools are compatible with running upstream, while heavy flows virtually assure your fish will hightail it downstream.
6. A trout hooked in a deep pool may well make its stand by burrowing down and circling in a restricted area. However, deep water may also be exploited by a fish only to gain momentum for jumps.,

In short, don't be shocked if and when trout in weedy streams take advantage of the weeds, if those in rocky waters use the rocks, if fish in rapids make you fight the currents as well as themselves. While a functional list of such evolutionary orientations could be compiled only by analysis of every trout fishery on earth, perceptive anglers can go a long way toward limiting the occasions they're caught flat-footed by learning to recognize in advance the most likely tactics to be employed by the trout on every river and stream they approach. Thus prepared, when the fish are about to do what for them comes naturally, the things they're programmed to do, it won't take long before they find out that their games have been taken away from them.

Regulars who fish the Letort, a famed limestone stream in south-central Pennsylvania, seldom get together without reviewing the classic confrontation between Ed Shenk, an exceptionally gifted local angler, and a gigantic brown trout that tested his will for a couple of seasons. As the story unfolds, the trout had apparently survived so long because, among other reasons, it occupied a small side eddy at the tail of which clung a brush pile of heroic proportions. Over the years the trout had collected a veritable beard of flies by running into the tangle and breaking anglers off each time it was hooked. Like the rest, Ed had lost the monster more than once, but he realized his best hope lay in finding a way to keep the trout away from its habitual haven.

Finally, Ed hatched a rather undignified but practical scheme to achieve his goal that included jumping into the eddy in front of the pile to try to spook the hooked fish into making its fight in the open, where it would be a relative "piece of cake." For weeks, perhaps months, thereafter, Ed could be spotted trudging up the road soaking wet.

"Ed's done lost that big 'un again," neighbors would hoot. "Hey, Ed, you cain't run faster'n a trout can swim."

Nevertheless, the angler continued to ply his maneuver unabashed and undaunted, knowing he was doing the only thing he could to land that fish. Time after time Ed lost the race and would be subjected to humiliation. But the long and the short of the story is that, in the end, he was either just a little bit faster or the trout was just a little bit slower than usual one day, and so today an eight-pound, eight-ounce brown hangs on Ed's wall as testimony to the value of strategy.

Although subtleties of strategy must be tailored to individual situations, anglers should not ignore the fact there are tactical rudiments that remain standard for playing every trout—the mechanics, so to speak, of subduing fish. It must be understood, for instance, that all trout, regardless of size, are best played directly off and on the reel, as line is taken by the fish and retrieved by the angler. Some heroes try to regain line by stripping it in by hand and holding it in coils. No fisherman, not even the bonafide expert (if there is such an animal) can guarantee to me that the loops he gathers won't occasionally snarl just as fish make unexpected runs. Don't let anybody convince you, therefore, that your fly reel is there simply for line storage. Such a notion is nonsense. A reel is a *tool* that should be used by the angler to peak efficiency. Given a choice between awkward alternatives, as a matter of fact, I'd rather take on big trout with no rod than no reel.

In a similar vein, it's beyond me why anyone would want to both cast and reel with his right hand, or vice versa for the southpaw, the traditional technique foisted upon generations of American and foreign fly fishermen by self-professed sages of the sport. Assigning one's dominant side both duties requires that the rod be passed from one hand to the other at some point, in order to play fish off the reel. Maybe the exchange can be accomplished successfully ninety-nine times out of a hundred, but what about the one-hundredth? Might it not coincide with the biggest trout of the season? The inescapable truth is that for the instant it takes to change hands, the angler isn't in control of his tackle or, therefore, of his fish. Further, most people will concede that their casting hands and arms are their strongest, and most reliable, the ones upon which they rely to do their most strenuous and meticulous work. Does it not make sense, then, that the dominant hand and arm take the brunt of battling fish? Or that the dominant side be the one back to which the actions of trout are telegraphed through the rod, enabling the angler to prepare the proper responses? In which hand and arm do you have the greatest confidence to manipulate the rod, which, after all, is used to guide every trout, up and down, in and out, and from side to side?

To crank a reel requires nothing more elaborate than learning to describe a simple circle. Not one person in a thousand, I'll wager, is incapable of that, and the one unfortunate would proba-

The author achieves maximum leverage against the run of a heavy brown trout by holding his rod at a steep angle of pitch. A right-handed caster, he nevertheless uses his right arm, his strongest, to manipulate his rod, while his left hand remains at the ready to reel in line as necessary.

bly still be better off redoubling his efforts to master the challenge since, if he's ultimately confounded by such an elementary task, what's going to be his lot when he undertakes to use his secondary limb to control frantic fish? As mentioned earlier, most quality fly reels are adjustable for right- and left-hand winding. The best advice I have to offer is to see that yours is converted appropriately, so that if you're a righthanded caster you reel with your left, or that if you cast with your left you reel with your right.

The intent of playing trout is to wear them down, to drain their energy until they become manageable. Taking the fight out of a fish is a function of applying relentless pressure to tire it out.

A trout must be alternately spurred and reined into sapping its own reserves of strength, a goal attainable only if the fish is persistently denied rest. Toward that end, the angler has two invaluable tools: his rod from which he gains leverage to influence the action of the fish; and his reel, which alternately inhibits and encourages the acceleration of a trout, depending on whether it's running or being drawn back. By adjusting the rod's angle of pitch, the fisherman can regulate the amount of pressure put to a trout. Both as a fish takes line or is reeled in the pressure increases as the angle of pitch is inclined toward the vertical. Because I don't believe trout should be mollycoddled, the optimum pitch of the rod, as translated into the degree of resistance it supplies, for me is the maximum exertable short of the extreme at which the hook pulls loose, the tippet breaks or tackle is damaged. When a trout flees, in other words, I raise my rod to make the fish earn every inch of line it gets, and when I have one coming back to me I see that it swims harder and faster than it might have a mind to without prompting from me.

Whether you palm (Fig. 1) or finger (Fig. 2) a reel spool depends largely on the reel design you choose. Palming is practical only with models constructed with revolving outer rims, such as the one shown in Fig. 1. Examples include the Hardy Marquis, and the Orvis C.F.O. and Battenkill series. For most other reels, like the Hardy Princess, shown in Fig. 2, fingering the spool is the best way to go. Note that in both instances, the author is careful that nothing interferes with the progress of his line off his reel. The thumb, extended when palming (Fig. 1), and tucked in when fingering (Fig. 2), can be especially troublesome if not kept out of the way. Note, too, that while palming, the author likes to keep his working hand well back on the reel rim, just inches, in fact, from the butt of his rod; and while fingering, he positions the tips of two fingers, the forefinger and middle finger of his left hand, behind his reel's line guide. Both tricks, you'll find, aid in insuring smooth resistance against running fish.

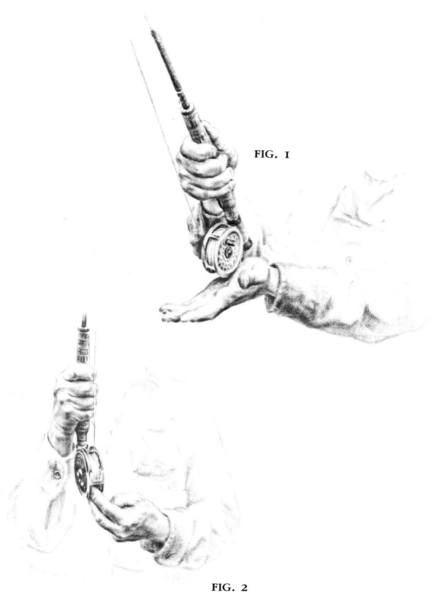

FIG. 1

FIG. 2

FIG. 1

FIG. 2

Fig. 1 demonstrates the posture employed by the author to counter long runs by trout on waters where there are a lot of potential snags. By holding his rod high overhead, two major things are accomplished: (1) the fish must earn every inch of line it gets, and (2) maximum line remains over the water where it is immune to obstacles. Note that his rod is positioned squarely over and in front of the author's head, thus enabling him to observe the course of the running fish directly. The rod is gripped by his right hand in the normal fashion, while his left hand is used to grip his right wrist for additional leverage and support.

Fig. 2 depicts how the author lowers his rod as a trout jumps. Note that the entire rod is lowered, not just the tip, and that the rod is lowered at arm's length. All this guarantees that his rod can be raised smoothly again in the wake of a jump. (When only the rod tip is lowered, an angler may tend to snap his rod up after the jump, thus causing his tippet to break.) Also observe that as he lowers his rod, the author leans sharply to his right, positioning his head as directly as possible over the rod to monitor the jump.

Altogether too much fuss is made, in my opinion, about adjustable drags on typical trout reels. While a smooth drag unquestionably can be helpful, I fear some anglers spend too much time engrossed in mechanical drag settings and too little attending to the antics of hooked fish. Thus diverted, all too frequently whatever potential benefits that might have accrued to them from being equipped with adjustable drags are hopelessly compromised. Far wiser than to be fiddling with tiny knobs, I believe, is to use good dragless reels or to set their drags at about one-half pound and then *leave them alone.* Alert anglers increase check on running fish without threat of distraction by learning either to palm reels or finger spools, both of which are depicted in the accompanying illustration. However, in both instances it's imperative that a sensitive "feel" for the measure and steadiness of tension be developed, since nothing is more likely to cause breakoffs than an oppressive or irregular touch on outwardbound line.

Trout seem particularly disposed to two stunts tailormade to whip themselves—the long run and the jump. Both are extremely taxing, even on bigger fish, and, handled by (1) holding the rod so as to guide your line away from rocks and other snags, as shown in Fig. 1 in the accompanying illustration, and by (2) dropping the rod tip to create slack to compensate for the latter (Fig. 2), both trout tactics often turn in the angler's favor.

Since you seldom gain anything (and may, in fact, lose something) by attempting to prevent trout from taking off, I let them rip, arching my rod to insure that each run becomes a painful and exhausting exercise. I'm especially pleased to see downstream flight, because trout can't breath efficiently while traveling with the current, and I've learned that the fatigue brought on by lack of oxygen, coupled with the burden of lugging a mile of fly line and backing through the water, can prove enough to break the spirit of many fish. Similarly, every jump debilitates, as effortless as it may appear, taking many times the quota of energy required, for instance, for unfettered swimming.

FIG. 1

FIG. 2

FIG. 3

FIG. 4

Shown is a reasonably typical, although hypothetical, encounter between angler and trout along a hypothetical stretch of river. The angler has carefully positioned himself to present a dry fly to a nice fish (Fig. 1). Note that he has waded sufficiently

266

close to his quarry to make an effective presentation. As hoped, the trout rises and snatches the fly (Fig. 1), and after being stung by the hook, turns and shoots downstream. Ideally, the angler has anticipated this run, and before it has even begun, has carefully backed into shallower water where he can be sure of his footing. Now he compensates for the run by picking his way downstream to stay abreast of his fish, while raising his rod high over his head to keep his line off the boulders and rocks (Fig. 2). Even after the trout's run is checked, the angler continues downstream along the shore, until he is securely stationed below his quarry (Fig. 3). Thus positioned, he knows he's in an ideal spot and lowers his rod after encouraging the trout to jump (Fig. 3). In the wake of the jump, the trout tires quickly, and so the angler leads it into calm water where, although the angler keeps the pressure on, he can safely permit the trout to make small circles until he's certain his fish is ready for the net (Fig. 4).

At the core of competent fish-fighting strategy is *positioning*. Throughout the course of a struggle between angler and trout, the essential test inevitably comes down to how astutely the angler perceives his optimum position at a given instant relative to that of the fish (see the accompanying illustration). He must use every conceivable trick to persuade the quarry to play into his hands. Only with very small trout, perhaps, does practical strategy permit the luxury of netting a fish while standing in the same spot from which you hooked it. In most instances, the angler must scramble to adjust location to compensate for, offset or anticipate the movements of fish. Those who plant their feet and try to crank trout back through strong currents exert negligible control and manifest even less skill. Most fish landed by such means should be written off to dumb luck, inglorious trout, or both. Luck, by the way, I'm convinced, has no place in trout fishing, least of all where it might be applied to managing fish from hookup to landing net. For besting trout, notably big ones, knowledge and finesse are the name of the game.

Here are several more elements that I've found can be exploited when playing most trout in moving water:

1. The flow of a river or stream may be turned to the angler's advantage. Never fight fish plus the force of flows, an issue that arises mainly when trout are allowed to get below disorganized fishermen. Whenever possible, maintain your position either across or across and slightly downstream of the quarry.

2. All trout respond to varying the angle of tension between the bite of a hook and the fisherman's rod. Note in the illustration that follows, by shifting the attitude at which pressure is exerted from the rod through the line and leader to the hook and the head of the fish, a trout can be prompted to perform all manner of predictable maneuvers, each enhancing the angler's purchase on the conduct of the battle. In every case, however, whether the intent is to nose a trout in a desired direction, to influence a turn, to plane a fish up or to encourage it to dive, it's important that the angler strictly beware of creating a situation in which his hook is tugged across the fish's jaws. The best way to avoid this risk is to learn to mark accurately where in a trout's mouth your hook is set and then to spot yourself accordingly as you move from place to place in the sequence of the fight.

Although integral to handling trout of any size, the principle of varying hook pressure points to modify the behavior of struggling trout is neither widely understood nor put to work by many anglers. Evidence the number of fly fishermen who maintain a uniform angle of rod pitch, regardless of the tactics initiated by the fish. Perhaps these anglers fail to recognize their fly rod as a lever, a guide if you will, utilized to peak efficiency only when adjusted as the situation evolves. Say that in Fig. 1 I am playing a trout that suddenly decides to run downstream from my right to my left two-thirds of the way across a broad river. Were I simply to plant my feet and point my rod at the fish, I would accomplish little or nothing to discourage that play. By reaching out and to my right,

however, while lowering my rod tip gradually, I exert
adequate inboard pressure on the fish to encourage it to turn
its head and to begin a broad swing to its left that will
culminate in the trout reversing its direction entirely and
swimming upstream again. In Fig. 2 the same trout is now
running upstream, and I have decided the time has come to
put the fish right in front of me. So, to turn the trout again, I
simply rotate my rod all the way across my body, thus altering
and intensifying the pressure exerted by the hook sufficiently to
incline my quarry to modify its direction once more, this time
to the right, until, finally, the trout responds by turning and
swimming downstream toward me. Following the same
principle, I can, in effect, influence each movement made by
my trout, until when it is whipped, I slide it into my landing
net.

FIG. I

FIG. 2

3. While long runs definitely wear trout down, from the stand-point of optimum control, there's nothing quite like keeping a fish close by. Therefore, after a trout has gotten a run or two out of its system, don't let it take a nap out there. Regain line as soon as possible and try to persuade the fish to remain in your vicinity for the remainder of the contest. The narrower the gap between you, you'll soon discover, the easier it is to keep a trout from sulking, and even when a fish does evidence such a stubborn inclination you'll find it comparative duck soup to start it moving again by tailoring the angle of tension, as depicted in the illustration on page 269.

4. Don't let a little slack line shake you up, particularly when your flies have barbed hooks. A tad too much slack is always preferable to putting too much pressure on a fish—the one certain way to lose a trout. Slack is actually beneficial on occasion, as when an obstinate fish is fooled into swimming up-stream by a bow in the line that creates the illusion the angler is stationed further downstream than he really is. Similarly, big bellies of slack can be used in desperation to dissuade large trout from leaving pools when by doing so they may be lost in more difficult waters.

Few weeks go by when I don't hear yet another depressing dis-course on "the one that got away," and although I've neglected to chronicle most of them, it seems that an inordinate percentage have revolved around the final seconds before trout were to be landed. Even among many anglers who take great pains to perfect fly presentation, hooking and fish-fighting techniques, somehow there persists an air of nonchalance concerning the landing of trout that is baffling to me. On occasion it's been stated by those who elect not to keep fish that losing them can be regarded, in essence, as a form of decorous release. In such a perspective, how-ever, there's inevitably an undercurrent of self-satisfaction suffi-ciently strong to make me question whether the concept isn't aw-fully long on rationalization and pretty short on chivalry. Given the noblest of motives, however, to shrug off the ultimate rendevous between angler and prey is in my view to miss, if not entirely dismiss, the indispensable fascination of sport fishing. For it's with the landing of a fish, the possessing of it, so to speak— whether or not you then release it—that the angler makes his definitive statement about success and failure, and, more important still, about his determination to see what he starts all the way through to the end.

The following section of drawings and accompanying text provides the best guidelines I can offer for landing trout by using a short-handled landing net, attached to a retriever that is fastened to the back of the fishing vest. Although some excellent anglers prefer to take fish in their hands or to beach them, I feel there's no equal to, nor substitute for, a tear-shaped net and the knowledge to use it effectively. Note that the technique calls for leading your fish into the calmest water possible, and then getting in as deep as you can, even to the level of your waist (you can always kneel in shallow water). It's also crucial, I believe, to keep a trout moving in lazy circles in front of you as you accustom it to the presence of your net, a function of the sensitive touch that results from coordinating the positioning of the net with the principles of varying angles of tension illustrated previously. Having settled a trout down, the trick becomes to guide it gently into the net and to lift the captured fish in a deliberate, uninterrupted arc. Never attempt to scoop a trout "on the fly," for the commotion created when the net enters and rushes through the water is apt to spook the quarry, while even the smallest miscalculation of the relative locations of the moving fish and the approaching net may lead to a broken tippet, or a trout jarred loose by hammering into the net frame.

1. NET AND RETRIEVER

Every fly fisherman seems to have his pet trick for rigging a landing net so it's always handy but stays out of his way until he's ready to collect him a trout. My friend Mike Kimball, for instance, has so much elastic cord strung all over him that his outfit brings to mind one of those uniforms Haile Selassie, the late emperor of Ethiopia, was prone to parade. Other anglers combine elastic cord and Velcro catches to fashion some truly ingenious Rube Goldbergs. And then there's the galoot who totes a folding net in a holster on his wader belt and looks all business until he draws and the net pops out like a springy snake from a can you'd buy at a novelty store.

I prefer something simple, and toward that end, use a spring-loaded, sliding net retriever, clipped to the ring sewn to the tab on the back of my vest by its manufacturer. Such tabs and rings, by the way, are generally standard. Outfitted thusly, my net dangles unobtrusively in the middle of my back, where it's ready and waiting when I need it, as depicted in Illustration 1.

The retriever I favor is manufactured by the Key-Bak Division of the West Coast Chain Manufacturing Co., Pasadena, Calif., and, although, as its name implies, it was probably designed for more everyday purposes, is readily available from tackle dealers across the nation. Incredibly sturdy, I bought the one I still use every outing from Walt Dette of Roscoe, N.Y., about a decade ago.

The landing net I like best is made of laminated ash in a teardrop shape with an opening approximately fifteen inches long and eight inches wide. It was purchased some twenty years ago at Folkerts Bros. in Phoenecia, N.Y., where the finest handmade nets have been sold for generations. Although expensive, such nets are, in my opinion, works of art and with care, including varnish occasionally and a new net bag every couple of seasons, should serve you for a lifetime. Similar models of excellent quality in an assortment of woods, some crafted by local artisans in the best Folkerts tradition, are now available from most distributors of quality fly fishing tackle.

2. THE LANDING GRIP

To bring a trout to your net requires some very delicate inclose work. With the possible exception of the instant the hook is set, more fish seem to be blown at this moment of truth than at any other time. For such fine work a considerable measure of rod and line control is vital. Such control is difficult to achieve—at least for me—when the rod and line are gripped in the normal fashion.

So, through the years I have experimented with a variety of grips and have found the one shown in Illustration 2 ideal for me. I hasten to add, however, that it may not be right for every-

273

2. THE LANDING GRIP

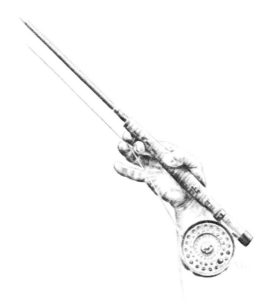

one; and even those who ultimately choose it will probably have to discipline themselves, even train, to develop the strength and dexterity required to use it without pain. Once mastered, though, most anglers should find this grip worth their efforts.

The painful part comes with developing the muscles needed to hold the rod, sometimes for considerable periods, in the position illustrated. Without becoming insufferably scientific, suffice it to point out that there are numerous extensor, flexor, abductor and adductor muscles in the forearm and hand that, like all muscles, can be built up with exercise. The muscle between my right thumb and the palm of my hand, called the adductor pollicis transversalis for anyone who cares to know, as well as my forearm muscles, have developed to abnormal proportions, the consequence of nothing more than the marathon fishing that I do. The resulting development is comparable to that observed among tournament tennis players. The relevance of this issues from the necessity for you to generate sufficient strength to be able to hold your rod comfortably by hooking the cork grip with your thumb and forefinger, as shown, while resting the butt of the grip in the groove formed by the meat near your thumb and the palm of your hand. Until such muscle development is attained, this can be agony.

Hand grip exercisers, or even squeezing a rubber ball, will help; but the best exercises of all seem to be hours of fly casting and sessions when you grip your rod as shown until it really hurts. With time you'll find that you can grip your rod thusly without the least discomfort.

The chief advantage of my grip is that every digit of your hand plays a key role in bringing trout to the net. Note, for instance, that your line is installed between your middle finger and ring finger where subtle pressure can be applied, whereas when additional line tension is required, your forefinger is right there to do the job. Meanwhile, your pinky is always available to be swung inboard toward the rod grip, along with your ring finger and middle finger, should it suddenly be warranted that you stop your line entirely. It should be further noted that this grip assures a free movement of your wrist to adjust the position of your rod as necessary in the critical moments prior to netting a trout.

3. LANDING AND NETTING A TROUT

Illustration 3 shows how I go about preparing to net a trout. The key elements to remember are timing, concentration and surprise. When a trout is in close, timing is critical, since your aim is to get the fish into your net as soon as possible without courting disaster by bringing it in too green. Likewise, concentration is important, as to be distracted, even for an instant, may just constitute the edge your trout needs to pull a stunt that will enable it to get away. The value of surprise should be self-evident, since ideally you seek to net the fish without it ever catching on to what is in store.

3. *LANDING AND NETTING A TROUT*

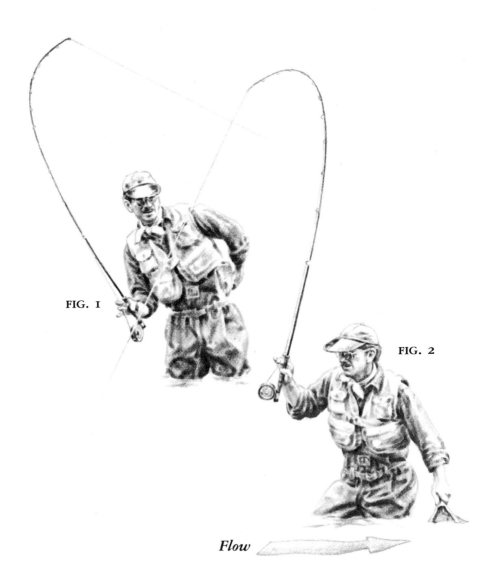

FIG. 1

FIG. 2

Flow

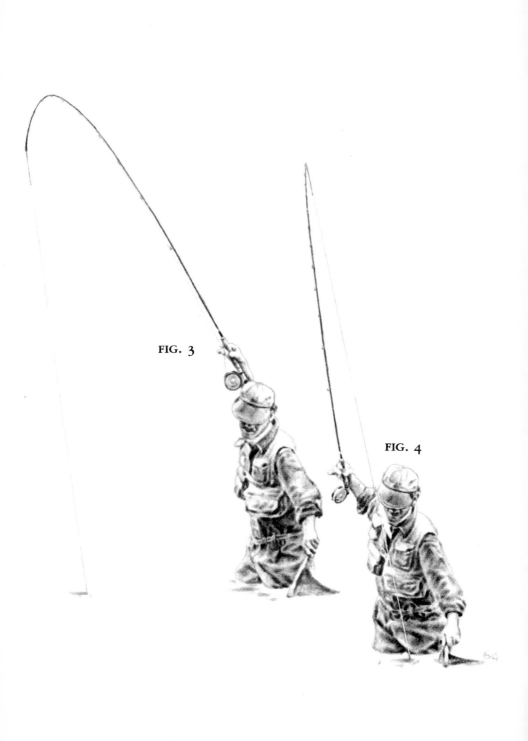

FIG. 3

FIG. 4

Although even experienced fly fishermen are duped occasionally by trout that play possum, fish generally manifest weariness by making tighter and tighter circles in front of you, until, finally, they show their sides when they can no longer maintain equilibrium. At this stage the trick is to keep your fish moving by leading it with your rod, according to the principles of varying pressure points discussed earlier in this chapter.

Bearing all this in mind, here's how to proceed:

1. As the end nears, convince the trout to turn in a counterclockwise direction, as shown in Fig. 1. (You should be gripping your rod as shown in Illustration 2.) Meanwhile, reach behind you and grasp your net firmly by the handle with your left hand (Fig. 1).

2. Now, without taking your eyes off your fish, lead it upstream past you from left to right (Fig. 2), and only when it is well above you, lower your net gingerly into the water in front of you and off your left hip (Fig. 2). The place where you spot the net must be chosen carefully, as it is there the net should stay until it is lifted from the water with the trout in the bag. It is important neither to let the fish see the net nor to permit the trout to take additional line.

3. When the trout has reached the limit of the line outside your rod's tip-top, try to alter the pressure point of the hook just enough to position the fish directly upstream from your net.

4. Now hold your rod firmly for several seconds to notify the weary fish that it will gain nothing further by trying to swim upstream (Fig. 2).

5. When the trout has settled, try raising your rod very gradually, first by inclining your forearm upward until it forms a right angle with your upper arm and then by rotating your arm rearward to a position behind your head. At this point you should ascertain whether or not the fish is inclined to back down tail first. If not, don't attempt to net the trout, but permit it to make another circle and then try again.

6. If the fish seems willing to play your game, continue raising your rod by straightening your arm out behind you and adjusting your wrist until you have reached the posture depicted in Fig. 3. At this point your rod butt can be braced against the un-

derside of your forearm for additional support (Fig. 3).

7. Finally, rotate your rod very slowly downward and to your left, as shown in Fig. 4. This will reduce the tension of the line against the fish and will encourage it to back downstream gradually into your net (Fig. 4).

~~~~~~

Epilogue:
A Half-Mile Farther On

THE FLOW OF THE BIG BEAVERKILL, the East's most popular
trout stream, below its junction with the Willowemoc, is in an
approximate east-west direction—a pertinent fact when you consider how a pool like Cairns' Eddy is surrounded at the height of
the season. A lineup follows the bottom contours out from the
beach along the north shore, fans across the tail, and forms a rigid
file on the rubble of the south bank below the abandoned Ontario
and Western Railroad right-of-way. A gut below the rapids at the
head, the easternmost end of the pool, is open only, it's certain,
because even a jumbo angler would drown trying to fill it up.

The condition is no better in the pocket water east of Cairns or
along the first pool westward, called Wagon Track. On a May afternoon you can count forty cars on the shoulders of Old Route
17 abreast of Cairns, which might be an enviable number for a
fast-food restaurant's parking lot but is obviously too many for

any trout pool or short stretch of river. From the tail of Wagon Track upstream nine-tenths of a mile to Hendrickson Pool, you can anticipate one hundred fishermen at the peak of a good weekend fly hatch.

Because it is a No-Kill stretch, where all trout must be released unharmed, there are always plenty of fish for the throng, although sloppy handling before release has left a lot of them looking like pugs with too much time in the ring. The fish are a tragic sight, snouts torn, maxillaries missing, one cruel consequence of the special regulations necessity. At first glance the boodle of anglers might seem surprisingly resigned, if not content, buzzing with comings and goings. It is, in fact, always just one uncomfortable flicker away from chaos, like family gatherings at holiday time. Punches aren't thrown, but there is evidence that some fishermen suffer a sort of General Adaptation Syndrome, the stress reaction manifested by any overcrowded species.

To onlookers who have experienced something better, the scene is depressing. Anglers are frozen to their places, as if afraid to leave them. The casting is jerky or mechanical, sometimes both. There is underlying tension, competition, too much looking around to see what the other guy is doing, too much oneupmanship. It's as if the worst a person leaves behind in the city for a weekend away greets him again on the river, that there is never a respite from it, and worst of all, that he develops a willingness to accept it. You don't have to be a psychologist to be certain it isn't healthy.

Perhaps no man before or since understood the essence of angling as Izaak Walton did. Any fisherman who hasn't read *The Compleat Angler* should do so before wetting another line. To Walton the essence was contemplation, something much deeper and more profound than the mechanics of casting and catching fish. He wrote:

> *Here, give my weary spirits rest,*
> *And raise my low-pitch'd thoughts above*
> *Earth, or what poor mortals love;*

Thus, free from law-suits and the noise
Of princes' courts, I would rejoice:

Bunching up on the Beaverkill, or anywhere else, is symptomatic of the essential sport, angling for its own sake, eroding like a stream bank with its alders torn away. Little by little science and technology supplant aesthetics. Tackle—who made it and how much it costs—assumes greater importance than how well it's used or how much fun it is to use it. Image outweighs satisfaction. New fishermen encounter too many other fishermen, and the individual is consumed by the fraternity, the fraternity by its pecking order. The pressure can be terrible.

It is easy to meet someone ready to sermonize on "ruined fishing." You will be told overcrowding is the inevitable price of making angling available to everyone. Such preachers are often so-called old-timers, overly prone to reflection. (One I know remembers the Depression as a grand adventure.) While retreat may have been easier forty years ago, peace can still be found by taking time to look around. Overcrowding is born of lethargy, perhaps, but not of necessity.

New York State, for instance, has about fifteen thousand miles of trout streams, most of which are public. Percentages in the West are probably even higher. Fisheries officials, however, report that ninety percent of anglers fish ten percent of the water, particularly if a stream carries some special regulations handle. Few anglers bothered with the Beaverkill near Horton until a couple of years ago when it was designated No-Kill. Then suddenly it attracted thousands. Above and below No-Kill areas you can hook scores of healthy unmarked fish without encountering other anglers for days. Similar privacy is available on the Willowemoc and other popular eastern waters, including the Ausable, Letort, Kennebec, Battenkill, Angroscoggin, Connecticut and the Delaware. While this is home turf, it's certain the same is true on well-known streams throughout the country.

You can have many lesser known streams all to yourself. That a stream isn't famous doesn't mean it fishes badly. (It probably means only that the stream has received minimum ink.) The Saranac River, for example, in New York's Adirondack Mountains can be better at times than the more popular Ausable, and in the Catskills the Mongaup may be the East's biggest sleeper.

Forty years ago the finest fishing may have been an easy cast from the car's running board. That's doubtful, though. Then, as now, better fishing probably existed around the second bend, or the third, just another half-mile farther on. Today's old-timers, who were young-timers then, simply didn't feel compelled to find it. Now, however, even adequate angling isn't so easy. It might be better, therefore, for sportsmen to spend more nights poring over maps than over tackle catalogues if they want better things to contemplate than highway bridges, cars and trucks, telephone wires, people and more people.

Nature can't talk to anyone too distracted to listen.

ABOUT THE AUTHOR

Art Lee doesn't know for sure whether he was yet old enough to walk when he caught his first fish, but does remember, vividly, his first fly-caught trout, wrestled as a child from a small stream in the foothills of the Berkshire Mountains in upstate New York. For about thirty years since that overcast spring morning, he has devoted himself to fly fishing in general, and fly fishing for trout in particular. Many flyrodders probably feel they know Art already through his dozens of articles and stories appearing in *Fly Fisherman* magazine, for which he has served as a field editor more than a decade. About him, John Randolph, managing editor of *Fly Fisherman,* said recently: "Of all those working in the fly-fishing field today, Art Lee is the *one* who combines the qualities of consummate angler and consummate writer." Writing and film assignments take Art and his wife, Kris, all over the world, and the resulting work, both non-fiction and fiction, has appeared in a host of publications, including *Sports Illustrated, Gray's Sporting Journal, Sports Afield* and *National Geographic.* He and Kris, their old shaggy dog, six cats and countless "critters" they're always feeding, now live and work where dry-fly fishing in America really began, in Roscoe, New York, within sight of Junction Pool, where the sacred waters of the Willowemoc and the Beaverkill merge, unquestionably the most famous trout pool in North America.